Developing the ICT-Capable School

What is ICT capability, why should a school develop it and how can it be achieved? *Developing the ICT-Capable School* responds to these questions from the perspective of school managers, ICT co-ordinators, teachers and pupils. It builds a vision of a type of school which is still very rare: a school where it is natural for everyone to apply ICT in the daily activities of teaching, learning and administration.

The authors analyse the current problems concerning ICT in primary and secondary schools. The focus is on developing a strong culture of ICT within schools without special technology funding, through strong management, effective co-ordination, radical changes in teachers' practices and providing continuity in pupils' learning between schools and between home and school. The book will provide readers with:

- greater understanding of personal ICT capability;
- knowledge of effective management, teaching methods and co-ordination strategies for ICT;
- understanding of the importance of a whole-school approach to improving ICT capability.

Developing the ICT-Capable School will be invaluable to senior management and governors in primary and secondary schools, ICT co-ordinators in schools, trainee teachers with ICT as a specialism and further/higher education lecturers concerned with ICT and school improvement.

The authors all work at the University of Wales Swansea. **Steve Kennewell** researches into ICT and learning, trains specialist ICT teachers and leads courses on teaching and learning. **John Parkinson** is involved in the initial training of science teachers, leads courses on school improvement, and his research interests include the use of ICT to promote pupils' learning. **Howard Tanner** trains maths teachers, leads courses in Curriculum and Assessment, and has led several nationally funded research projects concerning ICT and learning.

Developing the ICT-Capable School

Steve Kennewell, John Parkinson and Howard Tanner

London and New York

First published 2000
by RoutledgeFalmer
11 New Fetter Lane, London EC4P 4EE

Simultaneously published in the USA and Canada
by RoutledgeFalmer
29 West 35th Street, New York, NY 10001

RoutledgeFalmer is an imprint of the Taylor & Francis Group

© 2000 Steve Kennewell, John Parkinson and Howard Tanner

Typeset in Baskerville by
Keystroke, Jacaranda Lodge, Wolverhampton
Printed and bound in Great Britain by
Biddles Ltd, Guildford and King's Lynn

British Library Cataloguing in Publication Data
A catalogue record for this book is available from the British Library

Library of Congress Cataloging in Publication Data
Kennewell, Steve, 1949–
     Developing the ICT-capable school / Steve Kennewell, John Parkinson, and Howard Tanner.
          p. cm.
     Includes bibliographical references and index.
          1. Computer-assisted instruction. 2. Information technology. 3. Educational
     innovations. I. Parkinson, John, 1947– II. Tanner, Howard, 1951– III. Title.

LB1028.5 .K433 2000
371.33′4—dc21   00–030593

ISBN 0–415–23512–X (pbk)

Contents

Tables

Figures

Acknowledgements

We are very grateful for the contribution made by Helen Smith, who worked as research assistant on the Whole Approaches to IT Capability project. She provided much of the material for Chapter 4, and made valuable comments on many other chapters. We would also like to thank staff at ACCAC for their advice and support during our research, and the University of Wales at Swansea Department of Education for support during the writing of the book.

We would particularly like to thank all the headteachers and staff in the schools who so generously gave up their time to complete questionnaires, to talk to us about ICT and to help provide the insight we have gained into the development of ICT capability.

Introduction

'Information and communications technology' refers to the set of tools used to process and communicate information; to be 'ICT capable' is to be competent in controlling the situations in which those tools are applied. This book looks at how a school can generate a pervasive culture of effective use of new technology.

ICT is defined for curriculum purposes as

> the range of tools and techniques relating to computer-based hardware and software; to communications including both directed and broadcast; to information sources such as CDROM and the Internet; and to associated technologies such as robots, video-conferencing and digital TV.
>
> (QCA 1999a: 184)

Until recently, this field was known just as information technology (IT) in the UK, and some of our references to previous studies and documents will thus use the term IT. There is no real difference in the meaning. The *C* for Communications has been added to the National Curriculum subject title in England in order to emphasise the dramatic rise in significance of networked services. For simplicity, we will also use ICT to refer to the subject and key skill at KS4 (Key Stage 4) and beyond.

The term *ICT resources* will be assumed to cover all aspects of digital information handling, for it is the digital nature of data representation that has created the massive potential for change in education. The distinction between ICT *capability* and ICT resources is, as the QCA (1998b) points out, similar to that between *literacy* and text media, such as books. We might also extend the analogy to the distinction between *numeracy* and number – and we feel that the relationship with other basic or key skills is important.

Although we draw heavily on the literature and practices of the UK National Curriculum, our ideas are valid worldwide. The ways in which ICT capability is developed and applied will vary across different technological cultures and educational systems; but readers, irrespective of their cultural, ethnic and national origins, will be able to learn from this book.

What, then, do we mean by an ICT-capable *school*? How can an institution demonstrate an ability that is defined in terms of personal knowledge and skill? We claim that it is possible, and indeed helpful, to view an institution as demonstrating a capability which is more than just the sum of the capabilities of its members. We feel that this view reflects much of the research on school improvement, and adds an important perspective to that body of work. We will refer to schools, in line with common practice, as corporate entities that can think and act intentionally.

We do not, however, feel that ICT should be viewed in isolation. It influences, and is influenced by, the basic skills of literacy and numeracy, and other key skills such as *working with others* and *problem solving*. The issue of ICT capability development is best seen as part of an holistic, continuous approach to improvements in teaching and learning. While ICT has some special features that make it unique as a component of the curriculum, the ideas set out here in the context of ICT may be adapted and extended for the curriculum as a whole.

So why write a book specifically about ICT capability? First, we are acutely aware of the UK government's intentions in this field. The 1997 White Paper *Excellence in Schools* (DfEE 1997c) stated: 'We are determined to create a society where, within ten years, ICT has permeated every aspect of education.' Yet Lynch (1999) points out that 'there are few establishments where ICT has become indispensable to teaching and learning'. Consideration of the issue is thus particularly timely for teachers in the UK, who are experiencing

- large-scale funding of infrastructure and equipment currently being implemented in connection with the National Grid for Learning (DfEE, 1997a);
- training (both initial and in-service) being provided for teachers concerning the use of ICT in subject teaching (TTA 1998);
- a requirement in the National Curriculum that 'pupils should be given opportunities to apply and develop their ICT capability through the use of ICT tools to support their learning in all subjects . . .' (QCA 1999b: 36).

Second, it is the area of the National Curriculum in England and Wales that school inspectors have consistently found to be the least well taught (see, for instance, Goldstein 1997). It is in this context that ACCAC, the Curriculum and Assessment Authority for Wales, commissioned the authors to carry out research into whole-school approaches to developing IT capability (ACCAC 1999c) at the end of 1997. Having completed this work, which we refer to as the information technology capability development (ITCD) project, we are now in a position of having a particularly rich collection of data concerning ICT learning and application at all levels of school life: managers, teachers and pupils.

The third reason is our belief that ICT has an important part to play in the development of a school system that can contribute more effectively to the aspirations of a learning society (Ranson 1994).

Our purpose in writing this book is to help disseminate our knowledge of these important issues concerning ICT in schools. We write at a time when changes are being made to the National Curriculum – changes that are different in England and Wales. Although we comment on the issues raised by these specific changes, we attempt to ensure that the validity of our main arguments is independent of the particular specifications of ICT capability in different countries. (England and Wales shared the same National Curriculum for IT at the time of the research. Scotland, like Northern Ireland, has always had its own National Curriculum, and readers in those countries, as well as other parts of the world, will need to interpret our ideas in terms of their own terminology and structures.)

We bring together some of the ideas in the existing literature about the nature of ICT capability and the factors influencing the teaching and learning of ICT. We develop a framework for analysing ICT capability which is proving helpful in research, not just into the learning of ICT in curriculum contexts but into the use of ICT in subject teaching. We draw on the general literature of school improvement and staff development.

Readers will find that much of what we say mirrors the views expressed in the school effectiveness literature. This should not be surprising: we, too, have been studying the factors that influence success in schools. What, then, is special about this book? What we bring is a perspective based on the unique position in the curriculum of ICT, which is a subject, a Key Skill and a set of tools for learning. We are able to contextualise school improvement strategies in a specific component of the curriculum, while maintaining the whole-curriculum stance that we believe is important to the success of such strategies. This work would not have been possible for any other National Curriculum subject. It may well provide a model for studying whole-school approaches to the basic skills of literacy and numeracy, however, for despite the differences in the nature of these areas they share many of the general characteristics of a *capability*.

A number of key themes emerge through the book. In particular, we can identify the importance of

- having high expectations of pupils in their use of ICT, in and out of school, and of providing opportunities for disadvantaged pupils to spend as much time using up-to-date ICT resources as their more fortunate peers;
- focusing on teaching and learning higher order aspects of all key skills, throughout the curriculum, with a reduction in emphasis on low-level techniques and routines;
- purposeful assessment of attainment and use of assessment information to feedback to pupils and inform teacher planning;
- leadership from management and a cycle of ICT development within a culture of school improvement;
- supporting teachers in changing their teaching approaches to accommodate the potential of ICT as an educational tool;
- collaborating in response to challenge – management and staff, different subjects and age groups, teaching and support staff, teachers and pupils, school and home;
- a shared vision of what it means to be ICT capable, and a recognition that the process of developing ICT capability can never be complete.

The book augments the growing body of literature concerning the application of ICT in teaching and learning by focusing on what is involved in the effective use of ICT and how the ability to use ICT effectively develops. We do not attempt to examine in depth the role of ICT in supporting the learning of other subjects. This is a complex issue which is still under-researched in most subjects, and a thorough exploration of the issues would require at least one volume for each subject. We thus confine our comments to matters specifically concerned with developing ICT capability. Of course, the rest of the curriculum – and the rest of life – is the very reason *why* we wish to develop pupils' ICT capability. We know that ICT does not automatically enhance the learning of other subjects, and it needs engagement on the part of the learner in order for its potential to be realised. We feel that the emphasis on higher order processes, which we pursue throughout the book, is the most important factor in enabling learners to exploit the features of ICT in learning.

Who should read the book? It is intended to illuminate the field of ICT in schools for all involved or interested. It will be of particular value to

- headteachers, senior managers, governors and LEA (Local Education Authority) officers, who should gain insight into the mutual influence of ICT capability and school effectiveness;
- ICT co-ordinators, who will find guidance and support in carrying out their unique middle management role;
- classroom and subject teachers, who will find clarification of one of the key skills they are helping pupils to develop and can exploit in their teaching of other subjects;
- specialist teachers of ICT, who will find guidance on the teaching and assessment of ICT, and on their contribution to the whole curriculum;
- researchers in the field of ICT in education, who will find a range of relevant literature summarised and developed, and many matters considered in depth which elsewhere are dealt with only superficially, if at all.

In order to help readers optimise their use of the book, we provide, at the end of each chapter, a list of the key issues raised in the chapter and a number of points for reflection. These can be used by individuals or by groups of readers to help them relate the matters discussed in the chapter to their own context, and as prompts when planning improvements.

We attempt to cover readerships based in both the primary and secondary sectors. This is not easy; there are considerable differences in all aspects of school life between the phases, and particularly in curriculum organisation and teaching approaches. There is much evidence that this disadvantages pupils, and there have been many attempts to overcome the problems of discontinuity. We, too, hope to contribute to this goal, and have devoted a chapter specifically to these issues. The greatest need is for mutual understanding. Many of the key ideas are the same in each sector, and we have tried to avoid unnecessary repetition in the expectation that readers from one phase would read the chapters which concern the other phase, and then reflect on how the ideas apply in their own context. Although there can be no standard recipe which schools can follow to ensure success, there are some clear messages from our work which can guide those involved in their planning, implementation and evaluation.

We start in Chapter 1 with the necessary background to the ideas in the rest of the book, and in Chapter 2 we analyse in some depth the idea of ICT capability. This provides a good foundation for subsequent reading, and although we have designed each of the remaining chapters to make sense in isolation, readers will gain most from reading the whole book in sequence. Chapters 3 and 4 consider the respective roles of senior management and ICT co-ordinators, and then Chapters 5 and 6 examine classroom teachers' perspectives in primary and secondary schools. Chapter 7 focuses on ICT as a subject, but it includes a number of principles concerning effective ICT capability development which will be helpful to all teachers. Chapter 8 considers the pupils' perspectives – not just on the school context but on other contexts in which they are experiencing ICT – and Chapter 9 examines a particular issue for pupils, parents and schools: the discontinuity in learning at the transition from primary to secondary schooling. We conclude with a chapter which consolidates and develops the ideas found throughout the book concerning school improvement in relation to ICT, and focuses particularly on the role of staff development.

1 The context for ICT capability in schools

Policy, research and practice

In this chapter, we first set out the general context of education policy and practice in relation to ICT in UK schools. We then describe the nature of the research project which led to the writing of this book, and explain how the project characterised success in developing ICT capability.

The background to ICT capability in schools

Over the last thirty years, it has been argued regularly that the introduction of computers and information technology into schools would lead to developments and changes in the world of education as least as dramatic as the impact which had occurred in the world of work. For the last twenty years, the UK has been in the vanguard of the technological revolution in educational computing, but few would argue that the early utopian claims have been realised. Rather, most commentators agree that the computer has *failed* to permeate effectively into the school setting: 'The UK has a higher ratio of computers per schoolchild than almost any other country, including the US. Yet despite this lead and the fact that Information Technology has been on the agenda for almost thirty years, it is not clear that IT has made a significant impact on educational standards . . .' (Lovegrove and Wilshire 1997: 1). In recent years, computers have become a familiar feature of many UK homes and 5 million home computers were purchased between 1989 and 1997 representing 22 per cent of UK households (Lovegrove and Wilshire 1997: 1–2). This represents a significant foundation of technology from which to build.

On the other hand school provision varies widely. A high proportion of obsolete hardware is still in use in the classroom, with the result that children often meet industry standard hardware and software at home rather than in school. Usage in school is also very variable, and while in some schools computers are frequently used as teaching tools, in others they are hardly used at all (ibid.).

Pupils rarely use ICT in core areas of the curriculum such as mathematics and science (Cox 1997; Harris 1999), and the number of teachers in secondary schools using computers in their teaching has remained stubbornly constant 'at about 32 per cent' in recent years, suggesting that one of the most costly resources in these schools is being significantly under-utilised (Harris 1999). Primary schools appear to demonstrate greater curricular use of ICT, with 65 per cent of teachers feeling confident about this, but few primary schools make substantial use of ICT in teaching subjects other than English (DfEE 1998a). Word-processing and desktop publishing still predominate.

The relative failure of initiatives in the 1980s and 1990s to effect significant change in educational practice should not, perhaps, be all that surprising. Early developments in the 1980s consisted of industry-driven initiatives (Wellington 1989) which provided hardware for schools with very little support for teachers on how it might be used. The inclusion of ICT in the National Curriculum was something of an afterthought (DES–Welsh Office 1988), and the initial Orders (DES–Welsh Office 1990) placed ICT alongside design & technology as part of an umbrella subject called *technology*. These approaches may have placed too much emphasis on hardware provision and the development of abstract value-free skills. The aims of vocational education and the anticipated needs of industry, rather than the development of pedagogy, dominated the curriculum.

The Dearing review (1993) of the National Curriculum gave ICT the status of a subject in its own right, yet also placed it 'at the heart of the curriculum' as a cross-curricular skill. The subsequent (1995) National Curriculum orders required that pupils should be given opportunities to develop and apply their ICT capability in each subject. However, this conflicted with the *subject culture* of the National Curriculum. Given that many teachers were not convinced about the value of ICT for the teaching of their subjects and were being expected to pass on skills and knowledge which they did not have themselves, the failure to achieve the utopian vision is not surprising (Tanner 1992; Strack 1995).

During the last thirty years there has been a lack of clarity over the educational objectives for ICT, and this has exacerbated problems because of shortages of equipment and a lack of training for teachers (Tanner 1992; Strack 1995). As Lovegrove and Wilshire (1997: 3) have put it: 'We need to be clearer about what we want children to learn and whether learning should be about acquiring vocational skills or about learning for its own sake.'

Faith in the potential of ICT to improve standards in education resulted in the UK government's National Grid for Learning (NGfL) initiative. In an attempt to avoid repeating earlier mistakes, significant expenditure was also allocated for the in-service training (INSET) of teachers through New Opportunities Funding, and the ability to use ICT in subject teaching became a pre-requisite for 'qualified teacher' status.

The 1999 statistical release (DfEE 1999a) reported that schools themselves had spent large amounts (on average) on ICT resources, and the pupil–computer ratio had reached 18:1 in primary schools and 9:1 in secondary schools. Significantly, headteachers and subject heads indicated that 90 per cent of primary staff and 85 per cent of secondary staff reported having had some training in the use of ICT, and claimed that 65 per cent of primary staff and 61 per cent of secondary staff felt confident with the use of ICT in the curriculum. In the first part of the year 2000 we may be approaching the point at which a critical mass of technological resources exists in combination with appropriately trained teachers, so that it will be possible to begin to effect the changes predicted at the start of the 1980s.

However, politicians and perhaps some teachers appear too ready to believe that computers in the classroom are *inherently a good thing* and to accept skill-based notions of ICT capability uncritically: 'Our recommendation to Central Government is that they must make the act of faith and encourage the education sector to start using technology rather than talking about it!' (Stevenson 1997: 6).

ICT as a National Curriculum subject and as a tool for learning

It is strange that, of all the important assumptions behind the National Curriculum and the structure of knowledge implied within it, the notion of *IT capability* set out in the original National Curriculum orders (DES–WO 1990) is one of the least criticised (notwithstanding Birnbaum 1989 and 1990). The main problem which has been highlighted in the past is the difficulty which many teachers have in under-standing the ideas represented, because IT capability is written about at such a high level of generality (Murray 1992). The notion of *capability* itself, however, has not been challenged. The lack of clarity in objectives continues as the subject is renamed ICT in the new National Curriculum. Unless we clarify our objectives we are unlikely to arrive where we expect.

In the National Curriculum for Wales, however, the *subject* is to be called IT but the *resources* referred to as ICT (ACCAC 1999a). The distinction is unclear to many teachers and headteachers, however, and at the level of classroom interaction both subject and resources are certainly interdependent for activity and learning. We will use the term ICT to cover both the subject and the resources from now on, but there are three aspects of ICT which need to be distinguished.

1   There are the generic attitudes, beliefs, processes and strategies associated with the IT Key Skill. Key skills underpin learning in a range of subject areas within the National Curriculum and are generally learned on the way to learning something else. When key skills are learned in the context of another subject discipline it is likely that they will be learned in a form which is useful and useable within that discipline. Any definition of ICT capability should include within it a demand that pupils are able to employ technology appropriately in learning, employment and everyday life situations. It is this *use* of the knowledge, skills and understanding of the technology outside its own subject discipline which is being grasped at by the National Curriculum's authors through the term ICT. *ICT capability* is a useful term in this context in that it implies a capacity or power to act in as yet undefined situations, defining itself through its potential for application.

2   The IT Key Skill is associated with a discipline which can and should be seen as a subject area in its own right. However, ICT knowledge is different in significant respects from the formal knowledge required in the more traditional academic disciplines. Although there are low-level basic skills, routines and techniques that may appear to be at the heart of its subject content, progression within ICT requires understanding at a deeper level to facilitate the development of strategies and

processes, to identify opportunities, solve problems and evaluate solutions. These higher level objectives require far more than a basic skills' approach. Knowledge which is skill- and technique-based rather than concept-based tends to be specific to the context and the resources, making it difficult for students to transfer their skills to new situations (Blackmore *et al.* 1992: 252). Without an emphasis on understanding concepts, the use of computers in schools will always be limited (Herschbach 1995: 1). Conceptual understanding in ICT refers to the schemata or mental models which students develop about computer systems. The degree of abstraction characteristic of such mental models relates to the extent to which they could be applied to a range of differing ICT systems. There is evidence that abstract mental models support the transfer of knowledge and understanding, and thus underlie ICT capability (Twining 1995).

3   ICT may be viewed as a resource which can be used to support and extend pedagogy across the curriculum. The Industrial Revolution transformed society through its amplification of the power of the human muscle. The claim that ICT will revolutionise education through the amplification and emancipation of the human mind (Howe 1983) has yet to be demonstrated.

From ICT's first introduction into schools, claims have been made for its potential to facilitate the learning of other subjects and even for the development of students' thinking (see e.g.: Papert 1980; Pea 1985). It was thought that students who learned the programming language Logo would learn to think like a computer. They would immerse themselves in a mathematically rich environment and thus learn mathematics in a more natural and effective way (Papert 1980). Students pro-gramming computers were expected to reorganise and strengthen their own thinking (Pea 1985). Thus just by using a computer, albeit in a programming mode, learning would be improved. The pedagogy demanded by Papert and others who made claims for the power of programming to improve thinking was exploratory and individualistic, which then, as now, was very much against the dominant form prevailing in schools. Sadly, hard evidence for the development and transfer of such thinking skills has not emerged.

We may see tool software such as word-processors, spreadsheets, databases or graph plotters as adaptable tools of great utility. When students apply such tools to problems arising naturally in the contexts of other disciplines, they *may* develop ICT capability, although that might not have been the intention of the teacher or student in selecting the tool. The power of such tools lies in their ability to perform routine repetitive operations swiftly and accurately and allow the adjustment of variables in an exploratory fashion. This provides an opportunity to emancipate the mind from routine tasks, amplifying its power and allowing it to work at higher levels. For example, even young pupils producing a report about the school garden can quickly change the words and images used in order to cater for different audiences, such as pupils and parents. In developing the document, they can switch their focus between choice of words, images, sentence structure, syntax, and visual effect without having to rewrite the text each time. An older pupil using a spreadsheet to explore the effect of changing gradient and intercept in straight-line graphs is enabled to plot large numbers of lines quickly and accurately in order to make and test hypotheses. The pupil is thus enabled and encouraged to focus on the higher level mathematical processes rather than the mechanical skills of graph plotting.

The use of technology as a resource to support pedagogy across the curriculum *may* often provide opportunities for the development of pupils' ICT capability, but this need not always be the case. On the other hand, teachers may demonstrate *their own ICT capability* through the *appropriate* use of technology in their teaching.

There is a double bind here. If in a mathematics lesson pupils find difficulty in learning to use the graph-plotting software, the intended advantage of using a computer can be lost as the software becomes the focus of attention rather than the mathematics. The greatest advantage in subject learning may occur when the ICT used is familiar and routine. The *standards of achievement* (NCET–NAACE 1995) warn inspectors to distinguish between situations in which relatively low-level ICT skills are being used to support higher achievement in a subject and those where the main purpose is to develop mastery of ICT tools and their use. If you are a head of a secondary subject department or a primary subject co-ordinator, you will be focusing on targets for raising test and examination performance in your subject, and you are likely to be far more enthusiastic about the subject achievement than about the ICT capability.

Computer-aided learning using subject-specific software is usually based on a similar pedagogy to the old programmed-learning courses which proved to be such a dismal failure in the 1960s. For example, much attention is currently focused on a number of integrated learning systems (ILS) which are claimed to be useful in teaching numeracy and literacy. These systems tend to take a serial, atomistic view of learning based on an attempt to predict all possible misconceptions linked to particular incorrect responses. They emphasise *facts*, *right answers* and *correct methods*, ignoring intuition and stifling imagination. In contrast, the National Numeracy Strategy (DfEE 1999b) respects students' idiosyncratic methods. The two approaches appear to be mutually exclusive. Although it is not yet clear whether resources such as ILS develop subject learning effectively (BECTA 1999), they are unlikely to contribute positively to the development of ICT capability because of their highly directive nature.

ICT in the National Curriculum places emphasis on the development of a range of tools and techniques that can be used effectively

> to explore, analyse, exchange and present information and to support their problem solving, investigative and expressive work . . . being discriminating about information and the ways in which it may be used and making informed judgements about when and how to apply aspects of ICT to achieve maximum benefit . . .
>
> (QCA 1999a: 184)

Although the National Curriculum takes a functional approach to specifying the content of ICT, it expresses the aims in general terms rather than as specific ICT techniques. It adopts a vocational stance, with ICT contributing to the curriculum by preparing children to 'participate in a rapidly changing society in which work and other forms of activity are increasingly dependent on ICT' (QCA 1999a: 184). Yet the form in which the orders are written encourages an approach based on abstract skills, divorced from any specific technological context. There is an emphasis on higher level processes such as planning, analysing, predicting and evaluating, and an accent on pupil autonomy. It is only in the non-statutory examples that tool software such as spreadsheets, databases or word-processors are mentioned.

The vocational justification for ICT capability does not demand knowledge of specific skills, techniques or applications of ICT. Employers require a basic understanding of ICT rather than specific knowledge, which has a short working life (Wellington 1989). We see a need to prepare students for a life of constant change resulting from the progress of technology. Although we must prepare students to work confidently with the new technologies, we must also prepare them for a life characterised by ever-changing skill requirements and work patterns (NCET–NAACE 1995). Thus ICT capability is associated with attitudes which value life-long learning and personal qualities such as a willingness to explore, a sense of inquisitiveness, the ability to take responsibility for and to organise one's own learning (Benzie 1997: 59).

Unfortunately, all too often ICT activities in schools focus on showing pupils how to do a particular task using a particular ICT tool in ways that are typified by the exemplar activities (Benzie 1997: 56). In so doing the emphasis is often placed on particular context-specific skills rather than the more general ICT capability aspired to by the authors of the National Curriculum.

We see the dominant pedagogical culture in schools as directive rather than exploratory, and current government advice on the introduction of whole-class teaching approaches are likely only to reinforce this. Pedagogy based on the computer, however, is often individualistic and autonomous, clashing with the industrial nature of school (Thomas 1986; Goodson and Mangan 1995; Selwyn 1999b). In such circumstances, it is not surprising that the ill-defined aims of ICT are sometimes translated by schools into teaching pupils how to use specific tools in the context of artificial activities in order to exemplify and practise the specific low-level skills involved in the use of a particular piece of software.

It is not possible to be fully ICT capable: 'learning and re-learning are implicitly associated with IT capability' (Benzie 1997: 57). However expert a person may be, there will always be aspects of ICT that he or she has not yet fully embraced. Even familiar software has some rarely used functions, and in any case new resources are continually being developed. The learning never stops. It is the same for schools – there is no such thing as full capability, but they should continually strive to improve the way they use ICT along with all other aspects of teaching and learning. We have seen considerable differences in the level of ICT capability between otherwise similar schools, and we believe that it is important for those schools whose ICT capability is low to set about improving their culture and attainment so as not to disadvantage their pupils.

The ITCD project

During the spring and summer of 1998, we were funded by ACCAC to engage in research in a number of schools which had been identified as more successful than most in developing ICT capability. Our research aimed to provide a snapshot of what was happening in schools in Wales during the spring and summer of 1998, to identify successful practice and to formulate indicators of success which schools could use as the basis of targets for improvement (ACCAC 1999c).

The research was designed to illuminate our understanding of the relationships among factors at three levels: management level, teacher level and pupil level. It involved a mixture of quantitative methods, using questionnaires to sample groups from the populations of ICT co-ordinators, teachers and pupils, together with qualitative methods involving classroom observation and interviewing managers, teachers and pupils.

In our main study, we analysed questionnaires from 2,446 pupils, 450 teachers, and 33 ICT co-ordinators. We focused on a small number of schools where there was some evidence of success in developing pupils' ICT capability, selected in order to study the influence of a range of particular characteristics. In these schools we interviewed 6 headteachers, 12 ICT co-ordinators, 12 class/subject teachers and 9 pairs of pupils. We thus met a wide range of perspectives on ICT capability, and individuals' views differed on its nature and development. We were dealing with schools which had not been given any special status or funding. Our search for success in developing ICT capability provided much insight into the factors which either stimulate or inhibit progress, and generated the vision which we set out in the next section.

We refer to managers, teachers and pupils within schools. Prior to our research, we expected that there would be links between the effectiveness of management, the quality of teaching and pupils' attainments. It is not possible to quantify the strength of these relationships, but we are able to characterise qualitatively the features that seem to help bring about improvements. Not surprisingly, there are links between the ICT capability of teachers (and to a certain extent of managers) and the ICT capability of pupils. However, there are ways of overcoming limitations in the ICT capability of teachers and managers. During our research, we saw that the ICT-capable *classroom* can be generated in primary schools and in secondary subject teaching without the teacher needing a high level of personal ICT expertise, and we saw that a high level of ICT capability can be generated in secondary schools by the ways in which resources are made available for curriculum work both inside and outside the subject teaching classroom. We also saw ways in which some schools are able to exploit and build on the high level of ICT capability that pupils have gained from work on home computers. This brought into contrast observations in other schools where teachers seem to believe that they are the sole source of knowledge concerning effective use of ICT, and consequently discourage pupils from applying and enhancing the capability which they bring.

A vision for the ICT-capable school

We start with the premiss that the purpose of a school is to educate its pupils in order to meet the expectations of parents, the wider community and national government. These, however, go far beyond the narrow visions concerning test performance in particular subjects which characterise current performance measures. Expectations in ICT capability are concerned with preparation for work and leisure, fostering a commitment to moral and social values and providing a foundation for lifelong learning. The ICT-capable school will be successful in developing its pupils' ICT capability to the expected National Curriculum levels, but it will have broader aims and will expect to achieve much more than can be represented by mere numbers. Our study of ICT in schools has enabled us to appreciate just how complex ICT capability is, and how many factors at different levels impact upon the standard of pupils' attainment.

What exactly should we look for, then, to represent a school's success in developing pupils' ICT capability? In the ICT-capable school, we will see

- pupils with a positive attitude towards ICT, and a disposition to apply ICT to relevant curriculum tasks and to evaluate the outcomes of their use of ICT;
- pupils planning and applying ICT to tasks, describing and evaluating their work with ICT, with a high level of knowledge, skill and understanding in relation to their age;
- a strong role for ICT in the teaching and learning culture of the school, so that frequent opportunities are planned and provided for pupils to develop their skills in applying ICT to worthwhile tasks;
- teachers helping pupils to develop their ICT capability whenever there is an opportunity to do so, and provision for pupils to work on purposeful ICT tasks beyond the standard teaching times.

Further detail will be found in our Executive Summary from the ITCD project (ACCAC 1999b).

If we propose that all schools should have the goal of becoming ICT capable, we must justify this exhortation in terms of the educational benefits that will accrue. Are there not, after all, many schools which provide an excellent education, yet which are by no means ICT capable according to our criteria? Can our proposal be more than just the *act of faith* proclaimed by Stevenson (1997) and proselytised by the current UK government?

We think it can, but our belief is based on some assumptions, which we need to share.

All schools can improve on the education they are providing at present. It is still difficult to find clear evidence that will convince doubters concerning the general value of ICT in education (Lynch 1999). After all, the 'high school student who learns to write an effective research report on the environment by collecting evidence with peers in half a dozen countries may neither cost less to teach nor perform higher on a curriculum test' (Hirsch 1999: 100). Furthermore, Russell (1995) suggests that it is not fruitful to seek such evidence because the technology on which results are based will be out of date by the time widespread dissemination could be achieved. In any case, we do not want to suggest that an initiative to increase a school's ICT capability will make a difference in performance on its own. We see ICT capability as just one aspect of a general strategy for improving teaching and learning. It naturally associates with numeracy and literacy initiatives, in particular, as basic tools for learning and for life; it naturally associates with a focus on broadening the range of teaching and learning styles; and it naturally associates with a strategy of developing pupils' higher order thinking skills across the curriculum (McGuinness 1999). The ICT-capable school does not wait for empirical evidence of improvements in learning elsewhere before adopting ICT. It will embrace the technology as an integral part of its work and culture, and continually seek to improve the way in which ICT is used to enhance learning in the school's own context. A school which is performing successfully in terms of examination results, yet has a low level of ICT capability, will not maintain its rating without change in the direction of ICT capability development.

It is important for pupils to develop ICT capability as part of their preparation for adult life. This aspect of ICT capability involves learning *about* ICT. It does not happen automatically just because pupils are working on computers, however. Although practise of techniques is important, many subject-based ICT packages are deliberately designed to make it as easy as possible for pupils to respond to tasks presented on screen, so that lack of ICT capability does not form a barrier to subject learning. There is much more to the development of ICT capability, and this does not occur if pupils are merely pressing buttons in response to prompts. If pupils are to apply their ICT capability to goals in new contexts, they need to be able to reflect on their own and others' usage, generalise concepts and have opportunities to make decisions.

The use of ICT can provide a powerful aid to the learning of other subject matter, and this knowledge can then be utilised in non-ICT situations. We refer to this aspect as learning *through* ICT. It does not necessarily require a high level of ICT capability on the part of pupils or staff, but clearly the greater the ICT capability the more potential there is for the application of ICT to learning. Although we find that most teachers believe that ICT can improve learning, further probing reveals that this belief is based largely on pupils' motivation to engage in learning tasks with ICT, rather than on evidence that any knowledge gained may be applied in contexts different from the context of learning. There is a need for more specific research into what aspects of each subject can be learned more effectively through ICT, and what uses of ICT can help bring about such learning.

New subject knowledge at research level is now commonly generated with the aid of ICT, and thus pupils' own processes of constructing knowledge should reflect this. We refer to this as learning *with* ICT. The knowledge gained can no longer be considered as existing purely in the pupil's mind: in order to use the knowledge, the pupil requires the ICT resource. This mode of ICT application to learning does not require any expectation of transfer to non-ICT situations, but it does assume, of course, that pupils will have ICT resources available to them whenever they are to apply the knowledge. This is not merely a resourcing issue. It has profound implications for educational culture in general, not just of the school. It requires policy makers to resolve the conflicts in the messages they are giving to schools, whereby they are expected on the one hand to integrate ICT into their teaching and on the other to use so-called traditional teaching methods because they are to be judged on examination results that test traditional forms of knowledge.

Key issues

1   The subject-centred nature of the National Curriculum and the designation of ICT as a subject have restricted the development of ICT as a pervasive teaching and learning tool.
2   Confusion between ICT as a subject, as a key skill and as a learning tool has led to significant variations in approach and effectiveness in this field among otherwise similar schools.
3   Success in developing ICT capability within a school is seen in the products, practices and attitudes of pupils and staff.
4   A school's ethos and culture in respect of ICT are over-riding factors which can compensate for limitations in resources and skills.

Points for reflection

• What relationships do you see between developing ICT capability and using ICT in subject teaching?
• Do you know how ICT capable your school is in comparison with others of similar type? How could you find out?

2 Developing ICT capability
Providing opportunities and support

This chapter begins by considering how ICT capability has developed through successive National Curriculum orders over the last decade. From our analysis of the curriculum and our observations of classroom ICT activities, we identify five distinct components of ICT capability: basic skills or routines; techniques; underpinning concepts; processes; and higher order skills and knowledge – in particular metacognitive skills and metacognitive knowledge. We then consider how classroom practices might support the development of each of these components within the ICT-capable school.

A focus on progression

The term *IT capability* was coined by the authors of the original National Curriculum (DES–Welsh Office 1988; 1990). It was recognised that this did not represent a fixed body of knowledge, and the content was thus represented as five *strands of progression* (NCC 1990: C4):

1 developing ideas and communicating information;
2 handling information;
3 modelling;
4 measurement and control;
5 applications and effects.

Birnbaum suggested that

> IT capability consists in a rounded development in the five . . . [strands] . . . so that a pupil can:
>
> • recognise in which situations the use of IT is sensible;
> • use IT appropriately in such situations;
> • evaluate the effects of that use;
> • know and understand the range and purpose of applications of IT, and be able to evaluate their effects on individuals and society.
>
> (Birnbaum 1989: 5)

The IT component of the National Curriculum was expressed in these general terms to facilitate the *future proofing* of the Attainment Target and the Programmes of Study. The authors of the National Curriculum recognised the rapidly changing nature of the technology, and set out the requirements in very general terms. It should be noted, however, that progress in ICT capability as defined here involves far more than developing knowledge of more techniques and skills.

The range intended for ICT capability is indicated by the skills, knowledge and understanding identified in the revision to the National Curriculum for ICT in England for 2000 (DfEE–QCA 1999). The following strands appear in the Programme of Study:

- finding things out;
- developing ideas and making things happen;
- exchanging and sharing information;
- reviewing, modifying and evaluating work as it progresses.

In Wales, items relating to control technology have been placed in the design & technology order, while those relating to monitoring and measurement have been placed in the science orders to provide realistic and appropriate contexts for activities (ACCAC 1999a). Otherwise, the strands in the Welsh orders are very similar to the original ones.

Across the key stages, a progression may be identified in the knowledge, skills and understanding demanded by the Programmes of Study and Attainment Targets. Progression in ICT demands that pupils develop ever greater autonomy and confidence in their selection and use of information sources and tools. They are expected to develop into discerning users of ICT, with an increasing awareness of the benefits and limitations of the systems they use. They become able to present their ideas in an increasing variety of ways with a developing sense of audience. They use ICT-based models of growing complexity for increasingly complex lines of enquiry involving progressively greater decision making and personal autonomy. Their ability to evaluate their own work grows, and they become progressively more able to discuss and appreciate social, economic, political, legal and ethical issues (QCA 1998b).

In addition to progression within the skills, knowledge and understanding described above, the orders demand a breadth of study across each key stage. The breadth of study increases over the key stages, demanding that pupils be taught about an increasing variety of contexts, information sources and ICT tools. Pupils use these with increasing efficiency, to explore, develop and pass on information; to design systems and to evaluate their efficacy. Pupils' own use of ICT is also compared with their developing awareness of ICT use in the outside world (QCA 1998b).

Factors in progression

Progression in ICT capability is thus seen as including two major groups of factors, the first comprising strategies, processes and personal qualities relating to the application of ICT to the solution of problems, and the second depending on the range of problem contexts, sources and tools applied.

The first factor is related to the analysis of problem contexts from an ICT perspective; and progression emphasises increasing self-regulation, strategic planning, evaluation, deep understanding and transferable knowledge. It suggests both an ability to cope with the practical ICT demands of everyday life and also an *at-homeness* with computers. What is required is an understanding of the ICT potential of situations. This in its turn is dependent on the second factor – an experience of a wide range of problem situations for which an ICT solution has proved appropriate. Progression here involves the pupil solving increasingly sophisticated and abstract problems, constructing an increasingly rich and viable conceptual framework and developing fluency in the use of a widening range of techniques (Figure 2.1). In each case, this progression should parallel and assist similar learning in other domains, especially those which are directly supported by ICT.

ICT capability requires not only technical knowledge and skills but an awareness of this knowledge base, so that effective choices can be made. The choice of an effective strategy for a problem is dependent both on the knowledge that has been acquired and on one's awareness of that knowledge and the realisation that its use would be appropriate. Pupils must develop an awareness of the power and limitations of software and hardware systems together with a predilection to seek ICT solutions to situations.

To be ICT capable, then, is not merely to have secure knowledge and under-standing of a wide range of ICT skills, techniques, processes and strategies. It includes also the disposition to construct ICT solutions to problems which are appropriate to the context and are based on knowledge of the opportunities and

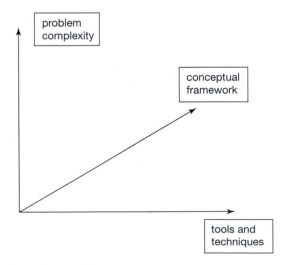

Figure 2.1 Dimensions of progression

limitations offered by the systems available. ICT capability therefore involves an interaction between technical facts and processes, strategic knowledge, meta-cognitive self-knowledge and affective aspects of mind including self-confidence and a disposition to use technology.

The authors of the National Curriculum used general ICT concepts to express their requirements so as to avoid writing a curriculum in terms of specific ICT techniques. The key elements of these concepts are relatively few, and we suggest a list below. In successful schools, careful attention is given to the teaching of these elements in a variety of contexts. Teachers increasingly prompt pupils to think for themselves how to apply ICT to a task, rather than dictating the ideas they are expected to employ.

The intention of the National Curriculum is also to reflect the higher order skills of planning to use ICT, making decisions concerning appropriate resources and techniques, monitoring progress and evaluating outcomes. The use of ICT throughout the curriculum is supposed to encourage 'critical thinking, imagination and creativity, problem solving, initiative and independence, teamwork and reflection' (QCA 1998b: 184).

Nevertheless, working with ICT certainly requires knowledge of particular techniques. These are very numerous, even for a particular type of software, and it is unrealistic to attempt to catalogue them here. They also tend to be highly specific to the resources used and have a limited lifespan. However, it is a feature of ICT that techniques do not have to be fully learned before they can be used, as usually the software provides prompts through on-screen menus and icons concerning what techniques are available and the options at each stage. ICT-capable users should be able to meet new software with a positive attitude and an inclination to explore. Using the concepts which they have developed from their experiences with other software, such as an object that can be *selected*, or a handle that can be *dragged*, capable users should be able to explore new systems and work out what to do next as they proceed. In fact it is characteristic of ICT-capable users that they *expect* to be able to explore new systems in this way with little assistance from manuals or instructors. It is important, then, when introducing a new software tool to pupils, that teachers start by discussing what it can do and how this might be achieved, rather than merely demonstrating a fixed sequence of techniques to achieve a single outcome.

Frequently used skills and techniques, such as *selecting objects* and *dragging handles*, eventually become automatised and no longer need conscious attention in order to carry them out. This process of automisation enables the ICT user to focus on the content of the problem in hand without having to monitor the progress of a technique. It is therefore locally important to develop such skills to an automatic level to facilitate current learning across the curriculum even if they are not at the heart of the subject and their longer term value is dubious.

Components of ICT capability

We conclude that ICT capability comprises five components.

Basic skills or routines

These are operations which are carried out without significant conscious thought. Basic skills include motor operations such as *moving the mouse* or tracker ball to point at a cell on the screen. Automatised routines include *dragging* a file from one window to another, or *double clicking* to open an application. Techniques such as copy-and-paste may become routines as a result of practice (mental automisation) or of developments in hardware and software (technological automisation).

The specific nature of many routines makes it difficult to transfer skills to different hardware and software. These difficulties may be lessened to some degree if skills and routines are underpinned by sufficiently abstract mental models of their use (Twining 1995). ICT capability demands an understanding or sense of technology as well as the basic expertise and skills:

> We should therefore look at computer expertise in terms of broad domains of transferable IT skills rather than the precise skills themselves . . . specific context based skills must be translated into higher-level areas of context free understanding in order to be of any lasting use for the learner.
>
> (Selwyn 1997a: 53)

Techniques

Techniques are procedures that still require a degree of conscious thought. They are methods known to achieve specified effects; for example: copying an element of a graphic design to make a regular pattern or selecting margins from the format menu in a word-processor in order to adjust the margins of a document to make a piece of text fit on a page. They are specific to the software tool used, but software designers often ensure that similar techniques can be used for similar procedures in different programs. Initially, techniques are likely also to involve an *ICT interference factor* (Birnbaum 1990). Since a part of the conscious mind must be allocated to controlling the technique, it is more difficult for learners to keep track of their goal.

One aspect of the learning of techniques is practising in order to achieve automaticity. The regular practice of techniques leads to *low-road learning* and the development of tacit understanding, skills and behaviour patterns (Salomon and Globerson 1987: 631). The development of automaticity through such low-road learning offers benefits in fairly short time as the mind is freed to concentrate on the problem situation rather than the cognitive overhead or ICT interference factor. When automatised in this way such techniques have become routine.

We have seen that techniques are often taught in a single context, which makes it difficult for learners to generalise. If, however, techniques are met in a variety of situations and contexts, the potential for reflection and concept development grows.

The *high-road learning* of techniques is supported by the progressive understanding of key concepts (see below) and general ICT principles, which enable ICT-capable learners to explore confidently when solving problems. If we encourage pupils to reflect on the use of techniques across contexts and situations, they are more likely to generate principles, ideas and strategies that are widely applicable (Salomon and Globerson 1987: 631).

It is much easier to use a technique than it is to describe or explain it. However, making techniques explicit or stateable is likely to support concept development and the possible transfer of techniques to new situations. The techniques we selected in a particular problem situation are a function of the context, the resources available and our strategic knowledge. They are underpinned by concepts, but their application depends also on the features and the structure offered by the technology, and the knowledge the user has of these.

For example, when we first show a child how to insert an image into a publication, it is helpful to talk about *selecting* the object by *clicking*, and to refer to *handles* and *dragging* when sizing or moving the object. If we use the same words in another context – or, better still, prompt the child to use the words – the concepts should start to develop.

Key concepts

The key concepts that underpin knowledge of techniques and processes are relatively few, and successful schools give careful attention to these and ensure that they are developed in a suitably wide range of applications and problem situations until they are well-integrated into pupils' knowledge. Table 2.1 represents a first attempt at identifying some of the fundamental concepts, understanding of which will have lasting value in solving problems with ICT and in learning the use of unfamiliar resources.

Processes

Processes are *multi-stage procedures* for achieving specified goals. For example, the process of developing a publication would, in the case of a desktop publishing package, involve a sequence of techniques such as:

* select the page to work on;
* create a number of frames;
* enter text into frames;
* choose text style;
* import images into frames;
* adjust size/position of frames.

The particular techniques and the sequence are not fully determined by the goal, and the user needs an understanding of both the goal and the tools available in order to make appropriate choices. Sometimes the choice made will not produce

Table 2.1 Fundamental concepts underlying ICT capability

Concept	Informal meaning
file	a unit of data which can be saved, loaded and printed
window	an area of the screen which can display part of a file
menu	a list of options which can be displayed and selected
text	a continuous string of characters, including formatting codes
object	something which can be selected, formatted, moved, resized, copied, deleted and transferred to other locations
presentation	a set of text and objects, animated suitably for communication in screen form
publication	a set of text and objects, positioned suitably for communication in printed form
database structure	a store of data which can be searched and selected information displayed
model	a representation of relationships amongst variables
spreadsheet	a grid each cell of which can contain a value or a formula
hypertext structure	a set of text and objects containing links which allow quick access to chosen options
procedure	a sequence of instructions which achieve a specified result
monitoring process	a system which records data automatically from sensors at intervals of time
message	a set of text and objects together with a destination and return address
web site	a hypertext structure which can be accessed remotely from any location

the desired effect, and a different technique will be tried. Reflection on this *mistake* will lead to learning which improves the user's ability to make an appropriate choice in the future.

Processes represent a significant part of the knowledge, understanding and skills described in the strands of the National Curriculum for ICT. It is the nature of these general processes that should be the basis for deciding which subjects might best incorporate pupils' work within the strands. They are often very complex and require a sound conceptual base in order to manage them effectively. Learning such processes requires a substantial degree of personal autonomy and active involvement on the part of the pupil. They are not associated purely with ICT, as they deal with the way in which ICT interacts with problem-solving situations in other disciplines or in the real world, rather than the technology itself. It is this aspect of ICT that distinguishes it from other subject disciplines – in its most significant aspects, it exists only in juxtaposition with other disciplines or real-world situations. That is not to say that ICT is not a real discipline: the lines of progression described by the National Curriculum are legitimate and meaningful. Rather it is to point out that progression in knowledge and understanding in ICT takes a form very different from progression in the other subjects of the curriculum, demanding both an authentic context and a far higher level of pupil autonomy and problem-solving skills than is usually the case in school. It is difficult to discuss the learning of such processes in isolation from the other higher order skills, knowledge and understanding involved in ICT capability: metacognitive skills and metacognitive knowledge.

Higher order skills and knowledge

Knowledge of processes and techniques is not sufficient for successful application of ICT to problem situations: the pupil must also choose to use that knowledge, to monitor the progress being made, and to evaluate the solution gained (Tanner and Jones 1994). The effective use of ICT demands such higher order skills as:

- recognising when the use of ICT might be appropriate or effective;
- planning how ICT resources, techniques and processes are to be used in a task;
- conjecturing, discussing and testing the strategies and data to be used;
- monitoring the progress of problem-solving activities;
- making and testing hypotheses;
- evaluating the outcomes of using ICT for a task;
- explaining and justifying the use of ICT in producing solutions to problems;
- reflecting on the leaning that might have occurred during the task.

These skills are relevant to all strands of the National Curriculum for ICT. We have seen that ICT also makes a particular contribution to the development of higher order skills in all areas of the curriculum by providing an interactive medium which is more supportive for many learners than other media they meet in the curriculum. These skills are to do with the selection, implementation, monitoring, control and evaluation of techniques and processes, and are meta-cognitive in nature.

Metacognition is a loose term that refers to the knowledge and control which individuals have of their own cognitive systems (Brown 1987). This dual nature is based on Flavell's commonly quoted definition:

> Metacognition refers to one's knowledge concerning one's own cognitive processes and products or anything relating to them, e.g. the learning-relevant properties of information or data. . . . Metacognition refers, amongst other things, to the active monitoring and consequent regulation and orchestration of these processes in relation to the cognitive objects on which they bear, usually in the service of some concrete goal or objective.
>
> (Flavell 1976: 232)

The concept thus includes both (a) the awareness that individuals have of their own knowledge of ICT techniques and processes, the opportunities and limitations offered by the possible use of those ICT techniques and processes, their beliefs about themselves as learners and the nature of ICT, and (b) their ability to regulate their own actions in the application of that knowledge.

The former aspect is *passive* in character and is characterised here as metacognitive knowledge or *knowing what you know*. It refers to the knowledge and beliefs that we have about our own cognitive resources in a situation, how well we are likely to perform in that situation, the ICT techniques and processes we might be able to use, and the nature of the situation itself (Flavell 1987: 22–3). Such self-knowledge, whether factual or not, is an important influence on behaviour and may be shaped by participation in day-to-day classroom practices.

Development of this aspect of ICT capability is significant for pupils' study skills, as they have to be able to make realistic assessments about what they can learn. Their ability to solve problems is also dependent on metacognitive knowledge, as 'problem solving calls for using efficiently what you know; if you don't have a sense of what you know, you may find it difficult to be an efficient problem solver' (Schoenfeld 1987: 190).

The issue is not always whether pupils know an ICT technique or process, it is often whether they *know that they know it* and are thus able to decide to use it. A further affective aspect of metacognitive knowledge is how pupils *feel* about using the technique or process: if they feel positive or confident about using an ICT process then they are more likely to choose to use it.

The second aspect of metacognition refers to the 'active monitoring and consequent regulation and orchestration' of one's thinking (Flavell 1976: 232) and is characterised here as a metacognitive skill. It has to do with 'when, why and how' pupils explore, plan, monitor, regulate and evaluate progress; and is influenced by pupils' metacognitive knowledge, including their attitudes and beliefs about themselves, and about ICT and learning with ICT.

Vygotsky (1962: 90) claims that 'consciousness and control appear only at a late stage in the development of a function, after it has been used and practised unconsciously and spontaneously'. This suggests that unconscious self-regulation should precede conscious self-regulation, and that teachers should thus operate in a coaching mode. A good coach guides the child's progress through a task by asking questions that focus their attention at critical points, but leaves the child believing that the plan was his or her own. The act of verbalising may then be associated with bringing the subconscious into the conscious and the consequent development of reflective awareness (Prawat 1989: 14). The significance of verbalisation in making processes explicitly available as objects of thought is confirmed by research. Several studies have included articulation by pupils as significant aspects of their approach (e.g. Tanner and Jones 1994 and 1999b).

We suggest, then, that teaching approaches focusing on the development of higher level skills and knowledge would emphasise:

- significant pupil autonomy in the selection of tools and resources;
- active participation by pupils in the process of planning and evaluating the use of ICT in problem situations;

- teacher intervention in the form of focusing questions to assist pupils in the formation of generalisations;
- the requirement that pupils articulate their thoughts about the opportunities and constraints offered by ICT techniques, processes and strategies which they have experienced (articulation might be verbal, written or via e-mail, but should be interactive);
- that teaching should develop pupils' enthusiasm and confidence about ICT;
- that pupils be given opportunities and encouragement to reflect formally on their ICT learning.

Teaching and learning ICT capability

In spite of the hopes of some of the early zealots, exposure to ICT is not in itself sufficient to ensure that learning occurs in either a curriculum subject or in ICT. There are already signs that, like television, ICT is becoming a familiar feature in children's lives and consequently is in danger of ceasing to be regarded as a serious medium for learning, and instead seen as a medium for fun (Robertson 1998). The lack of intellectual challenge found in mediocre lessons focused on little more than skills and techniques is likely to reinforce this trend.

Progression in ICT capability is facilitated through broadening and elaborating contexts and ICT environments, and using more sophisticated software in response to the demands of tasks. However, the increased use of sophisticated software *per se* does not constitute progression in ICT capability. This may constitute little more than the development of further computer-situated techniques. More sophisticated software should be used because the task demands it – not for its own sake. The aim is to broaden and elaborate contexts, and use more sophisticated software 'as a consequence of the increasing elaboration of curriculum contexts, not as an end in itself' (Birnbaum 1990: 91).

A pupil may find difficulties in some task or the problem situation itself, the use of the system or software, or the application of the software to the problem. The pupil must find, and overcome, difficulties for learning to occur. But if the IT interference factor is very large, the pupil will have little processing power left to use for the application of the software to the problem or to consider the issues arising in the problem domain (which may be another curriculum subject area). On the other hand, if there are only a few difficulties involved in either the use of the software or in its application to the problem situation, it is unlikely that ICT capability would be developed further by the lesson, although learning in the other subject may be successfully stimulated. The aim for teachers must be to maintain an appropriate balance between the factors according the objectives of the activity.

The development of ICT capability occurs in the interaction between social contexts, problem situations and ICT environments, as pupils engage actively and to some extent autonomously with problems in the pursuit of a designated goal. Clearly pedagogy is of the greatest significance (Kennewell 1997), but our ability to characterise the teacher's contribution to the learning process in the complex domain represented by ICT has often been limited by the lack of an adequate framework for analysis. The higher order knowledge and the skills demanded by the ICT National Curriculum do not sit comfortably with models of instruction based on behavioural objectives and individual cognition which pays no regard to context or situation.

Affordances and scaffolding

To analyse the development of ICT capability in the interaction between social contexts, problem situations and ICT environments we require a framework which takes into account the whole of the environment in which learning occurs. This includes the teacher, the other resources, the other learners, the cultural context, the prior knowledge of the individual, the opportunities offered by the technology, and the structural and constraining features of the problem to be addressed. The framework we use to analyse interactions in activity situations is based on a model of affordances, constraints and abilities developed by Greeno (1994), based on the work of Gibson (1977; 1986).

We use the term *affordances* to describe a potential for action, the capacity of an environment or object to enable pupils to achieve their goals within a particular problem situation. We assume that the pupils' contributions to an activity are not fixed but are dependent upon features of the environment and social context. Pupils' *abilities* are characterised by their potential to act within the particular environment. We thus view *learning* as a change in abilities (Greeno 1994; Kennewell *et al.* 2000).

The affordances of a particular environment include the opportunities presented to the pupil by the technology in support of a task, the social support for learning provided by the teacher or other pupils, and the contextual support provided by the setting in which the activity occurs. The affordances of the environment thus include intentional support in the form of the *scaffolding* (Bruner 1985), the *assisted performance* (Tharp and Gallimore 1988) or the *contingent support for learning* (Wood and Wood 1996) provided by the teacher and the other pupils or by the technology.

Although the metaphor of *scaffolding* has traditionally been used to refer to support provided by the intervention of an adult or a more competent peer in the learning process, in lessons involving the use of ICT this support may be provided by the technology itself. For example, when ICT is used to plot histograms and pie charts in a lesson on statistics, the affordances of the technology reduce the total cognitive load on the pupils by taking care of the mechanical aspects of the task, allowing them to focus on the conclusions that may be drawn from the data. There must of course be a *gap* to bridge between the pupils' abilities and the requirements of the problem situation if learning is to occur. This may be in the computer-intrinsic activity, i.e. using the spreadsheet to plot graphs, or in the task-intrinsic activity, i.e. making the link between the graph and the equation. The teacher may further reduce the gap by adding to the affordances of the environment, for example, by providing an information sheet to assist in the use of the software, by providing a clear demonstration on a big screen of the actions to be followed, by asking a series of structured leading questions, or by organising a class discussion of results.

For effective learning to occur, teachers will arrange the situation to meet the following conditions.

- On the basis of the students' current abilities, the affordances are insufficient for the learners to complete the set task.
- The teacher will then adjust the affordances of the learning environment to reduce the *gap* sufficiently for the students to be able to bridge it with effort. This may involve, for example, an explanation, the use of oral questions and analogies, structuring the task, an information sheet, a class discussion or brainstorm, or working in groups.
- Students' abilities change as a result of the experience (see Kennewell 2000 *et al.*).

We may analyse classroom situations of technological affordances, social affordances, problem contexts and pupils' abilities. This can help teachers to plan the combined teaching of ICT and other subjects. The teacher's role is to manipulate the contexts and affordances in relation to pupils' existing abilities in order to facilitate learning. If there is little or no gap between the abilities and affordances involved in the use or application of the software, but the use of the software reduces the gap between affordances and abilities to a manageable level in an activity drawn from a curriculum subject area, then learning in that subject is likely to be enhanced. However, progression in ICT is unlikely to occur. A manageable gap between affordances and abilities in areas of techniques and processes is likely to enhance learning in those areas. Furthermore, in order to encourage development in higher order skills and understanding, the affordances for planning, monitoring and evaluating the activity must not be too great.

This manipulation of affordances is central to the role of the teacher. It is also fundamental in management roles, too, and we will consider in the next two chapters how a school's senior management and the ICT co-ordinator can recognise and influence affordances for ICT activity.

We have found that there are predominant sources of learning for each component of ICT capability:

- Routines are developed primarily through practice.
- Techniques are learned primarily by copying a teacher or other pupils, or by trial and error.
- Concepts are developed through verbalisation of activities and by reflection on experience – particularly experience which is carefully structured by the teacher to engage the learner explicitly with examples and non-examples of the concept.
- Processes are developed by the supported combination of techniques into multistage procedures in a range of problem situations, with an increasing degree of personal autonomy and active involvement on the part of the pupil.
- Higher order knowledge and skills are developed in an environment which encourages exploration when opportunities are presented to decide which software to use and how to use it, to make plans, to monitor progress during

extended tasks, to evaluate and reflect on solutions and the contribution made by ICT. They are unlikely to be learned without significant teacher intervention and support.

Assessing ICT capability

The question of assessment in this area of the curriculum has been a vexed one since the inception of the National Curriculum, and we do not believe that there are straighforward procedures which will lead to a valid assessment of a pupil's capability.

Different assessment methods assess different aspects of ICT capability, and the ITCD project found that a combination was needed to provide a full picture:

- Tests were used to assess factual and conceptual knowledge.
- Observation during ongoing activities was used to assess techniques and routines.
- Observation during ongoing activities was used to assess the use of processes and higher order skills and understanding, but such observations were supplemented by systematically collected sets of work, showing development from draft to final version.
- Oral questioning was also used to assess the development of concepts and higher order skills and knowledge.

In order to gain a valid judgement of progress and provide timely feedback for pupils, it is important to integrate assessment with teaching and learning, rather than rely on the summative evaluation of pupils' work or on tests following a unit of study. It is not necessary for the experienced teacher to use a clipboard approach, in which every time a pupil successfully uses a technique a tick is entered on a chart. It should be possible to make judgements – and give feedback – naturally during the course of a lesson. A record can then be made after the lesson of a broad assessment of the class's progress, together with notes on particular pupils' attainments (or lack of them), which can be used in planning the next lesson.

The implementation across a school of a co-ordinated approach to ICT assessment will be discussed in Chapter 4, and we will consider some specific techniques in Chapter 8.

Success in developing pupils' ICT capability

The most successful schools in the ITCD project were clear about the nature of progression in ICT capability. Rather than teaching more and more techniques for their own sake, or requiring pupils to use more complex software, they provided tasks which increasingly required sensitivity to information requirements, sophisticated decision making, knowledge of available tools and accuracy in evaluation. Techniques were then taught at the stage where the task provided a suitable context. Extra practice in routines was provided if necessary to supplement the work in context.

Teachers were better able to develop pupils' ICT capability when they knew why they were using ICT in their teaching. For example, some teachers were aware that the use of a particular piece of software would demonstrate or explain aspects of a topic far more clearly than would a traditional lesson by exploiting the affordances of the technology to provide dynamic display. Others exploited the computer's capability for instantaneous re-calculation to allow an exploratory approach which would otherwise have been too time-consuming. They were then able to draw the attention of the class to the reasoning behind their approach.

The most successful teachers questioned the whole class or group prior to activities using ICT to clarify their expectations, focused pupils on what they were going to do and generated ideas on how they might go about it. They identified when it was helpful for pupils to plan their work first on paper so that they would have a clear view, for example, of the layout of a document or the structure of a database. In other situations, such as the writing of a book review, pupils were expected to use the computer immediately to draft ideas and then develop them on screen. Successful teachers made the reasons for making these choices explicit through questioning and discussion.

Where highly structured tasks were used to introduce particular techniques, staff ensured that pupils had the opportunity to use those techniques subsequently in more open tasks in which they could make decisions about the choice of techniques.

Furthermore, successful teachers recognised that an activity usually has more than one learning purpose. Where teachers had integrated ICT into their thinking about other subjects, they were able to combine the ICT and other subject issues in their discussion and questioning of the class or group.

As with any subject or activity, the teacher's role while pupils were working on tasks and at the end of a period of work was important in bringing about learning. Work on a computer screen has a more public nature to it than work on paper, and teachers moved systematically around the room monitoring what pupils were doing and intervening when requested or when they noticed pupils were pursuing an unfruitful or inefficient strategy. The most successful teachers drew the pupils' attention to the issues through focusing questions, rather than taking over the mouse or keyboard.

They were also aware that ICT resources would not always perform as expected. They had a very high degree of familiarity with the software being used by pupils and had considered the potential difficulties pupils might experience. In addition, they made contingency plans to ensure that pupils were able to pursue alternative tasks which contributed to their learning.

Successful teaching strategies used in schools included:

- whole-class teaching with a large screen;
- pupils working independently on structured tasks at different rates using help sheets;
- pupils working individually or in groups on extended projects involving planning, reporting and evaluating;

- manual tasks which represented the concepts involved in an aspect of ICT such as database structure or giving instructions in sequence.

Some specific principles for teaching ICT concepts are discussed in Chapter 7.

Whole-class briefings were successfully used to clarify the task, generate ideas and demonstrate techniques. Many teachers felt that they should minimise non-interactive periods for fear of losing the attention of pupils and holding back the more capable, but the use of a large screen often enabled the teacher to involve pupils for a worthwhile length of time in strategic thinking through whole-class questioning.

Computer rooms are generally set out differently from other classrooms and do not support the ways of organising a class that are familiar to experienced teachers. Transitions in lessons between pupil computer activity and teacher talk needed to be particularly carefully managed to ensure that pupils attended to key points. Some teachers successfully used a form of monitored instruction where the whole class was taken step-by-step through the techniques required for a task. This enabled the teacher to discuss with pupils the purpose of each step and gave them a feeling of whole-class collaboration. Where used successfully, the more capable pupils were involved in monitoring and helping others to ensure that all kept up with the instructions. It was usually less successful when pupils worked on their own from printed materials immediately after a short verbal briefing.

Another successful form of organisation was to provide a workshop environment for extended tasks once pupils were familiar with the important techniques. This approach is common in specialist ICT lessons at KS4, and successful secondary schools employed this strategy with some activities in KS3. It was also successful in primary schools where the teacher or classroom assistant was able to give the same attention to the group using ICT as to other groups in the classroom, rather than leaving the pupils on their own when using the computer.

In primary schools, the most successful methods included:

- a whole-class briefing on the context and activity;
- a detailed explanation to each group when its members are ready to work on the activity;
- a careful choice of pairs to work on the computer in turn;
- a review of key points with each group afterwards.

We develop these points further in Chapter 5.

Key issues

1   Progression in ICT is in three dimensions:

- development of concepts;
- the level of knowledge, skill and confidence applied to tasks; and
- the range and type of problems tackled.

2   As well as the strands of ICT capability, it is helpful to identify the routines, techniques, concepts, processes and higher order skills as components for planning and monitoring progress.
3   These components require a variety of conditions for their development, and higher order skills and concepts need supported exploration and reflection.
4   Assessment of ICT capability is an inexact process requiring holistic judgements against broad criteria.
5   Successful teaching for ICT capability comprises a variety of strategies that show sensitivity to how pupils learn in this field.

Points for reflection

- Consider an example of pupils' learning in ICT in some context. Which components were developed? How did the pupils learn? How were they stimulated and supported by the resources? By the teacher?
- How can teachers be stimulated to move from showing pupils how to do a particular task to creating an environment in which pupils can be inquisitive, willing to explore and able to take responsibility for their own learning?
- Identify the various assessment procedures for ICT in your school. Do they assess all components satisfactorily? What changes might be made, without making the task unmanageable?

3 The role of senior management
Driving the change

In this chapter we start to examine in detail the factors that influence the development of ICT capability. We suggest that, for it to use ICT effectively, a school must possess a culture that incorporates a strong belief that using ICT can help pupils to learn, increase the efficiency of the day-to-day activities within the school and generally improve the quality of the school's performance. Some schools already have such a culture, but they are in the minority. Most schools are still considering how they can come to terms with a rapidly changing, and expensive, technology. For these schools, there needs to be a major culture shift, and that, we believe, can be brought about only by clear leadership from the senior management.

An ICT culture

The culture of a school is difficult to describe, being a combination of the realisation of relationships, beliefs, attitudes and ideologies of all those that work in the establishment (Stoll and Fink 1996). School cultures clearly do exist and can be visualised through the norms and routines of the school day, the behaviour of the pupils, the range of academic and non-academic activities on offer and the ways in which the school relates to the community at large. Although clearly intangible, it is a very powerful force in determining the direction of a school. Some schools have a culture that is open to change: they are experimental in their approach, with the hope that new ideas will revitalise the learning experiences on offer. Others have a culture that favours a traditional approach, with an emphasis on the value of tried and tested techniques. Clearly there are positive and negative aspects to both of these cultural dimensions, but if a school is to move forward along with the changing nature of the world of work, it must be prepared to adopt a culture that prepares its pupils for change.

A school's culture is shaped by its history, and by the influences of the local education authority, the community and the teaching staff. The headteacher and the senior management play important roles in building a professional culture of teaching which is responsive to change (Hargreaves and Dawe 1990). These senior members of staff help to set the values for all, and attributes such as commitment and hard work can be made to filter through all aspects of school life.

The way in which ICT is used is becoming an important facet of school culture, with some schools seeing it as a key subculture that can empower pupils' learning and make radical changes to the way the school operates (Goodson and Mangan 1995). A subculture such as this can arise because of the interests of a group of staff. This group would recognise the value of using computers in lessons and regard ICT as a way of solving problems rather than causing them. It could be said that, if a school is to move forward with its use of ICT, such a subculture must be embedded in the structure of the school. This may be problematic if the traditional subcultures of the school are such that the introduction of ICT is seen as a new – and alien – force (Goodson *et al.* 1998). But what if a school does not have a subculture that promotes the use of ICT? Is it never going to have an all-pervading technological climate? The culture should be such that it supports the principles detailed in Chapter 1 and creates opportunities for pupils to build on their knowledge of basic skills to become critical and imaginative thinkers. Clearly, cultural changes are difficult and time-consuming, and may provoke considerable anxiety among all teaching staff (Schein 1997). A conscious decision has to be made to transform the culture of the school by challenging existing views concerning the nature of ICT. Such changes can be brought about as a result of an inspection report highlighting deficiencies in the use of ICT, or through the leadership of dynamic staff who are able to stick to their convictions and take others with them.

In the ITCD project, we noticed the extent of the impact which the headteacher could make. In one school that had developed its ICT culture over the last few years, the headteacher ensured that financial support was available to maintain and update the equipment on a rolling programme. She made a point of using ICT herself in her administration and in her occasional teaching. Staff were encouraged to attend courses to learn new ICT skills. Staff used ICT when they thought it would improve the lesson, e.g. by making it more interesting, providing differentiated learning, and by enabling pupils to draft and redraft written work. They looked upon ICT as a help and not something that needed to be done merely to satisfy National Curriculum requirements. They were beginning to see the use of computers as just one of the many teaching tools available to them.

Leadership

Even the most inspiring ICT co-ordinator is going to make little impact on a school without the support of the headteacher. Headteachers continue to be the powerful definers of the culture, ethos and organisation of their schools, and it is through working with small groups, or even individuals, within the school system that they are able to build the momentum and involve others in the process of change. Grace (1995) considers that educational leaders should be involved in the practice of reflective and critical thinking about the culture and organisation of their schools, and about the ways in which this culture may need to change. Imposing a new order is at best slow and cumbersome, and at worst impossible. Fullan and Hargreaves (1992) identify seven possible consequences when experienced teachers are subjected to imposed change. The teachers might:

- continue to work as before;
- form cliques, factions and enclaves;
- leave for another job;
- use the opportunity to gain promotion and develop a new teaching career;
- offer general resistance to or even sabotage the change;
- shift the balance of their lives to other things; or
- grasp the opportunity to implement the change.

Clearly there are plenty of opportunities for the imposition of change to lead to low morale, dissatisfaction and reduced commitment. The head needs to consider how it will affect individuals within the school, whose reactions might vary from fear of being unable to use the technology in front of pupils to a questioning of the value of using computers to help pupils to learn. The change must involve winning over the hearts and minds of the teachers to the extent that they feel in control and have ownership of the new order. In the ITCD project, we found that success in some primary schools was facilitated by the deputy-headteacher and other subject co-ordinators demonstrating effective personal use of ICT, and classroom organisation for pupils' use of ICT. Where senior staff are seen as lead teachers, it is important that they are positive about integrating ICT rather than relinquishing responsibility to the ICT co-ordinator.

In one of the secondary schools involved in the project, the headteacher took an enthusiastic interest in developing ICT in the curriculum and worked closely with the ICT co-ordinator to check the extent to which the agreed policy and schemes were being implemented in various departments. The headteacher recognised the need to pursue many other initiatives as well, and in order to sustain this level of support for ICT, he was planning to involve a new deputy increasingly in the monitoring process.

There are lessons to be learned from some of the changes imposed on schools in recent years and how they have altered school life. Some, such as the introduction of the National Curriculum, have made a substantial impact on the operation of schools and have met with little resistance (Grace 1995). Where initiatives have failed, they have generally done so because the curriculum developers have failed to win over the hearts and minds of the classroom teachers (Proctor 1987).

It is a bold step for a headteacher to introduce any change, but to ask all of the teaching staff to radically rethink the way they teach requires great courage. When the headteacher further considers that such a move could have detrimental consequences for the school's position in the *league tables* and a possible consequential drop in revenue to the school, it could result in a curriculum with ICT on the periphery. Teachers will use ICT because it is mentioned in their subject National Curriculum or because they have found a useful piece of revision software that will keep the pupils occupied for a long lesson. This kind of tinkering with ICT will not permit pupils to benefit from the significant number of learning opportunities opened up by using computers.

While there are differing viewpoints on educational leadership, most schools have adopted an approach that involves some type of collaborative management. In this way schools are able to maximise the skills, commitment and energy of their staff to create a 'potent and catalytic mix for successful change and development' (Whitaker 1993: 67). Adequate time and resources are essential ingredients for successful collaborative process, but so too is pressure. If there is no pressure to move, then there is a tendency to stick to the status quo. It is important to have deadlines and clear targets, as well as the support required to achieve them (Fullan 1992).

In the ITCD project we found that teacher collaboration through the formation of an ICT committee or advisory panel helped to promote an ICT culture. This group can play an important role in influencing teaching strategies throughout the school, and is in a position to monitor the implementation of ICT. The group should be made up of members who can represent the interests of each of the key areas. In secondary schools, membership usually includes a representative from each department or faculty and one or more members of the senior management team, as well as the ICT co-ordinator. In primary schools the group may be the whole staff or, in large schools, the task may be delegated to the head, the ICT co-ordinator and other key subject co-ordinators. Involving staff in this way helps to develop team spirit and a sense of ownership of the decisions made, and hence an increased acceptance of how ICT should be implemented in the school. However, heads need to be aware that some staff will see this process as time-consuming and, being an aspect of management, not part of their business (Yukl 1989).

Headteachers wishing to embed a positive ICT culture in the school must make their intentions clear to all through the processes that take place on a daily basis. This will manifest itself in a number of ways:

- How much attention does the headteacher give to the use of ICT in subject areas on a daily basis and how does she/he comment on what is observed?
- What financial resources are given to ICT and to what extent does the headteacher go out in search of additional funding?
- To what extent is the headteacher a role model in the use of ICT?
- How does the headteacher support staff development in ICT?
- Does the headteacher take into account a person's ICT capability when selecting and promoting staff?

Caldwell and Spinks (1992) suggest that the creation of a culture capable of promoting and sustaining excellence has a number of implications for school leaders:

- It is necessary to be able to describe and analyse the culture of the school.
- It is necessary to ensure consistency between the values and beliefs the school proclaims and the manifestation of the school's culture.
- We need to recognise that changing school culture takes time.
- It is helpful to be able to make links between the different developments in the school – seeing the larger picture.
- The capacity to cope with continual change needs to be built into the culture.

- Leadership must function at technical, human and educational levels as well as the cultural level.
- As there are few individuals able to fulfil all these requirements, empowering others is necessary for the development of the organisation. It is also desirable for the development and motivation of individuals.

Generating and maintaining an ICT policy

In order to clarify and disseminate the ideas represented in the culture of the school – the vision of the school leadership, and the actions expected of staff and pupils – most schools have written policy documents. Policies for ICT are an essential basis for

- effective design, organisation and management of opportunities for pupils to develop their ICT capability in a coherent and progressive manner;
- clear communication within a school, between neighbouring schools, between a school and its LEA, its local community, etc.

As ICT is something that every teacher will use, it is important to have a policy to hold together the ways in which ICT is involved in lessons throughout the school. And if this policy is going to influence practice, it is vital that all teachers share the values expressed within it and that they understand its implications. It follows that every teacher should have some involvement in the production and upkeep of the policy. In secondary schools, this is most likely to happen through departmental discussions or through representatives on the ICT management group. When the ICT policy is written by a single person, usually the ICT co-ordinator, other staff are unlikely to have ownership of the document and are unlikely to implement its principles into their work. Harris (1994) suggests that developing an ICT policy is a valuable exercise in its own right, as the least valuable type of policy is one that has been obtained from an external source such as the LEA, another school or a web site. While these may give indications as to layout and what to include, the lack of ownership makes the document almost worthless.

A policy should not be regarded as static and will need to be reviewed annually, as teachers' expertise grows. Pupils' ICT skills are changing rapidly through the use of computers at home and it is essential to give this due credit and to have a policy that supports their continued development.

The ITCD project found that a number of factors are likely to help frame the ICT policy, including the school's overall aims, policies and plans; the views of parents and community representatives; LEA policies and support provision; national policies and initiatives; research on effective teaching and learning; and developments in technology. Policies were more successful when seen as serving three purposes:

- setting out the aims and values for ICT which had been agreed by the staff and supported by the headteacher;

- making explicit the principles behind the effective learning and application of ICT;
- identifying other principles that the school needed to address, and which formed the basis of a development plan with specific targets.

BECTA (1998a) suggests that policy is created through a number of stages:

1 a statement of intent for teachers, governors and parents;
2 the identification of a rationale;
3 a curriculum audit of ICT usage;
4 the setting of goals.

1 *Statement of intent.* It is important that the aims and objectives of the policy are clear and have been understood by all the staff. It needs to be accepted as being practical, manageable and likely to lead to improvements both in pupils' performance and in the general attitude towards ICT. It is important that these goals are clearly communicated to governors and parents.

2 *Identification of a rationale.* There will always be members of staff who believe that ICT is the answer to most, if not all, curricular problems, although there are clearly times when using ICT is unnecessary or inappropriate. There will be others who think ICT can never contribute to their work. It is a valuable exercise for all those concerned to think about why they are using computers and what are the benefits to pupils.

3 *Curriculum audit.* The ICT co-ordinator needs to gain a clear picture of the ICT use across the school and must find out any mismatches in resources (TCT 1997). Smith (1995) describes a series of steps that teachers could use to get a full picture of what is going on in the school, fundamental to which is the process of finding out

- what software is used and for what purpose;
- the skills and attitudes of teachers and pupils towards ICT;
- the extent to which the ICT National Curriculum is covered;
- the hardware available and its use.

4 *Setting goals.* In this section the staff sets out where it wants to be in twelve months time. These statements will be linked to the targets set out in the school development plan. They will be centred around improving pupils' learning and will look at how

- ICT will be distributed across the curriculum;
- pupils' work will be assessed and how the assessment informs future teaching;
- the efficiency of ICT use can be maximised.

The contents of a policy are generally organised under some or all of the headings in Table 3.1. The process of producing a policy is valuable in itself as it gives the participants the opportunity for cross-fertilising ideas and developing a picture of

Table 3.1 Policy headings

- Background details, including the date of adoption
- The nature of ICT and ICT capability
- Aims
- Curriculum
- Administration
- Links to the scheme of work
- Pupils' experiences
- Access – entitlements, equal opportunities and ethical use
- Assessment, recording and reporting
- Roles, responsibilities and management structure
- Teaching and learning – styles and methods
- Hardware – purchase and maintenance
- Software – purchase and development
- Networking – internal and Internet service provider
- INSET
- Links to the school development plan
- Monitoring and review
- Funding
- Staffing – specialist teachers, technician
- Future planning

pupils' learning experiences in different subject areas. By regularly reviewing the policy the school can be assured that staff are making progress in terms of their ICT development and that ICT is kept at the forefront of the school's agenda.

Target setting

Target setting is a key activity for improving schools and it involves everyone in the school community from the LEA through to the pupils. Targets are not ends in themselves, but they provide a focus for planning changes and for monitoring progress towards personal or institutional goals. Targets that focus on outcomes, e.g. examination and test results, attendance, participation in extra-curricular activities, are usually clearer than those that focus on processes, e.g. policy implementation, teacher approaches and pupil activity. But clarity will be of no value unless the targets correspond to the real goals, and simple numeric measures may not represent fully what a school is seeking to achieve. In writing targets it is worth bearing in mind that the primary aim of the whole process is to help individual pupils perform to their best. It is important to be ambitious but realistic about the pace of change. In order to achieve their goals, schools may have to tackle habits and attitudes that are deeply ingrained in their culture, and they may take time and tenacity to accomplish.

Lawley (1999) has identified how the process of target setting can help to sharpen up issues that at first may seem nebulous. He suggests that targets should fulfil the five characteristics summarised by the SMART acronym: Specific, Measurable, Achievable, Realistic and Time-related. Targets should be devised to provide a common framework for all staff and to give a unity of purpose to the work of the school. Everyone can participate in the formulation of targets as well as sharing the responsibility for carrying them out. We suggest some specific ideas for use in target setting for ICT development at the end of this chapter.

The school development plan

The development plan represents specific activities which the school intends to carry out in order to implement its policy and achieve its targets. ICT will undoubtedly form a part in each school's development plan and will probably continue to do so as the technology improves and our knowledge of pupils' learning with computers grows. The purpose of the plan is to help the school to improve its use of ICT through reflection on existing practice and the development of new ideas.

Heinrich (1995) suggests that a good ICT development plan should contain:

- a statement of intent for teachers, governors and parents;
- a commitment to equal opportunities regarding both culture and gender;
- strategies for monitoring and assessment;
- specifications for selecting, funding and purchasing hardware;
- specifications for selecting, funding and purchasing software;
- a consideration of resource availability, access, safety and maintenance;
- plans for ongoing replacement and development of equipment;
- a curriculum map of proposed ICT usage including clear progression and continuity issues;
- consideration of training needs for teachers, support staff and technicians;
- procedures for the monitoring and review of the policy.

Figure 3.1 shows how one school has set out its long-term plan relating to ICT. Although some of the tasks given in Figure 3.1 do not meet the SMART requirements, they are valuable in giving direction to the school's senior management and in identifying priorities. More frequent medium-term planning can add the specific focus and detail once the broad goals are established.

Advice from the DfEE (1997b) on planning for improvement indicates that schools need to go through the process of finding out *where they are now* and identifying *where they wish to be* after a set time interval. Frequently, this process can be aided through discussions and comparisons with other schools of a similar nature, and with support from the LEA. A staged cyclical process is suggested that must be carefully planned and monitored for effectiveness. Such a process has been applied to the ICT situation in Figure 3.2. A key element of the development process is the drive needed to ensure that the cycle is completed effectively and regularly. This can be provided by a particularly enthusiastic ICT co-ordinator in a relatively small school, but the co-ordinator will need the support of the headteacher. The ITCD project found that in the most successful schools, the drive is maintained at the level of the headteacher or other member of the senior management. Furthermore, a reserve *driver* is needed in order to maintain momentum and direction if the usual one leaves.

PRIORITY: To develop a curriculum which meets the needs of all students aged 11–19
TARGET: To implement a whole school information environment
TIME SCALE: 1997–2002

SMT CO-ORDINATOR: Headteacher
TEAM MEMBERS: Head of IT, IT Working Party
GOV. COMMITTEE: Curriculum Committee

	TASKS		SUCCESS CRITERIA	PR C	OG P	RE S	SS L	INDICATORS/COMMENTS
(a)	To install a school network which will ultimately serve all departments.	(i)	Computers purchased, installed and fully operational.					
(b)	To incorporate IT into all schemes of work.	(ii)	Computers in maximum use.					
(c)	To implement a strategic approach to IT development within the school.	(iii)	IT working party meeting regularly and taking policy forward.					
(d)	To implement a programme of staff development to ensure that all staff develop IT skills.	(iv)	Staff skills improving.					
(e)	To monitor closely curriculum development arising from expenditure on IT.	(v)	Schemes of work and practice reflect increased use of IT.					
(f)	To monitor closely the use of IT within the school in order to ensure that resources are deployed efficiently.	(vi)	IT used across departments as tool to raise standards of achievement.					
(g)	To produce a written whole-school IT policy document.	(vii)	Pupils of all ages develop and use appropriate IT skills.					
(h)	To provide appropriate and adequate technical support.	(viii)	Technician's log indicates effective use of time and significant support within curriculum. Teachers' and pupils' time not wasted by technical matters.					
	RESOURCE IMPLICATIONS		INSET REQUIREMENTS					
(a)	Five-year commitment to lease (£30,000 per annum).	(i)	Training in specific skills for large number of staff.					
(b)	Appointment of IT technician.	(ii)	Advice/support for staff in classroom.					
(c)	Purchase of software and peripherals.	(iii)	Network management training.					

C = COMPLETED   P = PROGRESS ACCORDING TO PLAN   S = SLOW PROGRESS   L = LITTLE OR NONE

Figure 3.1 An example of a page from a school development plan

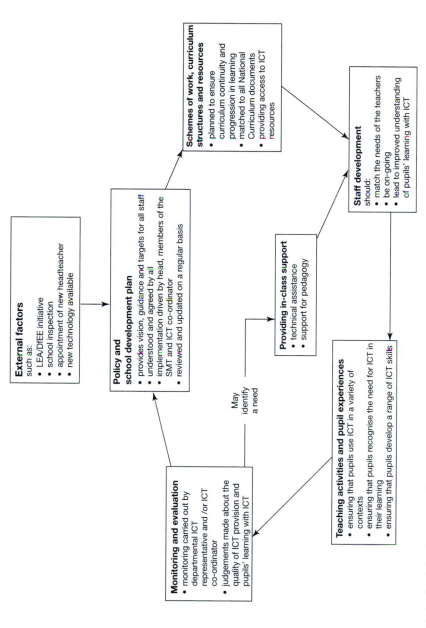

External factors
such as:
- LEA/DfEE initiative
- school inspection
- appointment of new headteacher
- new technology available

Policy and school development plan
- provides vision, guidance and targets for all staff
- understood and agreed by all
- implementation driven by head, members of the SMT and ICT co-ordinator
- reviewed and updated on a regular basis

Schemes of work, curriculum structures and resources
- planned to ensure curriculum continuity and progression in learning
- matched to all National Curriculum documents
- providing access to ICT resources

Staff development
should:
- match the needs of the teachers
- be on-going
- lead to improved understanding of pupils' learning with ICT

Providing in-class support
- technical assistance
- support for pedagogy

Monitoring and evaluation
- monitoring carried out by departmental ICT representative and/or ICT co-ordinator
- judgements made about the quality of ICT provision and pupils' learning with ICT

Teaching activities and pupil experiences
- ensuring that pupils use ICT in a variety of contexts
- ensuring that pupils recognise the need for ICT in their learning
- ensuring that pupils develop a range of ICT skills

May identify a need

Figure 3.2 A school development cycle

Achieving and sustaining ICT capability

Clearly, an ICT policy and the inclusion of ICT in the school development plan will not on their own bring about the desired change in teachers' perspectives. For many schools the process of becoming ICT capable requires a root and branch change, where teachers' thinking is challenged and which, as we suggest in Chapter 6, may involve more than just the use of ICT. Teachers frequently go through a period of uncertainty when confronted with something new. Whitaker (1993) points out that managers need to be sensitive to three particular clusters of feelings that teachers may experience when confronted with change:

1   *Loss of*

   • firmly held beliefs and ideas;
   • established patterns and behaviours;
   • comfortable habits;
   • confidence and self-esteem.

2   *Anxiety about*

   • required levels of understanding;
   • new skills;
   • what the future will be like;
   • being able to cope;
   • being seen as different.

3   *Struggle to*

   • survive intact;
   • acquire new competence;
   • gain respect and recognition.

A key element in successfully achieving and maintaining an ICT culture is the establishment of a cycle of development (see Figure 3.2) where policy and whole-school planning are put into practice through integrated schemes of work. Here teachers recognise the importance of undergoing certain types of training, depending on their needs, and understand the importance of reflecting on the effectiveness of their use of ICT in lessons. The challenge for managers is to create conditions which will help individuals and teams to achieve their goals and the overall goals of the school, recognising that perfection is beyond reach and that what matters are the significant events that are accomplished on the way.

The ICT co-ordinator plays a significant part in ensuring that the development process is maintained, but he or she will need the support of the headteacher or a member of the senior management in secondary schools. These individuals must drive the change process forward and ensure that it does not lose momentum by keeping ICT on the agenda of key school committees and by their sheer energy and enthusiasm for the subject.

In the ITCD project we found that in successful schools, policies and schemes of work were reviewed annually and developed in response to new technologies, educational initiatives, inspection findings and internal evaluation. It was recognised that not only could policy changes lead to improvements in practice, but that often policy needed to be developed to reflect and disseminate successful practice that had been implemented and evaluated informally.

Monitoring progress

Senior management in the most successful schools had a broad view of the extent and quantity of ICT use, but systematic information on pupils' progress, their range of experiences and frequency of ICT use was rarely available. It is dangerous to assume that teachers will invariably follow the scheme of work for ICT, and in the successful schools the ICT co-ordinator would keep a close eye on what was happening in subject departments.

Improving both quantity and quality is a daunting task and needs to be thought of in terms of both short- and long-term goals. For schools embarking on a review of their policy, the normal starting-point is the auditing of current teaching and learning activities involving ICT. It is important to identify a baseline for development through an audit process for ICT and to monitor progress towards the goals or targets set.

The ITCD project found that partial auditing had been carried out in many schools. Most headteachers tended to assume that teachers and their pupils followed the scheme of work. Most ICT co-ordinators were aware of gaps in implementation and barriers to progression, and in the more successful schools they were able to work with the headteacher or deputy-head to plan how to overcome the deficiencies.

The headteacher or deputy-head played a key role in monitoring the inclusion of ICT in schemes of work for other subjects and in the actual teaching of those subjects. In successful whole-school approaches, senior managers were able to convey to teachers their accountability for ICT in the curriculum in a way which conveyed support rather than threat. In large schools, a clear management structure (covering the roles of the headteacher, other senior managers, the ICT co-ordinator, other curriculum managers and external support) for this process of policy implementation and monitoring was particularly helpful.

We found in the most successful schools that senior managers were not concerned merely with the quantity of resources and opportunities for pupils to use them: they were concerned primarily with evaluating the quality of the teaching and learning of ICT. Following on from this, they considered whether the schemes of work were coherent and complete, whether the staff had sufficient knowledge of teaching ICT and whether the resources were adequate to support the teaching required.

In some successful schools there was an expectation that policies would be reviewed annually by the relevant co-ordinator. The advent of new technology and initiatives such as the NGfL (DfEE 1997a) were perceived as the main reasons why changes were needed, but the increasing experience of pupils at home and at previous schools were also bringing about change in policy. Other successful schools at primary and secondary levels were reviewing their ICT policy as part of their whole-school focus on teaching and learning. This would enable them to consider the co-ordinated development of higher order skills by planning literacy, numeracy and ICT capability together (CCW 1992).

Successful development of ICT capability is unlikely to result from coercion. Pupils and teachers who are forced to do something which does not meet their needs will produce poor results. But once the proposed change is matched to teachers' goals, there is much value in being specific about targets. Clearly, each school must set its own targets which reflect the starting-point and the needs of the school. The ITCD project produced a set of – what we have called – *success indicators*. Table 3.2 shows this set of statements, which we feel will help schools determine their baseline in ICT capability and set targets for development from whatever point they are starting.

Although written as statements, they should not be seen as items in a list to be ticked off. They represent qualitative and quantitative variables by which those concerned with monitoring progress can track changes over a period of time.

Key issues

1   The role of the headteacher and the senior management team is central in the establishment of an ICT culture.
2   It is important to formulate policy, establish goals, set targets and plan activities to achieve the goals collaboratively rather than by direction from the top.
3   As well as planning specifically for developing ICT capability, schools should consider how ICT capability contributes to all aspects of school improvement.
4   ICT capability development is not a once-and-for-all initiative. Progress should be monitored and goals reviewed regularly.

Points for reflection

* How was policy developed in your school? Has it changed to reflect current developments and thinking about ICT? Has it influenced the school development plan?
* Do you set specific targets in relation to ICT? How far in the future should you look when technology is changing so rapidly?
* To what extent does senior management drive ICT forward in your school? To what extent does management influence day-to-day practice?
* Do you have plans for staff development in ICT beyond the National Opportunity Fund (NOF) programme?

Table 3.2 Success indicators

Policy and schemes of work
- There is a written policy for ICT which includes, among other matters, the school's aims and values in respect of ICT in the curriculum
- All staff know and support the principles embodied in the policy
- The headteacher, senior management and governing body are explicit in their support for the policy
- Schemes of work for ICT and in other subjects set out programmes of teaching and learning activities which provide for progression in skill development and continuity of skill application

Planning, monitoring and review
- There is a development plan for ICT, which includes targets for developing pupils' ICT capability, together with the staffing, resource provision–distribution–management, lesson scheduling and staff development required
- Funding is allocated to implement the plan
- Systems are in place for monitoring the implementation of the plan, for evaluating its effectiveness and for reviewing the policy, schemes of work and development plan accordingly

Role of the ICT co-ordinator
- A realistic set of tasks is specified for the role of ICT co-ordinator
- The ICT co-ordinator provides an effective model of teaching and is familiar with the teaching style of other staff
- The ICT co-ordinator has senior status within the school together with the explicit support of the headteacher and other senior managers
- An adequate amount of time and staff (including technical support) are made available to the ICT co-ordinator

Staff skills in ICT and in developing ICT capability
- All teachers have an agreed base level of personal ICT capability and confidence in helping pupils use their ICT capability for at least one activity in their teaching
- Support in the classroom is available for staff who are building their knowledge and confidence
- Agreed targets are set for staff reaching higher levels of personal capability and using a wider range of ICT activities effectively in their teaching
- All teachers believe that they should help develop pupils' key skills and are incorporating recommended approaches into their teaching

Coherence of the curriculum
- Schemes of work, for ICT and for other subjects, show planned progression in new skills and continuity in opportunities to apply these skills in the curriculum
- Liaison activities between primary and secondary schools are designed to promote continuity of learning across phase transition

Expectations, opportunities and access for pupils
- All pupils have planned opportunities to develop and apply their ICT capability
- Pupils are expected to employ higher order skills as well as ICT techniques in pursuing worthwhile tasks in the curriculum
- Pupils are given opportunities to develop and consolidate their ICT capability in school at times outside their normal lessons

continued

Table 3.2 continued

Pupils' approach to learning ICT	Assessment and feedback
• Pupils are keen to develop their capability and value the teaching they receive • Pupils are prepared to take the initiative in applying ICT to relevant tasks • Pupils are motivated to persevere with challenging tasks	• Procedures are in place for staff involved in developing pupils' ICT capability to assess pupils' progress against statutory levels or expectations for their age • Teachers use their knowledge of national expectations in feeding back regularly to pupils on their progress and in setting expectations of improvement in their work

Pupils' ICT attainment
- A rising percentage of pupils are attaining the level of ICT capability expected for their age
- A rising percentage of pupils are attaining a level of ICT capability above that expected for their age
- In secondary schools, a rising percentage of pupils are gaining a recognised qualification in ICT

4 Co-ordinating ICT

Linking policy and practice

We continue the exploration of a school's ICT capability by focusing on a role which is particularly important in generating the right attitudes and practices concerning ICT in the school. In setting up procedures for co-ordination, head-teachers will need to consider a number of related issues, and we examine the main ones in the course of this chapter. Senior management have little direct impact on the day-to-day activities of teachers and pupils; it is middle managers who play a vital role in converting the vision and drive of senior management into effective teaching and learning environments. As a middle-level role, ICT co-ordination still does not impact directly on pupils' learning, but the way in which the staff responsible effect the vital two-way links between senior management, subject leaders and class/subject teachers (see Figure 4.1) has the potential to make a great deal of difference to pupils' attainment (Harrison 1998).

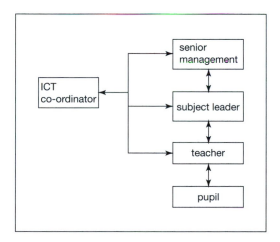

Figure 4.1 Linking role of ICT co-ordinator

What we mean by co-ordinating ICT

The role is a unique one in both primary and secondary schools. ICT has a different range of tasks and responsibilities from any other subject leadership role. In the

ITCD project, we found that in primary schools the most frequent aspects of the role were staff training, co-ordinating the teaching of ICT and classroom support for colleagues. This contrasts with science co-ordinators: Bell (1992) found only a small minority of practitioners who perceived these aspects to be part of their role. In secondary schools, the cross-curricular role of the ICT co-ordinator is necessarily very different from that of a head of department with responsibility for a team of specialist subject teachers. We found much commonality in the roles of ICT co-ordinators across the phases, however, and we shall deal with both differences and similarities in this chapter.

When we consider the wide variations in schools' attempts to implement the statutory requirements of the National Curriculum for ICT, it is perhaps surprising that there is one aspect of strategy that has been adopted almost universally: nearly every school has an ICT co-ordinator (DfEE 1998a). Although this role was already established in many schools prior to the National Curriculum, it was seen mainly as a source of advice concerning the use of ICT resources. A definite impetus towards the focus on ICT capability was provided by the non-statutory guidance on implementing ICT in the National Curriculum (NCC 1990; see also CCW 1990). This was reinforced by the requirement of Ofsted, the schools' inspection body for England, and of the equivalent organisation for Wales (Ofsted 1995a; OHMCI 1996) to report both on the teaching of ICT and on the application of ICT in the curriculum. Clearly, the headteacher was perceived to require a member of staff who could take responsibility for the policy, schemes of work and assessment in this aspect of the curriculum.

The non-statutory guidance, furthermore, suggested that co-ordinating ICT might involve a number of staff. In a small primary school, ICT may be just one of many responsibilities assumed by the headteacher. In larger schools, some aspects would be the responsibility of the headteacher or senior managers, while others would be taken on by another teacher or teachers. Our research has found, however, that in most primary and secondary schools there is one person, clearly identified as the ICT co-ordinator, who is expected to deal with all matters concerning ICT – in the National Curriculum, and as a resource for learning and teaching, and for other aspects of teachers' professional activity.

One of the most important factors affecting their work is the nature of the assistance the headteacher and class teachers expect this person to provide (Webb 1994). The non-statutory guidance for England sets out separate lists of respon-sibilities for ICT co-ordinators in primary and secondary schools, though under the same headings:

- co-ordination (of policy, schemes of work and assessment);
- resources (purchasing, organisation and maintenance);
- staff development and support (advice, INSET, dissemination of information);
- monitoring and review (of policy implementation, of resource provision, of teaching practices, of assessment practices);
- external liaison (personal updating, advisory services, other schools).

More specifically, the non-statutory guidance for Wales (CCW 1990) identified the following co-ordinating tasks as necessary for effective ICT provision:

* the integration of ICT into schemes of work and learning activities across subjects (in secondary schools) and years/key stages;
* the provision of appropriate support and INSET for staff;
* monitoring and recording pupils' experiences of using ICT;
* assessment of ICT capability and the moderation of those assessments;
* the provision and deployment of ICT resources;
* the provision of technical support (internal or external);
* liaison with parents and the local community;
* communication and collaboration with other schools;
* whole-school curriculum developments related to the use and application of ICT;
* the processes of monitoring and reviewing the implementation of the school's ICT policy.

However, Webb (1994) has pointed out that primary co-ordinators in general feel that there is a large discrepancy between the rhetoric surrounding the role and the reality of what they are able to achieve. The list of tasks looks a daunting one if each item is considered separately. They naturally overlap in practice, however, and should not be seen as a series of distinct jobs to be worked through one-by-one over a particular period of time. Instead, the list may be seen as an aide-memoire to co-ordinators and senior management for planning and monitoring purposes.

The qualities and tasks required of co-ordinators

The way in which co-ordinators approach their tasks is important if the work is to be effective. The non-statutory guidance (CCW 1990) suggested that ICT co-ordinators should:

* possess a broad vision of the potential of ICT and a good grasp of whole-curriculum issues;
* have credibility as successful classroom practitioners;
* be able to work productively and sensitively with a variety of people, and to lead/manage teams effectively;
* exhibit a positive and supportive attitude to colleagues;
* be well organised in their approach to tasks.

These qualities are very similar to those identified by Bell (1992) for the co-ordinator of science. The non-statutory guidance (CCW 1990) was also clear that 'the possession of technical skills is less important to ICT co-ordinating roles than being a good ICT practitioner and having a good understanding of curriculum issues together with appropriate interpersonal skills' (CCW 1990: C7). The interpersonal skills are detailed further by Harrison (1998), who clearly expects to find exceptional qualities in the successful ICT post-holder.

Prior to the National Curriculum, schools had been encouraged to use ICT as a medium for teaching and learning. A number of central and local government schemes had been devised to promote this idea, some involving the provision of equipment. As a result, many primary schools had on their staff an individual enthusiast for ICT and had given this teacher some responsibility for developing this aspect of the curriculum. Most secondary schools had a head of computing who had responsibility for computer studies/science and had tended to assume responsibility for ICT resources, which were largely gathered in computer rooms.

In most schools, then, there was a single person with some combination of responsibility, knowledge and interest in ICT, and it was natural to give him or her responsibility for the co-ordination of ICT as a subject area to be taught, as well as the co-ordination of ICT as a resource for learning. Indeed, the two roles were not distinguished in the non-statutory guidance, despite the suggestion that more than one teacher could be involved. There is a high degree of overlap in the co-ordination of ICT teaching and ICT application, particularly if ICT is taught (or partially taught) across the curriculum as was envisaged by the non-statutory guidance. Both roles are likely to involve collaborative curriculum planning, staff development, monitoring and evaluation.

The role that may be separated in many secondary schools, particularly the larger ones, is the responsibility for examination courses in ICT. As well as reducing the burden on the co-ordinator, separating off the major specialist subject responsibility should make clearer to other staff the school-wide nature of the role of the co-ordinator. Indeed, some secondary headteachers, when seeking a suitable ICT co-ordinator, have rejected the head of computing and appointed a teacher with less technical knowledge but better interpersonal skills.

Most secondary ICT co-ordinators are now expected to carry out the following major tasks:

- resource allocation;
- system maintenance;
- co-ordination and monitoring of ICT usage across the National Curriculum;
- co-ordination of assessment of ICT capability;
- staff training;
- classroom support for staff (Kennewell and Selwood 1997).

Furthermore, their task involves working with senior managers and subject teachers in guiding and planning developments in resource acquisition, promoting effective use of ICT across the curriculum and exploiting new technological developments (NCET 1998). The ITCD project also found that liaison with primaries was part of most ICT co-ordinators' role. Most secondary co-ordinators were also responsible for specialist teaching of examination courses.

How demanding are these tasks? In a 1995 survey, cross-curricular co-ordination was most frequently rated one of the two most difficult tasks faced by respondents

(Kennewell and Selwood 1997). This survey found that the size of the school also affects the nature of the ICT co-ordinator's role and the difficulties they face. A larger school means less contact with individual teachers and more need for contact at departmental level – not necessarily with the head of department. A larger school also usually means a greater focus on strategic resource issues and less contact with minor technical problems – they can afford a technician to deal with these.

ICT co-ordinators' comments in the Kennewell and Selwood survey (1997) make it clear that it is not the *nature* of the tasks that makes them difficult, but their sheer *number*. They do not see any one task as particularly difficult, but the fact that one person is often expected to do all of them, as well as being a specialist teacher either of ICT or another subject, poses a challenge. They have inadequate non-contact time, often no technical support, and frequently encounter a lack of understanding of the issues on the part of senior management.

Perceptions of the status of the co-ordinator

Much is thus expected of ICT co-ordinators, yet generally they feel that they lack the status warranted by their whole-school responsibilities. Despite the CCW's (1990) argument that the ICT co-ordinator should be a member of the senior management team, studies consistently report a lack of status being attached to this role (Owen 1992; Yeomans *et al.* 1995; Kennewell and Selwood 1997). They are usually appointed at the same level as the head of a small department, yet they have a very different and much bigger role. Kennewell and Selwood (1997) report that few of those who carry out the usual role of a head of department find this aspect as difficult as they did the whole-school responsibilities. Furthermore, they feel that senior management does not understand the nature of ICT capability, its place in the curriculum, or the demands that its co-ordination makes on the post-holder. In the more successful secondary schools identified in the ITCD project, however, the co-ordinators did feel that the headteacher accorded them a status at least as high as that of head of department, although other teachers did not always see them as having such high status. A similar pattern was found in primary schools, but with co-ordinators feeling that other staff viewed their status as equivalent to that of other subject co-ordinators.

The responsibilities of primary ICT co-ordinators have been less extensively studied. Although they have similar titles to those of secondary co-ordinators, they are clearly of a different nature and there is a different balance of demands on their time.

Cooke (1998) finds that a large proportion of the job entails solving technical problems, yet less than half of the primary ICT co-ordinators feel confident in these trouble-shooting activities themselves. They have received no formal training on this aspect of their work. Furthermore the vast majority have no non-contact time in which to carry out their tasks. The CCW (1990) suggests that primary schools should budget for external technical support.

The role of co-ordinator does not involve direct teaching of pupils. In small secondary schools with specialist lessons, however, a co-ordinator may actually teach ICT to every pupil personally; at the other extreme, the co-ordinator may have no teaching timetable at all in a large school, where ICT teaching is integrated into the rest of the curriculum. Primary school co-ordinators normally carry out the full role of class teacher, and possibly other roles as well, but in larger schools they may *float* so as to provide support for other teachers and some specialist teaching for pupils. In all schools, however, it is important for the ICT co-ordinator to provide a good model both of classroom organisation for ICT and of a range of teaching methods appropriate to the development of pupils' ICT capability. The ITCD project found that the co-ordinator's style had an informal influence over other staff and that it is possible to formalise this dissemination of good practice in teaching ICT.

Most primary ICT co-ordinators were expected to co-ordinate teaching and assessment, carry out staff training, provide classroom support, and allocate resources. A smaller number, but still a majority, were expected to co-ordinate assessment and to maintain resources. Very few had liaison with secondary schools specified as part of their role.

Subject co-ordination is not necessarily a senior role. Indeed, Harrison (1998) highlights research which finds 90 per cent of primary school teachers have *at least* one co-ordination role. Clearly, the amount that can be achieved by a multi-subject co-ordinator is likely to be limited. Harrison suggests that if the role is taken on by a relatively inexperienced teacher, then only some of the tasks may be delegated to the co-ordinator initially, with others being carried out by the senior management. The role could then grow with the experience of the co-ordinator. There is a danger, however, that this will reinforce the image of the ICT co-ordinator as a technical, rather than pedagogical, expert.

Recently qualified teachers often have greater personal ICT capability and may be asked to take responsibility quite early in their careers. Indeed, the fresh view of matters which this may bring can be helpful. In one of the ITCD project primary schools, the ICT co-ordinator was in his second year of teaching. He had identified a number of staff, at different levels of expertise, who were receptive to developing their ICT work, and was initially focusing his support on these staff. He recognised that the pupils taught by other teachers would have less well-developed ICT capability, however, and the next target would be to help all staff achieve a basic level of personal ICT capability, and to incorporate a limited range of ICT-based activities into their classroom work.

However, it is not easy for a relatively junior ICT co-ordinator to convey to other staff that they should have higher expectations for pupils' work. Although some co-ordinators were bringing about higher standards of work from pupils, this was achieved by taking over the teaching of ICT rather than influencing the ICT-related endeavours of the other staff. There was some success where the ICT co-ordinator discussed the assessment of ICT capability in the context of comparing work their children had done with material designed to exemplify particular levels, so that the other teachers could appreciate for themselves the difference between what their children were doing and what was expected nationally for the age-group concerned.

It is also clear that ICT co-ordinators see ever-more powerful and easy-to-use computer systems coming on to the market, but are often expected to keep old and idiosyncratic equipment running rather than to update their knowledge of new resources. Many schools now have a variety of 'makes' of computer, some with different operating systems, and ICT co-ordinators are under pressure to train other staff on unfamiliar computer systems while attempting to update their own knowledge. There is still a degree of *fire-fighting* in the nature of the support for ICT in schools, and this may inhibit ICT co-ordinators from conceptualising the place of ICT either as an element of the curriculum in its own right or as a means of improving teaching and learning generally. Keeping equipment running from day to day is seen as a necessity, whereas curriculum matters are less pressing.

The ITCD project found that success in whole-school co-ordination of ICT often did rely primarily on the characteristics of the ICT co-ordinator. Typically, an effective co-ordinator has an assertive yet approachable personal style, an ability to understand how other staff think and teach, and a teaching style that seems to provide a good model of how to manage an ICT-based classroom. These characteristics were seen by headteachers as more important than technical knowledge.

It was not essential for the ICT co-ordinator's interpersonal skills to be exceptional, however, and in any case these skills alone may be effective only in a relatively small school with a stable staff. Some schools had developed successful co-ordination through careful thinking about structures and procedures, with strong support from senior management which enhanced the status of the ICT co-ordinator.

This was particularly important in large secondary schools, where the teaching–learning culture was generally heavily based on subject disciplines and loyalties (see Chapter 6).

In primary schools, similar issues of status were found to arise, and success is more likely to be gained when the ICT co-ordinator can influence numeracy and literacy co-ordinators as well as supporting class teachers directly.

Models of curriculum organisation for ICT in secondary schools

In secondary schools, the role of the ICT co-ordinator depends on the way in which the teaching of ICT is organised in the curriculum. Models of delivery for ICT in secondary schools may be characterised in terms of being either *cross-curricular* or *discrete*. Neither of these are standard approaches, however. A cross-curricular model may be an *integrated* one, with ICT adopted by other subjects as appropriate to their schemes of work, or a *hosted* model, where ICT is added as a scheduled sequence of lessons within the timetable for another subject. A discrete course may be planned in terms of competences, study skills, topics, or subject demands as the basis. ICT may be scheduled as a brief intensive input, often at the start of KS3 (the *kick-start* approach), in regular modules throughout that Key Stage, or a regular lesson throughout each year. The regular lessons may provide the whole of the planned ICT provision (the *centralised* approach) or merely a basic preparation for co-ordinated application throughout the curriculum (the *core skills* approach) (NCET 1995 and 1996; Smith 1991).

A DfEE survey (1998a) found that few schools now have fully cross-curricular models for Year 7, but around 30 per cent use this approach in Years 8–11. The ITCD project found that the most common reason schools give for the discrete lessons in Year 7 is that their intake from different primary schools has received very different levels of ICT teaching and that they feel that all pupils should have a standard ICT skills' course regardless of previous experience. An inadequate understanding of relevant ICT concepts among teachers of other subjects (Selwood and Jenkinson 1995) may be the reason why schools with a high level of curriculum integration presented the greatest challenge to effective co-ordination. Policies of permeating ICT throughout the curriculum pose particular difficulties in ensuring that pupils develop ICT concepts and skills, and in assessing their developing capability.

There are advantages and disadvantages to each model, of course (NCET 1996). From the inception of the National Curriculum, an integrated cross-curricular model was seen as the ideal: 'Given the inherently cross-curricular nature of IT, it is not intended that IT should be regarded as another subject' (CCW 1990: A3).

It is clear from our own analysis of ICT capability in Chapter 2 why this model was advocated. However, headteachers, co-ordinators and teachers in schools that have attempted to implement a fully integrated model have met with con-siderable difficulty in realising the intended aims. As Chapter 8 shows, large numbers of pupils experience the application of ICT in only a very small number of subjects, and a significant minority of pupils do not encounter ICT at all unless discrete lessons are scheduled. Headteachers are thus faced with a major challenge to the entitlement of pupils which they set out in policy documents, and school inspections have revealed that 'Cross-curricular delivery of ICT works only when subject teachers are also confident with ICT, pupils' progress is monitored and structures are in place for motivating and effectively co-ordinating delivery' (Ofsted 1995b: 3).

In the face of such reaction, it is not surprising that the ITCD project found that many schools have abandoned their ambitious initiatives and returned to a pattern for teaching ICT which is similar to the favoured approach for traditional subjects. Many schools adopted the discrete approach at the inception of the National Curriculum and have maintained that approach ever since, often because the ICT co-ordinator wished to ensure that all pupils were taught by specialists. However, Ofsted also notes: 'Where ICT is taught as a separate course, coverage of the programme of study is more rigorous; but often there are insufficient opportunities to apply the ICT skills so acquired to work in other subjects' (Goldstein 1997).

As discrete delivery increases, such comments arise with increasing frequency. The existence of discrete lessons elsewhere on the timetable seems to teachers of other subjects to remove much of the rationale for including ICT in their own lessons. Although this reaction is partly a reflection of those teachers' view of ICT as a discrete activity in their subject in any case, it still means that pupils' experiences of some aspects of ICT in the curriculum can be in a single context or even without a meaningful context at all. Furthermore, ICT co-ordinators are given only limited curriculum time for discrete lessons, with the result that the lessons are either brief or infrequent. Both alternatives are seen as unsatisfactory for effective progression.

Secondary headteachers are thus grappling with a fundamental curriculum dilemma, and the role of the co-ordinator is vital in resolving it. An approach based on specialist teaching and subject application requires sensitive encouragement, thoughtful scheduling and systematic monitoring of the opportunities for pupils to use their ICT capability across the curriculum; an approach based on cross-curricular integration requires collaboration with subject departments to devise schemes of work to include teaching opportunities and subsequent application opportunities, and to provide staff development programmes and classroom support for teachers charged with teaching aspects of ICT.

Models of curriculum organisation for ICT in primary schools

The primary sector does not experience the same curriculum scheduling issues because a class teacher has the same pupils for most of the time. However, primary headteachers often face similar dilemmas to those faced by secondary headteachers, for many primary teachers find it difficult to incorporate ICT into their teaching, either as an aid to learning other subjects or as a focus of study itself. DfEE statistics (1998a) indicate that the majority of schools combine the two approaches, with very few teaching ICT only as a separate subject.

A good scheme of work and the support of an effective ICT co-ordinator can together help considerably in overcoming the difficulties and enabling class teachers to see how to structure the ICT learning of their pupils and how ICT can aid learning of other things. But there are also various alternatives to the class-teacher-only model of organisation:

- The co-ordinator (or another teacher with confidence in ICT teaching) is freed from his or her own class at certain times in order to work in the classroom with a less confident colleague. She does not take over the teaching completely, but provides a model which the class teacher can gradually incorporate into his or her own teaching.
- A variation on the above is for the ICT-confident teacher to take one group of pupils separately from the rest of the class, either in the classroom or in a resource area with a cluster of computers. While this enables the ICT-confident teacher to give a lot of attention to individual pupils, each group of pupils will gain access to the ICT teaching very infrequently, and it does not help class teachers to develop their ICT teaching expertise.
- The ICT-confident teacher swaps classes with each teacher in turn at certain times, and takes the whole of the class to work on ICT activities in the room where all the school's computers are based. While this maximises the access of pupils to the ICT-confident teacher, it has the secondary school centralised model at its heart and separates the use of ICT completely from the rest of the curriculum.

In parallel with the move towards discrete lessons in secondary schools, we have seen a similar tendency in primary schools to concentrate resources in a computer room. This is an understandable short-term response to the requirements of school inspectors to improve the consistency of ICT teaching and learning (Goldstein 1997). In the longer term, however, all class teachers need to develop the skills to plan and manage ICT in their teaching, and schools will need to equip each classroom with computers of sufficient quantity and reliability to give each pupil regular and frequent access in the context of a coherent curriculum.

Schemes of work and collaboration within teaching teams

Just as the ICT co-ordinator is the vital link between the headteacher and the class teachers, so the scheme of work is the vital link between general policy and classroom practice. It needs to be realistic, practicable and useful.

The purpose of a scheme of work is to show how ICT capability will be progressively and continuously developed through the school. NCET–NAACE (1997) suggest that it will include all the elements of the Programmes of Study, but divided into sections so that each class teacher knows what needs to be covered during the year. It would also include ideas for activities, sample lesson plans, assessment criteria and the resources which may be used. It should be drawn up in consultation with all teachers, and should reflect their actual and intended classroom practices. Various alternative approaches are suggested:

- formalising existing practice;
- developing a strand of ICT;
- starting from the Programmes of Study;
- developing chronologically.

A scheme of work can never completely specify what activities are to be carried out in the classroom. The most effective scheme of work is one that is used continually by teachers for reference and guidance. One that is hidden away is clearly not serving a useful purpose. Nor should it be restrictive: teachers will have new ideas and improved software and hardware, and they should be able to incorporate innovative activities in addition to those agreed. In order to take account of new ideas, new requirements and the results of evaluations, the scheme should be reviewed and updated regularly.

The ideal scheme of work is a working document to which teachers feel able to refer, one they make use of and contribute to on an ongoing basis. In most areas of the curriculum, a well-established staff may need only limited guidance, while more detail may be needed by inexperienced teachers. In the case of ICT, however, few teachers are confident in their knowledge of the subject, and a fairly detailed structure will be appreciated by staff. Bennett (1997) thus suggests a number of questions to be considered when developing a scheme of work. These include the following issues:

- How prescriptive should it be?
- Does it cover the National Curriculum Programmes of Study in sufficient depth?
- Are the activities set in the context of work in other subjects?
- Which are the strongest areas of the curriculum for supporting ICT work?
- Is the scheme of work achievable in terms of the planned resources, staff development and available time?
- Is the assessment built into the scheme feasible and useful?
- How will the scheme be monitored and reviewed?

The ITCD project found that many schools have obtained ready-made schemes of work from their LEA or from publishers, or have downloaded them from the internet. These included the exemplar scheme of work for primary schools from the QCA (1998b), and the very comprehensive Association for Computing and IT Teachers' scheme for secondary schools (ACITT 1997). In successful schools, these generic schemes of work were not adopted as a substitute for curriculum planning, but were rather adapted by each individual school, according to the specific resources available and schemes of work for other subjects. Nor were they kept static: they were developed in the light of new resources, research about effective teaching and learning, and new National Curriculum requirements. Co-ordinators were conscious that schemes should not become overloaded, and that care should be taken to ensure that important aspects of ICT are not cut out completely.

Harrison (1998) emphasises the importance of sharing the load in order to develop more effective use of ICT in the classroom. Co-ordinators need to promote the notion that ICT is a shared responsibility between different stakeholders. We see much potential for collaboration at all levels between the ICT co-ordinator and teachers charged with co-ordinating literacy and numeracy work.

In one of the ITCD project schools where numeracy and literacy hours were being introduced, the headteacher and the co-ordinators for numeracy, literacy and ICT had planned together how activities might be organised during these periods to ensure that ICT was included. They had identified which of their existing software would be suitable, such as a multimedia dictionary. The headteacher had agreed to purchase new resources, where needed, in order to make effective use of ICT within the numeracy and literacy activities.

In many primary schools, staff work in year-group teams to establish schemes of work, and to decide what should be assessed and when (Passey and Ridgway 1992). The most successful ITCD schools set out clearly what was expected from each year group in relation to the scheme of work and the activities used in their school. In the absence of a statutory requirement to report on pupils' attainment at the end of KS2, however, many schools did not carry out a systematic assessment of each pupil's capability in ICT. Indeed, we found that many ICT co-ordinators did not have a realistic view of the levels expected of pupils at age 11, which led to difficulties for continuity and progression during transition from primary to secondary schools (see Chapter 9).

Co-ordinating assessment

We discussed in Chapter 2 the integration of formative assessment into teaching and learning, and the ICT co-ordinator has an important role to play in helping colleagues to do this. The assessment process in primary schools has been supported by converting the level descriptions into *expectations* for the end of Years 2, 4 and 6 (QCA 1997). In one ITCD primary school, the ICT co-ordinator had listed expectations for each year or two years, and indicated, using terms that would be easy for staff to recognise and use, what progression was expected. Thus, for example, Year 2 pupils are expected to *begin to draft and update work*; Year 3 pupils are expected to *choose the most appropriate font and style*; and Year 5/6 pupils are expected to *show an awareness of audience*.

For summative assessment, ACAC (1995) has recommended the use of exemplar portfolios. An exemplar portfolio contains a set of work from a particular pupil for whom there is general agreement about the level of attainment. The work thus provides a point of reference for teachers to use in comparing other pupils' performance and thereby to develop a common understanding of expected standards. A primary school could have portfolios at levels 1, 2 and 3 for KS1, and for levels 2–5 at KS2.

Such portfolios need more than just isolated pieces of work, however. If teachers are to assess the pupil's attainment, rather than the outcomes of tasks, they will need to consider the process involved in producing the task outcomes and the affordances available to the pupil. The portfolio should thus contain, for each task represented, information concerning:

- the task context and objectives;
- the process of development for the work – plans, drafts, comments on decisions made, etc.;
- the resources available;
- the help given by teacher and peers concerning ICT (not concerning other subject matter for which the pupil might have required assistance).

The contents should be discussed during meetings of staff, rather than being presented as a *fait accompli*.

The ITCD project found that this was particularly successful where the ICT co-ordinator was able to discuss with the non-specialist the features of the work which characterised progression from earlier attainment, and the degree of independence shown by each pupil in the process of achieving the outcome. It is also important that the approaches to assessment are designed to support the teaching approaches adopted, and we examine this idea in more depth in Chapter 5.

In order to make effective judgements about capability, it is important for teachers to consider not just the quality of pupils' response to a task in terms of the choices made and techniques used, but the complexity of the task, the way in which they have tackled it and the help that they were given. Guidance concerning assessment of pupils' ICT capability has emphasised the matching of evidence of a pupil's performance to one of the level descriptions in the National Curriculum orders (ACAC 1996; SCAA 1996).

In secondary schools, the ITCD project found three successful approaches to schemes of work at KS3, based on different models of curriculum organisation:

- In a *discrete* model, ICT was treated the same way as other subjects, and the ICT department had its own scheme of work and assessment procedures which were designed to provide progression and continuity in discrete lessons. Other departments then referred to this scheme and assessments of pupils' attainment, in order to plan how they could take advantage of pupils' ICT capability in their own schemes.
- In a *cross-curricular* model, ICT learning and assessment were integrated into other subject schemes. The ICT co-ordinator's role was to map the plans of other subject leaders, negotiate adjustments to ensure progression and continuity in ICT for pupils, and advise other teachers on how to assess ICT capability in their subject context.
- In a *core skills* approach, each module of ICT teaching was followed by application in a subject context. This was planned jointly by the ICT co-ordinator and a representative of the subject department, so that task specific criteria for assessment were agreed.

The schools found that where teaching was based on a cross-curricular approach, a carefully designed assessment system was needed. If a combination of discrete teaching and subject application were employed, different groups of teachers could use the assessment process to contribute to pupils' ICT capability development (Figure 4.2). The ICT co-ordinator developed the recording system, liaised with

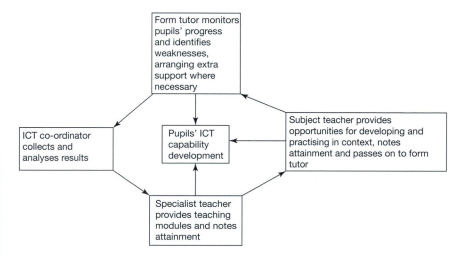

Figure 4.2 An approach to monitoring and assessment in secondary schools

subject leaders over the timing of ICT work, planned the scheme for specialist teaching, and planned support for subject teachers who were not confident with developing pupils' ICT capability. The form tutor could have a role in collecting assessments from different subject areas and identifying pupils' overall progress, alerting the ICT co-ordinator to general weaknesses in aspects of their class's progress and specific difficulties with particular pupils.

We have identified three levels at which assessment, recording and reporting are carried out. Each has a different purpose, focus and methods. With experience, the first two levels may be conflated for the majority of pupils. The ICT co-ordinator will need to give advice to class and subject teachers concerning expectations of pupils. It may also be helpful to provide recording frameworks with task-specific prompts, as long as the assessment process does not become just a box-ticking exercise.

Lesson-based assessment

Purpose: to monitor the progress of individual pupils, to evaluate the effectiveness of the lesson, and to plan specific oral feedback to pupils for the next lesson.

1   Identify the learning objectives for the lesson.
2   Devise opportunities for pupils to engage with the objectives.
3   Set criteria for success in terms of process and outcome.
4   For each pupil, note whether success was achieved independently, with some help, with much help, or was not achieved.
5   Note the implications for the next lesson.

This process need not require detailed records for each pupil, and lengthy checklists are inappropriate.

Task-based assessment

Purpose: to ascertain the National Curriculum level of pupil's work and to provide written feedback to pupils on their skills and needs for development.

1   Identify the purpose of the task outcome (e.g. a poster to advertise a school concert).
2   Determine the features required for (National Curriculum related) levels, marks, grades in terms of particular aspects of the process and the outcome.
3   Review each pupil's response to the task, together with lesson-level assessments, to produce a level, mark or grade.
4   Give feedback to the pupil in the form of suggestions for improvement (process and outcome) as well as a level, mark or grade.

Again, detailed records are not necessary for each pupil. It will be helpful to record particular strengths and weaknesses, however, in order to inform the planning of future work.

Annual report

Purpose: to provide a summative report on the pupil's strengths and weaknesses in relation to expected progress.

1　Review records of task-based assessments (and possibly the complete folder of each pupil's work).
2　Decide the overall National Curriculum level as the description which best fits the pupil's attainment.
3　Summarise the comments made about task process and outcome during the year for this pupil.

For this report, the needs of parents must be considered, and a balance is needed between being informative and being brief.

Working with other staff

For many teachers at the initial stage of using ICT in the classroom, technical skill is what they feel they most lack, and their demands for technical support can overshadow more important aspects of the ICT co-ordinator's role. There is a need to foster technical independence in other staff, and this should be incorporated into any training which is provided. Technical aspects should not be the main focus of work with other staff, however, and the co-ordinator must build on these basic support needs to raise awareness of teaching and learning issues. If a technician can be employed, full or part time, according to the size of the school, then the pressure on the co-ordinator can be relieved considerably.

In secondary schools, teachers have tended to indicate a strong preference for training from their ICT co-ordinator, rather than from specialists external to the school (Williams and Moss 1993; Michael 1999). But many teachers perceive subject-specific barriers to effective utilisation of ICT (Pelgrum and Plomp 1993; Kennewell 1997), and it is hard for co-ordinators who lack appropriate knowledge of content and pedagogy in other subjects to overcome those barriers. This is particularly the case for 14–16-year-old pupils: ITCD project teachers found it hard to integrate the more advanced ICT skills expected at this stage with subjects that have their own demanding syllabuses. Furthermore, many ICT co-ordinators saw the professional development needs of colleagues as a problem rather than an opportunity.

It is important that other subject leaders, especially those concerned with core subjects and basic skills, incorporate ICT activities into their own schemes of work (OHMCI 1999). In primary schools, the deputy-head and subject co-ordinators could be influential in demonstrating effective personal use of ICT, teaching of ICT and classroom organisation for pupils' use of ICT. Similar effects were evident in secondary schools: where the head of a department used ICT in the classroom and discussed this with colleagues, ICT was more likely to be adopted by other staff in that department. Alternatively, this role can be taken by a more junior member of the department as long as he or she is seen as a successful teacher in general rather than just an enthusiast for technology.

Harrison (1998) suggests that the primary school ICT co-ordinator should tackle classroom management issues at an early stage, and arrange to go into other teachers' classrooms. The class teaching commitments of primary teachers means that it is rare for co-ordinators to work alongside other staff (Webb 1994), but it can provide a much greater impetus for change and subsequently can be more helpful because the co-ordinator is able to contextualise their advice.

Our research indicates that this is no less valuable in secondary schools, although much care is needed by the ICT co-ordinator to recognise the different subject cultures and work with the values and practices specific to each subject area (see Chapter 6).

The idea of teaching collaboratively, and working with other adults in the classroom, is increasingly familiar. In primary schools, particularly, the idea of teachers sharing the teaching of a class is quite natural. The way in which a teacher works together with a co-ordinator is rather special, however, since the co-ordinator's aim is to help the teacher develop his or her own skills, rather than taking over part of that teacher's role or taking responsibility for particular pupils. In this case, the co-ordinator must ensure that the affordances provided are not too great and leave a gap for the teacher to bridge.

The same considerations apply to assessment: it is unrealistic to expect the co-ordinator to assess all pupils directly. Formative assessment involves monitoring pupils' progress against expectations in each element and strand of ICT capability. The ICT co-ordinator can assist teachers by providing a structure and prompts. The class or subject teacher can then give an assessment of pupils' progress in relation to the expectations of the class and the amount of help given to each pupil.

Improving the effectiveness of ICT co-ordinators

Although the ICT co-ordinator's role is not concerned directly with the teaching of pupils, the co-ordinator's effectiveness must ultimately be judged in terms of pupils' attainment in ICT. It is important to focus any evaluation of effectiveness and plans for improving effectiveness upon pupils' learning, while recognising that there are many ways in which a co-ordinator may influence the quality of learning.

We suggest that the following core responsibilities will provide a good framework for developing the co-ordination process:

- Be aware of developments in ICT itself.
- Be aware of published research and professional advice on ICT teaching.
- Identify staff development needs and providers.
- Provide, or facilitate, in-house staff development where ICT is appropriate.
- Revise schemes of work for ICT and advise other subject leaders concerning ICT in their schemes of work, so as to ensure an appropriate range, frequency, challenge and progression in pupils' learning of ICT.

- Monitor the implementation of schemes of work and report to senior management.
- Evaluate the quality of ICT teaching through comparison of assessment results.
- Monitor the quality of ICT resources and report to senior management.
- Monitor the frequency and range of pupils' active use of ICT across the curriculum and report to senior management.

It will be helpful to clarify where these responsibilities lie, and what skills are needed to meet them. Some of them involve a leadership role in the school, and should be carried out by a senior member of staff with the status to ensure that staff take notice. Others may be delegated, where the size of the staff permits, with senior management providing affordances for this delegated activity.

While schools find it valuable to have one person who deals with all matters involving ICT, we have seen that the complexity of the role is daunting and it may be expecting too much of one person to take all the responsibilities concerning ICT.

In a small primary school, none of the tasks of ICT co-ordination need assume major proportions. The technical demands may be the most challenging in terms of time and expertise, and it may be best to contract these out so that the teacher with ICT responsibility can focus on planning the curriculum and monitoring pupils' learning. They will no doubt have responsibility for these tasks in other subjects as well, and the ICT responsibility can easily fit in to a well-designed curriculum management system.

In the medium-sized or large secondary school, on the other hand, all the tasks will impose significant demands, and it is sensible to distribute them around a number of staff. The main aspects are summarised in Table 4.1.

Primary schools, too, should consider the potential for distributing the role according to the strengths of different teachers.

The precise allocation of these responsibilities to two or more staff will depend on the size of the school, the qualities and interest of available staff, as well as the potential for appointing new staff. It is important, too, that a particular member of the senior management is responsible for all initiatives and monitoring concerning these responsibilities in order to ensure that the overall effect is developmental, coherent and supported. It should also be expected that some tasks which are currently seen as a specialist's responsibilities increasingly become part of the role of subject leaders, and some should be adopted by all teachers. NCET–NAACE (1997) have provided an activity in which key staff in a school consider a set of sixty tasks related to ICT in schools, and identify whose responsibility each one should be. This should lead to a clarification of roles for all involved.

Overcoming obstacles and identifying successes

There are many potential obstacles to successful ICT co-ordination, and it is helpful to identify these, set targets for overcoming them, and seek the support of those people who can help. Table 4.2 lists some of the obstacles we have found, and suggests how they may be overcome.

Table 4.1 Suggested division of responsibilities for ICT

Title	Responsibility
Subject leader for ICT	Teaching and assessment of ICT as a subject (the nature of this role will depend on whether examination classes are offered and the delivery model for National Curriculum ICT, but specialist qualifications in ICT would be expected for this role)
Curriculum co-ordinator for ICT	Whole-school planning, and support and monitoring of the use of ICT in subject teaching (less depth of ICT knowledge is required for this role)
Staff development co-ordinator for ICT	Planning, arranging and evaluating INSET for ICT (this may be assumed by the school's staff development officer, or may be combined with curriculum co-ordination or resource management)
Resource manager for ICT	Planning, implementation, support and monitoring of hardware, software and communications' provision at strategic level (may include administrative function of ICT, and may be contracted out as part of managed service provision)
ICT technician	Day-to-day support for maintenance of equipment and basic operational support for pupils and teachers (maintenance aspect may be contracted out as part of managed service provision)

It is important to set out goals for co-ordination and identify successes when they occur. Examples of success may include:

- a feeling of staff supporting each other rather than relying on the co-ordinator to solve problems;
- assessment systems providing feedback about progress to teachers and pupils;
- pupils transferring skills and practices from one context to another without prompting;
- senior management and governors recognising the improved results and the enhanced school ethos that can result from a co-ordinated approach to ICT capability development.

Such successes are harder to recognise than are those in teaching a particular subject, however. It is important to set attainable goals, and to work with the culture and stated aims of the school (Harrison 1998). Targets should be incremental in order to chart achievements along the way.

Table 4.2 Overcoming obstacles

Obstacle	How to overcome	Who might help
Unsupportive senior management	Explain to the senior management how the development of ICT will help improve teaching and learning generally in the school, and seek to include ICT in the school development plan	Governors
Reluctant staff	Build on the belief of most staff that pupils should use ICT in learning across the curriculum. Incorporate this principle in the school ICT policy Support staff in using ICT for subject teaching Ask pupils to help staff who are not confident, and ask staff to let pupils help them	Senior management, subject leaders, pupils
Antagonistic staff	Plan opportunities for pupils to learn ICT from other teachers Team teaching	Senior management, subject leaders
Excessive technical demands	Insist on technical support (internal or external)	Senior management
Excessive administration	Simplify systems to ensure that you only record what is important and useful Use ICT where possible for record-keeping; ask pupils to maintain records of their progress	Senior management, pupils

The drive to develop the use of ICT in subject teaching is focusing co-ordinators on developing teachers' basic ICT skills and on providing technical support. Ofsted (1995b) has suggested that headteachers should encourage ICT co-ordinators to think at a more long-term, strategic level. There seems to be little opportunity, however, for co-ordinators to undertake professional development themselves to improve their own teaching approaches for ICT or their interpersonal skills in working with colleagues.

Staff development for ICT co-ordinators

The ITCD project found that many ICT co-ordinators have identified their own needs and priorities for staff development, but these are not always provided for since the reduction in the role of LEA ICT support centres (Kennewell 1997; NCET–NAACE 1997). ICT co-ordinators feel a need for updating on technical developments, personal ICT skills and curriculum resources. These are the aspects that are seen as of most immediate value in supporting ICT in schools and advising other staff. Most sources of advice are not rated highly, however, and many ICT co-ordinators do not use the full range of sources (Kennewell and Selwood 1997). Personal contacts with colleagues in other schools or with LEA advisory staff were quite highly rated, along with those publications which provide updates on hardware and software developments, and practical advice on a particular aspect of ICT in the curriculum. Many respondents also highlighted the value of advice from equipment and software vendors. The Department for Education and Employment's 1997 survey (DfEE 1998a) found that of all sources such commercial suppliers were the most widely used. This reflects the need for technical advice, but there are dangers in over-reliance on this source, of course: vendors are likely to quote reviews and research findings selectively in order to show their own products in the best light.

In the ITCD project schools, most primary co-ordinators valued opportunities to explore and discuss resources with the aim of disseminating to others, but time for this type of activity was limited. A few ICT co-ordinators were technical enthusiasts, however. They were happy to move ahead of other staff, acquiring new resources for their own classrooms and spending their time developing these to the detriment of support for other staff. Some headteachers thus rotated the role of ICT co-ordinator in order to ensure a greater spread of expertise. We also found that staff in small schools, where specialist co-ordination was unrealistic, particularly needed more specific guidance concerning the management of ICT, with priorities highlighted and checklists of key points to be considered at regular intervals.

Ultimately, it is teachers and pupils who make the difference, but the ICT co-ordinator is a vital link between the initiative and drive that should be provided by senior management, on the one hand, and the teachers who will bring about the improvements in the classroom, on the other. It is important to identify exactly how that linking role might best be achieved in each particular school.

Key issues

1   ICT co-ordination forms a vital bridge between management and classroom practice.
2   The ICT co-ordinator's role is complex and demanding. It is subject to a variety of interpretations concerning tasks and status.
3   Collaboration between the ICT co-ordinator and teaching teams is important when producing schemes of work and assessment procedures to support the effective teaching and learning of ICT.
4   Senior management should recognise that ICT co-ordinators have particular needs for professional development, and they should monitor and support the process of co-ordination.

Points for reflection

•   How important are the personal skills of those involved in co-ordinating ICT? Should the personalities of individuals affect the allocation of responsibilities?

- Is it necessary to link responsibility for ICT capability development with responsibility for ICT resources? Is it helpful?
- Is general subject leader training appropriate for the role of ICT co-ordinator? What specific professional development should be sought?

5 ICT in the primary classroom

Yet another subject to teach?

We have examined the impacts of headteachers and ICT co-ordinators on the development of ICT capability within a school, but clearly the main influence on day-to-day learning in the classroom is the teacher (Bennett 1997). Class teachers in primary schools generally have the responsibility of teaching all curriculum subjects to a particular group of pupils, often of quite a large age-range. They are expected to develop their pupils' ICT capability, and to incorporate ICT into the teaching of all other subjects. In this chapter, we consider the role of the class teacher in creating an environment that fosters ICT capability. Children gain much from their use of home computers, but the teacher's activity planning, structured whole-class teaching, grouping of pupils for tasks, assessment of learning and feedback to pupils can add considerably to the learning that occurs outside school.

Planning the incorporation of ICT activities into the curriculum

Primary teachers are faced with a quandary when planning an ICT-based activity. They must ensure that pupils have the support they need for developing their ICT capability, while providing them with contexts which stimulate learning in other subjects as well. This is a challenge that requires clear thinking, and teachers should consider:

1   What is the educational purpose of the activity – to develop ICT capability, to support learning in another area of the curriculum, or both?
2   Will the children need to be monitored to identify opportune moments for teacher intervention to enhance their skills?
3   Does it provide children with experience of using ICT as a tool?
4   Are there opportunities to assess children's ICT competence?
5   Will the children work co-operatively or collaboratively? How will this be introduced and supported?

(Bennett 1997: 65)

The ITCD project found that schools commonly used a grid to help ensure a balance of coverage across the curriculum and to maintain coherence and continuity. Typical headings were:

- year-group;
- date;
- theme/topic context;
- description and purpose of activity;
- ICT strand and learning objectives;
- subject learning objectives;
- assessment criteria;
- resources.

Other schools successfully used a termly forecast for medium-term planning, sometimes combined with the planning grid. Each of the subject areas was addressed in turn, providing detailed information about aims and objectives, intended practice and resource requirements. Schools found this highly detailed approach very useful for subject areas with which a teacher is unfamiliar or lacking in confidence – which was often the case with ICT work.

We have noted the danger of adopting a ready-made plan as opposed to developing a plan for the particular curriculum of the school and the needs of its teachers. This can easily lead to an ICT curriculum that is divorced from the learning of other subjects. The QCA (1998b) scheme, for instance, is ICT-led rather than theme- or subject-led, in order to exemplify progression in ICT concepts and processes. For example, units in the modelling–control strands include:

- understanding instructions and making things happen;
- routes: controlling a floor turtle;
- exploring simulations;
- modelling effects on screen;
- graphical modelling;
- introduction to spreadsheets;
- controlling devices;
- spreadsheet modelling;
- control and monitoring – what happens if?

Successful teachers had carried out further development work on these units to relate them to schemes of work for other subjects, to incorporate their own ideas and to add detail of how they would work in their own classrooms.

Plans for ICT activities have a limited lifespan, in any case, and teachers in successful schools recognised the need to replace some of the activities they had used for years in order to take advantage of new resources and research. For instance, the advent of the internet affords the free exploration of remote information sources. Pupils can visit sites that would otherwise be inaccessible, and this can stimulate the reading of text and the writing of e-mail messages by pupils reluctant to engage in traditional literary forms. Paradoxically, we found that this degree of emancipation increased the need for planning. Web research can lead to pupils becoming frustrated, and there is no value in pupils simply downloading quantities of information without understanding the content. It is thus important for teachers to structure the work and preview relevant pages to ensure that pupils have a chance of success. When effectively managed, pupils can develop higher order skills of independent learning and research (DfEE 1999c).

All teachers face the same challenges, and most successful schools formed planning teams (either formally or informally) for a particular year-group or topic. As we have seen (Chapter 4), these teams enlisted the support of the ICT co-ordinator to advise them or provide ideas for ICT-based activities which built into a progressive scheme of work for the whole school.

We found that where teachers' knowledge and confidence in ICT were low, individual discussion with the ICT co-ordinator helped them to understand the role of the computer in learning and to identify where the learning of ICT could be recognised and supported.

Building on pupils' use of ICT at home

An increasing number of pupils in today's primary classrooms are confident, competent and regular users of computers in their own homes. Yet schools' inspectors in Wales note that in around half of primary schools 'teachers often underestimate what pupils can do and much of the work lacks sufficient challenge' (OHMCI 1999: 3). Indeed, Downes (1998) found that pupils preferred their ICT work at home to that carried out in school. In order to gain most from their ICT work in school, it is important that pupils' activities are interesting to them and structured in such a way as to engender understanding that may be difficult for them to achieve unaided. In planning these activities, it is thus important for teachers to appreciate the extent and the nature of children's computer work at home.

Downes (1998) identifies specifically that, in contrast to the short periods of time for which pupils were able to use ICT in school, children work on the computer at home in an uninterrupted fashion for as long as they need. This helps to build their confidence. Furthermore, many of the children regularly engaged in writing and drawing activities, and used information-based programs for leisure as well as school-related work. This reveals some gaps in the expressive use of ICT, however, which schools should attempt to fill by teaching pupils to construct databases, models, hypertexts and multimedia presentations, and by setting relevant homework.

Downes also warns us of the potential inequities produced by an over-reliance on home activities in pupils' learning, and recommends the adoption of strategies to provide opportunities, inside and outside of lesson time, for those pupils who do not have home access to good ICT facilities (Downes 1999). In the ITCD project, however, we found that extra-curricular provision was quite rare in primary schools, and what there was tended to be provided by ICT enthusiasts for pupils who were already the most ICT capable.

We found that it was these most capable pupils who made the greatest use of ICT in lessons, too. It is thus essential that schools should consider how they can make ICT facilities available outside of lesson time for those who are currently missing opportunities to learn.

Stimulating and structuring learning

In order to build on informal use at home, the more formal learning in school should be based on clear objectives, involve structured activities and have high expectations of all pupils, with an appreciation of the problems likely to be experienced by pupils and planned strategies to deal with them.

The ITCD project found that the most successful teaching methods were similar to those recommended for literacy and numeracy teaching. In particular, the following sequence was used effectively:

1   whole class briefing on the context and activity;
2   detailed explanation to each group when they were ready to work on the activity;
3   careful choice of pairs to work on the computer in turn;
4   a review of key points with the group afterwards.

The most successful teachers thus worked with the whole class or group beforehand to clarify their expectations, focus their attention on what they were going to do, generate ideas on how they might go about it and demonstrate any new techniques involved. They identified when it was helpful for pupils to plan their work first on paper so that they had a clear view, for example, of the layout of a document or the structure of a database. In other situations, such as the writing of a book review, pupils were expected to use the computer immediately to draft ideas and then develop them on screen.

Many teachers over-estimated the extent to which pupils could develop understanding merely by working on tasks themselves. Important learning activities need to be introduced by explanation and questioning of pupils, and concluded by further questioning and a clear summary of what has been learned.

In one of the ITCD project schools, for instance, the Year 4 teacher planned the activities and the pairs at the beginning of each week. The activities were taken from the scheme of work, which included the learning objectives, techniques to be used, assessment opportunities and resources needed. For one activity, pupils had been finding out how to preserve fruit in a fruit salad. They had used 6 fruits and tested 4 different ways of preserving them. The teacher explained to all the pupils that they were going to record their work in a table using a familiar word-processor. She worked with the first group and showed them the techniques of creating a table, with the appropriate number of rows and columns. She proceeded to show them how to move from column to column. She then chose the first pair to work on the activity. She knew the needs of the individual pupils and carefully chose the pairs, usually one capable pupil to work with a less capable one.

At the end of the session, one pupil from each pair explained to the class what they had done and suggested ways of improving their work. In order to do this, the pupils had to clarify their ideas and formalise the knowledge they had gained. The teacher structured questions before and during the feedback to focus attention on the processes that had been used – both in science and ICT – as well as the results.

In extended work like this, successful teachers did not try to cover every point during their introduction. They found it more effective to plan interventions during the activity at the stage when pupils meet a need for the relevant knowledge. These planned interventions can be written into the activity sheets which teachers use as the basis for the work, and pupils can be asked to see the teacher when they reach a particular stage. These interventions will be additional to the normal unplanned interventions when pupils need help with more basic points.

Teachers also set targets for completion of tasks. Time was allowed at the end of periods of work to bring pupils together, in order to evaluate the products and the processes involved. This evaluation stage was used systematically to communicate expectations concerning what constituted a high quality outcome and to compare different techniques and resources.

Monitoring progress and intervening to help pupils learn

The most effective teaching seen in the ITCD project was both well planned and capable of responding to the *ad hoc* opportunities that arose to stimulate learning at important moments. Pupils benefited from the praise, feedback and support that included guidance on how to improve. The timely intervention of the teacher had a beneficial effect on the development of children's technical skills and knowledge of ICT, and was used to help develop children's higher order thinking skills. Children seemed to make more rapid progress and become independent more quickly when teachers provided assistance at critical moments. It is thus important to monitor pupils' work frequently in order to make decisions about when intervention will be effective. This is particularly important with ICT for two reasons:

- it is common for pupils to appear to be usefully occupied with the task when in fact they are working very inefficiently and failing to exploit the potential of ICT;
- because of the richness of the resource, pupils may divert from the intended task without it being obvious from their behaviour.

What, then, should teachers be looking out for, and how should they intervene? In Chapter 2 we suggested that ICT capability may be characterised in terms of routines, techniques, processes and higher order skills.

- *Routines* may be recognised by the ease and speed with which familiar techniques are carried out. For each age-group, a brief checklist of techniques that pupils should be able to use routinely will be helpful. Pupils who struggle with routines that are characteristic of their age-group will require specific attention and extra practice. Practice in specially designed activities should be supplemented by opportunities to apply the techniques concerned to worthwhile tasks which involve other areas of the curriculum. It is important to keep this list up-to-date in relation to the hardware and software available. Some ICT resources automate routines that in other situations need practice. For instance, the technique of *drag-and-drop* becomes routine more easily than *cut-and-paste*, and may be expected at an earlier age. The combining of words, pictures and sounds in programs written especially for children is easier than using some Windows packages.

- *Techniques* which have not become routines may be carried out in different contexts using the affordances on the screen (icons, menus) or with help from adults or peers. It is useful again to have a checklist for each class to enable the teacher to keep track of which pupils are confident in using the technique. It is important to give those pupils needing help only the minimum of support. Pupils can often remember techniques or work them out themselves with a little prompting concerning where to look for options. This support should be withdrawn as soon as possible.

- *Processes* are more general and are made up of several techniques. An understanding of relevant concepts is needed in order to analyse a situation and identify the particular techniques required to reach the desired goal. Pupils need to work on a task which is not set out step-by-step, so that the teacher can let them try out their ideas, observe their approach and intervene when they fail to make the expected progress. Again the minimum level of support should be given. The idea of *scaffolding* may be helpful – the teacher initially structures their activity by questioning, prompting and showing if necessary, and then withdraws as much support as possible to see what the learners can achieve unaided. However, the pupils' understanding of a process such as developing a poster using a desktop publishing program, or modelling with a spreadsheet, cannot be represented by a checklist. It requires a description of the way in which they approach a task and the support that they need, for which the National Curriculum levels should provide a convenient shorthand system. The level description which best matches the pupils' approach can be recorded, together with an indication of the degree of help required.

- *Higher order skills and knowledge* are independent of the tools and the context. They enable pupils to carry out complete processes themselves when the *scaffolding* provided by the teacher is removed. A number of key teaching strategies can aid their development. First, the teacher can *model* the techniques of strategic planning by thinking out loud in front of pupils to show the questions which might be asked during the process. Second, the teacher gives groups of pupils responsibility for planning a task and *coaches* them by asking focusing questions at intervals to guide pupils towards a viable plan. Third, the teacher involves the pupils *socially* in planning, monitoring, evaluating and reflecting through whole-class teaching.

Information handling work is a particularly suitable context for developing these higher order skills, and NCET (1995b) identifies the following sequence or *process loop* for teachers to use as a model for effective information handling:

1   Starting-point: identify the context and the prerequisite skills, knowledge and experience.
2   Engagement: establish interest, define purpose, decide on data needed, gather and explore data.
3   Look for connections: sorting/classifying/ browsing through data.
4   Ask questions: inquisitively look at the data, ask purposeful questions and suggest possible relationships.
5   Look for answers: interrogate the data, looking for relationships and counter-examples; decide whether the evidence provides answers to the questions.
6   Interpretation: question the validity of the findings; try to explain the answers/relationships.
7   Product: new knowledge has been acquired in domain of enquiry; greater ICT capability.

These observable aspects are underpinned by concepts, which are more difficult to evaluate. Specific questions should be asked to probe these concepts and stimulate reflection. Opportunities will arise during pupils' work to identify and challenge inappropriate assumptions. Pupils will naturally try to apply existing knowledge to a new program, and this can lead to errors and frustration where their assumptions and ideas about the features of the program are inaccurate. When starting to use a spreadsheet program, for instance, users will be concerned that most of their text is lost if they type a long heading into a short cell.

The ITCD project found that *The Logical Journey of the Zoombinis* (Broderbrund 1996) was a popular activity on multimedia computers. This involves a series of challenges for pupils, who must solve logical puzzles in order to guide the Zoombinis through a number of hazards. However, the need to discover a rule or principle to solve each puzzle was not clear to many pupils, and they continued to work on a trial and error basis. In order to help develop their concept of a computer model, the teacher asked the children to talk about, or write down, the rules which led to success on each puzzle, and then to explain how they had worked out these rules.

Teachers' knowledge of the resources

Having a clearly defined purpose for the task will help sharpen the focus of a teacher's interventions. Being familiar with a program will help the teacher identify the circumstances when pupils are ready to move on to a new feature or to use the software for a more demanding purpose (Bennett 1997).

This familiarity involves more than just knowing how to use the program for a variety of tasks. It means reflecting on the processes it helps the user to carry out and the techniques with which particular effects can be achieved. It then requires consideration of how the pupils will be introduced to the program, what ideas need to be clear before they start and where they might find difficulties.

It is thus more important for teachers to be very knowledgeable about one program that their pupils will use than to have an acquaintance with a large number. This does not limit the pupils' development, however. It is also better for the pupils to work with a small number of versatile programs and progressively develop skills and confidence in these through carefully structured activities than it is to try to learn how to use a large number of programs superficially (Bennett 1997).

During the multimedia for portables initiative (BECTA 1998b), the teachers were encouraged to become familiar with one piece of software at a time and to use this with their class, if appropriate. In the same way, it was important that they had visited the sites on the World Wide Web that they wanted their pupils to use in studying a particular topic. Initially, they found it valuable to prepare help cards so that the pupils could quickly access and explore the specific aspects of the sites that would give them relevant information. The focus in ICT capability at this stage is on learning from information displayed in hypertext databases. Greater autonomy could be allowed subsequently in extended information handling projects, following the process loop described above.

Assessing, recording and evaluating the development of ICT capability

Daugherty and Freedman (1998) have noted that primary teachers have used diverse strategies to carry out National Curriculum assessments, and that they see them primarily in summative and evaluative terms rather than as a means of supporting pupils' learning. It is perhaps particularly difficult for teachers continually to keep track of each pupil's attainments and development needs in ICT, when their own subject knowledge may be quite limited.

Planning, monitoring, assessment, record keeping and reporting are so closely related that they are best addressed together to help ensure that each aspect supports the others. Although assessment may seem more difficult for ICT than for other curriculum areas, it is achievable if activities are planned to include opportunities for assessment. Assessment should be closely linked to forward planning (NCET 1991). Figure 5.1 shows an example of a school's activity planning sheet, which sets

---

Year 6 Autumn	**Communicating Information**
Topic: *Big Swig and Fling*	Subject: English/Art/D&T

Activity: Pupils will use *Publisher* to produce a book review. They will learn to scan their own illustrations and import them into their page. Pupils will add text and develop their word-processing skills to present their review of the book according to the audience they choose – parents or children. They will save, retrieve, edit and print their work independently if possible.

Grouping: Pairs

Assessment: Effective choice and combination of images and text, use of font/style/colour of text to add clarity and emphasis for the audience they choose. Independent management of work.

Figure 5.1 Activity planning sheet

out what to look for in pupils' work as well as specifying the nature and purpose of the activity.

This sort of record can be used

- by senior management and the ICT co-ordinator in monitoring the implementation of ICT;
- to assist the teacher with future planning;
- to inform the teacher of the next age-group of what work has been covered;
- to inform supply teachers.

It can also show any discrepancies between what was planned and what was actually taught.

In order to gain evidence for pupils' attainment, teachers select from a number of methods that are appropriate in different circumstances. These include observation, listening, discussion, marking and testing (Bolton LEA 1999). It is important for the approach to assessment to fit in with the teaching approach, and our recommendations for teaching fit well with these suggestions for assessing children's ICT capability:

- Devise methods of enabling the children to monitor and record their own progress e.g. self-assessment sheets of skills accomplished in illustrated or written form e.g. *I can print a page*;
- Question children and ask them to demonstrate how they went about a task;
- Set occasional prescribed challenges e.g. *Can you write a caption and print it out for me?*
- Make use of well-briefed parent helpers to work exclusively with children at the computer, recording the amount of help each child received with a piece of work;
- Vary pairings to see how children work with other partners;
- Encourage children to save their first drafts as well as final drafts of each piece of ICT work.

(Bennett 1997: 68)

In each case, it is important to provide feedback to the pupils by making explicit what they have done well, in addition to suggesting how their work could be improved.

Keeping records

Keeping track of the precise progress of every pupil can become an unmanageable task. The broad descriptions of pupils' levels used in the National Curriculum and the supporting advice (ACAC 1996; SCAA 1996) are helpful in characterising major aspects of progress, though teachers will find it valuable to have more specific guidelines relating to their particular scheme of work and software. Ager (1998) sets out, for each National Curriculum strand, examples of criteria for each level which

Table 5.1 Progression in modelling

Level	Action
1	Not applicable
2	Use the Logical Journey of the Zoombinis and find out what happens when you choose different things
3	Type prices into a prepared spreadsheet model to find out whether you can afford your Christmas presents
4	Use Logo to try to draw a triangle with all sides the same length
5	Use a prepared spreadsheet model to investigate the perimeter and area of rectangles; for a rectangle with perimeter 20 cm, change the length systematically to find what length and width will make the greatest area

relate to curriculum activities, and these could be adapted for the school's software. Table 5.1 gives an example for the modelling strand.

In general, we found that teachers' record-keeping systems reflected two perspectives – the areas of the curriculum that their teaching has covered and the progress of individual children. The recording of progress in ICT needs to be manageable within a system for the whole curriculum.

NCET (1991) suggests two further recording sheets which follow on from an activity planning sheet (see Figure 5.1). The purpose of the first is as a checklist to indicate whether the pupil has carried out an activity. Records are far more informative, however, if they include an indication of the skills pupils have used in the task (OHMCI 1999). The main techniques could be listed, and a code recorded for each child to indicate independent or aided use of the technique for an appropriate purpose. The second sheet is for the teacher to record anything significant concerning a particular pupil's progress. This dual system should not impose too onerous a task because this second sheet would not need to be specific to the activity. It could be used to record aspects other than the coverage of techniques and pupils' confidence in their use. Pupils' higher order skills (such as planning, choosing, hypothesising, evaluating) and understanding of processes (communicating information, handling information, modelling) should be recognised and notes made concerning their development.

Pupils may be involved progressively in the assessment process. This helps them to take more responsibility for their learning and develops their higher order skills (Tanner and Jones 1994), as well as helping the teacher keep track of their learning. We discuss how this process can contribute to primary–secondary transition in Chapter 9.

In one of the ITCD schools, the ICT co-ordinator was piloting in Year 6 a system where pupils kept their own records of progress. Each pupil had a sheet containing statements such as:

- 'I can analyse results and present the information in a variety of forms.'
- 'I can access information for the internet.'
- 'I can program a sequence of instructions (traffic lights) using a control box.'

Pupils were able to indicate whether completed tasks were done *by myself* or *with help*. They used this self-assessment as a basis for talking to their teacher about their work when they completed a task. Further examples of documents to support this process are given in Chapter 9.

Organising the classroom

We observed in the ITCD project that the way in which a classroom was organised made a considerable difference to the potential for ICT capability development. If access to ICT resources was difficult, irregular or conditional on the completion of other activities, the ICT application gained the status of something special. This formed a barrier to the development of the ICT-capable classroom.

It is essential that computers are placed in a classroom so as to maximise the opportunities for curriculum activity. Pupils should be able to move to and from the equipment as necessary to undertake various tasks. There needs to be room, not only for the peripherals such as a printer and scanner, but for two to four children to be able to discuss the activity, work together at the computer, and write on paper by the side of the computer when appropriate (NCET 1991).

If the activities are well planned, good ICT work can be achieved with one or two computers per class. These are sometimes augmented by desktop PCs on trolleys which can be moved easily from class to class, and by portable computers which can be booked for particular purposes. The addition of a large screen, multimedia projector or electronic whiteboard – as these become more affordable – enables the activities to be demonstrated to the whole class at the beginning of the lesson and can be used for a plenary session at the end.

Most schools in the ITCD project felt that they had a satisfactory level of resources for the work they are attempting. Overall, the number of computers available did not appear to be the decisive factor in determining pupil performance. However, we found that old and outdated equipment was still in use in many schools. Effective use of these machines resulted from clear planning concerning the age-group or the curriculum activity for which they were best suited.

We found that most schools had specific procedures to ensure that all pupils used ICT. However, the most able and confident pupils were often those who had additional access to computers, when they had finished other work, or else had computers at home. Some pupils, on the other hand, avoided using the computer because they felt they were not good at it; having finished their other work, these pupils preferred to draw. A system for ensuring regular access together with sufficient time and support for such pupils is vital if they are not to miss out on basic ICT capability development.

Grouping pupils and resources

The more successful schools had given careful thought to the teaching strategies for ICT, and this had influenced the way in which resources were allocated and pupils grouped for ICT activities.

One of the schools in the project organised the computers into banks of four which were used in open areas linking two classrooms in the same age-group. This enabled a group of approximately eight pupils to work on an activity together immediately after an initial briefing. Discussion and evaluation could also take place immediately after the activity, rather than waiting until all the group members had taken a turn. In addition, pupils from both classes worked on similar activities and both class teachers gained from planning and working together. Such clusters could serve a larger group of classes, and allow one computer to remain in each classroom.

Where there were only one or two computers available, a rota was used to ensure that each pair of pupils in the group had an opportunity to work on the task shortly after the briefing and demonstration. The pairing of pupils needs to take account of various factors:

- *Differences in ICT capability.* When a pairing positions a more capable child as *mentor* to one who is less capable, the less experienced child learns more if the mentor has a clear idea of the role and the teacher interacts occasionally to reinforce this role (Underwood *et al.* 1990).
- *The personalities of the children.* Dominance by one of the pair can lead to disengagement from the task by the other, and dominant pupils should be paired together when possible (Kennewell 1993; Downes 1998).
- *Sex.* Single-sex pairs generally co-operate more successfully, but some pairs of boys tend to take turns rather than work together. The gender mix in groups of younger children is less important to learning than it is with older children (Hayward and Wray 1988). Pairing boys with girls can have benefits, though boys are less inclined to benefit when working with girls on language activities, whereas girls benefit when working with boys on spatial tasks (Hughes and Greenough 1989).
- *The nature of the task.* Will both children be collaborating on one outcome, or will they be assisting each other with their individual pieces of work? (Bennett 1997)

It is difficult for a single teacher in the classroom to give adequate attention to groups of pupils working on different activities. We found that in successful primary schools, assistance with pupils' ICT capability development was often provided by adult helpers. The briefing and deployment of these adults is an important consideration. The British Computer Society (BCS) Schools Committee (1999) gives this advice to adult helpers on using strategies in ICT activities:

- Invite the children to plan ahead.
- Listen to what the children say and encourage them to share their ideas.
- Help the children to understand that it is acceptable to try out their ideas and to make mistakes.
- Give the children time to work out their answers.
- Take every opportunity to praise the children's success when completing an exercise or developing a computer skill.

Pupils naturally turn to their more expert peers for help in the busy classroom, however, and it is possible to use this feature to everyone's advantage. The more capable pupils can develop clearer concepts about the processes by having to analyse what they do in order to explain it to their friends. This does not apply if they just do the work for them, of course, and the pupils will need to be briefed about how to support learning rather than taking over.

The demand on these 'class experts' (Kennewell 1995b) can be considerable, however, and successful primary teachers are aware that the potential demand for help could distract the more capable pupils from their own work. The teachers minimised this problem by allocating mixed-ability pairs when there were important ICT learning objectives for the activity.

Teachers in the ITCD project schools found that time was short for pupils working on ICT activities. To make the most of children's computer time, successful teachers recognised the value of group or whole-class teaching for the briefing and review of the work. They found it important for all pupils to be aware of what each group had achieved so that they could learn from the experience and ideas of others, rather than depend directly on the teacher for all their learning.

Evaluating ICT teaching and learning

Teachers should consider whether each ICT-based activity is appropriate within the curriculum as a whole. Tasks should not involve repetition of techniques just for the sake of practising unless there is a specific need, otherwise ICT can become a chore. Nor should ICT be used merely to present existing work in a different way. The work should contribute to pupils' learning, not simply be an excuse to use ICT.

Teachers' own evaluations of their teaching can take place at two levels:

- reflecting on the effectiveness of a particular activity or unit of work in relation to objectives for developing pupils' ICT capability and for other learning;
- the overall evaluation of how pupils have progressed during the course of a year in relation to expectations.

Records of pupils' progress can help to evaluate the teaching as well as informing the planning process. If pupils' work does not meet expectations, teachers can then try to identify what might help to improve progress – training, help with planning, increased resources, better classroom organisation, or a change in teaching approach.

Application of ICT capability

We noted in Chapter 4 that the majority of primary schools use a mixture of separate ICT teaching and cross-curricular application. In this chapter, we have suggested how this may be planned effectively. But there are many different ways in which pupils use ICT in other subject work, and the contribution to ICT capability varies tremendously. We can classify these ways under three broad headings, each of which makes different demands on pupils and teachers.

The computer is in control

Pupils are restricted to either a specific response to what the computer decides to show them (as for example, with ILS – see Chapter 1) or drill and practice software. This requires minimal capability on the part of pupils, but may require more from the teacher in order to access and analyse the records of pupils' progress. ILS studies have found that this use of ICT to monitor and diagnose pupils' progress in other subjects has been a significant factor in developing teachers' ICT capability (BECTA 1998b). The use of ILS for other subjects will, however, do little to develop pupils' ICT capability. Its value is designed to be in effective learning of the subject matter, but the difficulty for the teacher is in planning how it can be integrated with other teaching in the subject.

The computer provides a structure for the activity

Pupils have some control of the computer but not complete freedom (for example, simulation or multimedia database). This requires decision making by the pupils. It can stimulate and scaffold the ICT processes and higher order skills, thus providing opportunities for the teacher to explain and review the processes carried out in order to help pupils develop more general concepts of modelling, information structure and logical enquiry. Thus teachers themselves need a good understanding of these concepts and higher order skills, together with a clear picture of the content and purpose of the package.

The computer provides tools

Pupils have almost complete control over the computer (for example, content-free and generic application software such as desktop publishing or spreadsheet packages). Tool software can itself be used in many different ways, and the demands and possibilities will depend on whether the main objectives are to learn ICT techniques, to develop understanding of processes, or to apply familiar techniques/ processes in learning other matters. It may not be fruitful to combine too many of these into one piece of work. Bennett (1997: 20) summarises these ideas as follows:

> When the purpose of an activity is to support or enhance work in other areas of the curriculum – to provide experience of colour and shape-matching or to practise spelling for example – the level of computer control is likely to be very high. There is a place for this type of computer-based activity provided, of course, this is not the only ICT experience the children receive. To develop children's ICT capability to the full, they need to be given opportunities to use more intellectually challenging *content-free* software such as word processors, painting and drawing programs or databases where the child's level of control and decision making is quite high. Clearly, this has implications for the teacher in planning work and organising activities which puts control more into the hands of the child.

Bennett suggests a number of questions which might help evaluate the educational potential of content-free software:

- What features and facilities does the software provide which might be used to extend children's learning?
- How easy are these features to use?
- Will the children need to be instructed in their use before or during their use of the software?
- What is the educational purpose underlying the child's use of the software? (e.g. To develop ICT skills? To learn how to use the software? To use the software as a means to an end? To develop communication skills and knowledge?)

(Bennett 1997: 21)

As well as technical skills in how to use the computer, pupils need understanding of processes to decide when it might be appropriate to use a computer for a task. This is best achieved through purposeful activities in meaningful contexts.

ICT capability and literacy

The ITCD project found that teachers tended to respond to the introduction of ICT into their teaching by assimilating the technology into their pre-existing system of beliefs, attitudes and approaches. Thus those favouring whole-class approaches tended to continue with these when incorporating ICT. Others who favoured individualised working were generally happy to allow pupils to work alone on computer-based tasks while the rest of the pupils continued with their own tasks. This is very much in line with other research (e.g. Moseley and Higgins 1999).

We found also that most teachers are still confident only with word-processing or desktop publishing software among the range of generic tools. Teachers' confidence in using ICT personally for improving the presentation of their work was significantly higher than it was for searching for information, developing or testing ideas. It is thus apparently easier for teachers to assimilate ICT into literacy work than it is for any other subject. Indeed, we observed a particular desktop publishing package being used by Year 2, Year 4, Year 6, Year 9 and Year 10 pupils. This program was easy to use, yet powerful, and was able to support use at very different levels of literacy and of ICT capability, in pupils' first and second language. But there was no clear progression in what was expected of pupils, and their work depended on the teacher's personal knowledge of the potential of the program and the techniques of operation.

The extent to which ICT was used effectively to support the development of literacy or numeracy depended to a large extent on the teacher's own personal capabilities in ICT and in literacy and numeracy teaching. When teachers felt their own skills in ICT were lacking, there was sometimes only a haphazard development of ICT skills. The most effective lessons which supported the development of literacy through the use of ICT made effective use of the provisionality inherent in ICT.

In such cases, ICT was used to draft and re-draft work using spellchecking and grammar checking to improve the text. In the very best cases, pupils drew on material from CDROM or the internet as sources for writing, sometimes copying pictures into the text. Teachers who were ICT capable and confident in the teaching of literacy felt able to allow pupils the freedom to explore and develop their work in this way. Unfortunately, when teachers lacked such confidence, we often observed pupils drafting and re-drafting work away from the computer and only using ICT to provide a tidy copy of the final draft.

The Literacy Hour provides a clear opportunity for pupils to develop ICT skills which are firmly located within another subject. However, the emphasis on whole-class teaching and specific tasks which last a fixed amount of time may seem counter to the spirit of ICT capability. Government guidance has given little help to teachers seeking to integrate ICT, but the recommended mixture of focused short tasks and integrated projects matches the principles of effective ICT teaching.

Teachers with more advanced ICT skills are sometimes willing to explore teaching approaches that integrate their use of ICT with the spirit of structured literacy teaching. For example, confident teachers are able to use a large screen to model drafting and re-drafting to improve language to a whole class. Others are more willing to encourage shared writing using ICT, and this is later presented to the class. Presentation software offers opportunities for whole-class activities that focus attention on aspects of story writing, grammar or comprehension (Moseley and Higgins 1999).

With large screens and multimedia projectors, teaching whole classes or large groups with ICT is realistic. Children do not always need to have their hands on the computer to develop their ICT capability: understanding of concepts and higher order skills will be enhanced by whole-class questioning by the teacher; group discussion of processes will be carried out, as will the teacher's modelling of planning, hypothesising and evaluating.

Children's practical use of ICT will be most likely to take place within the twenty minutes allowed for independent work. These sessions may be planned to provide, over a period of time, a mixture of tasks in which

- ICT and literacy skills are developing concurrently;
- literacy skills are being developed but ICT skills consolidated;
- ICT skills pertinent to literacy such as word-processing or DTP are developing but other literacy objectives are secondary.

Moving beyond communicating, presenting and exchanging ideas

Generic tools for other strands of ICT capability seem under-exploited in the primary classroom. The use of flatfile databases to store and interrogate information collected by the pupils, and of Logo for sequencing instructions in a mathematical or story context, are less common now than a few years ago, before professionally written multimedia packages became available (Robertson 1998). While there is much that pupils can gain from interacting with multimedia software which allows them to explore, hypothesise, and evaluate the information they have obtained, there must still be a place for devising sequences of instructions to achieve a particular goal and for structuring information for retrieval. Multimedia authoring is not yet widely taught, although the prospect of web publishing and of producing CDROMs is having a motivating effect in those schools which have attempted to look forward. Science, geography and history are subjects with facets which may be investigated and represented by pupils using these tools. Furthermore, even spreadsheets are still not commonly used in primary schools for either exploratory or expressive modelling (see Mellar *et al.* 1994). There seems to be a feeling that notion of *formula* is too difficult for the primary age-group, yet the National Curriculum holds no expectation that primary pupils will need to devise formulae themselves. Prepared spreadsheets, created by the teacher or obtained from other sources, can provide models for pupils to develop their skills of systematic investigation and hypothesising.

ICT capability and numeracy

The numeracy National Curriculum provides an ideal opportunity for utilising these ideas. For example, we observed a class of Year 6 pupils using a simple spreadsheet (see Figure 5.2) which had been prepared by their teacher to investigate number patterns. Pupils were initially asked to examine the spreadsheet and find out how the numbers 3, 63, 7, 27 and 100 had been calculated. They were then challenged to re-arrange the numbers from 1 to 9 in the square pattern to get the biggest possible total and the smallest possible total.

The task required no theoretical knowledge about spreadsheets on the part of the pupils. The lessons were not *about* spreadsheets, although the pupils had gained

	A	B	C	D	E	F
1						
2		1	2	3		3 (B2 * D2)
3		4	5	6		
4		7	8	9		63 (B4 * D4)
5						
6		7 (B2 * B4)		27 (D2 * D4)		
7				Total		100 (F2+F4+B6+D6)

Figure 5.2 Square one

significant knowledge and skills by the time the tasks were completed. The spreadsheet was used as a tool to do mathematics. The tasks exploit the power of spreadsheets to offer instantaneous re-calculation of a set of numbers.

The main part of the task requires only that pupils are able to enter data into one cell of the spreadsheet. Later extensions invited pupils to set up their own formulae to create new challenges for their friends. When groups of fast-working pupils reached the point at which new skills were required, this teacher was able to provide the information and skills at the moment of need. In any case, many of the techniques seemed to move around the room of their own accord via pupil to pupil communication.

The teacher called the class together at the end for an effective plenary in which the key skills and knowledge acquired were summarised by asking the pupils to make a list of the things they had learned in the lesson that would be useful on another occasion. The list, which was brainstormed, included higher order knowledge as well as mathematical and ICT processes and techniques.

Again, it was those teachers who were most confident about their ICT abilities and their mathematical abilities who were the most willing to allow pupils to experiment with such open-ended tasks.

The *Ways Forward with ICT* study (Moseley and Higgins 1999: 95) reports significant links between mathematics value-added and the reported use of computers for class demonstration and for the study of patterns and connections through spreadsheets and databases. The authors suggest that a part of this effect is due to the teachers being willing to develop their professional skills in an area they feel will make a difference to pupils' learning. While this may well be the case, we would agree that 'if computers and other forms of ICT are to become powerful educational tools, they will have to be managed by effective, enthusiastic and challenging teachers. ICT can indeed be effective when used purposefully' (Moseley and Higgins 1999: 95).

The automatic features of ICT have had fundamental effects on the value of written algorithms for calculation. The curriculum changes required go deeper than merely replacing exercises in long multiplication with exercises in pressing calculator buttons, however. ICT capability in the field of number involves much more than merely the ICT techniques needed to perform number operations and produce graphs. Such capability also involves the higher order skills needed to identify when ICT is the most effective way of achieving a goal and which tools are appropriate to the task. Furthermore, this decision involves more than ICT knowledge. It requires knowledge of mathematical concepts and processes, and metacognitive knowledge of one's own speed and accuracy with numeric techniques and routines. If we ask children to find the total cost of 68 pens at 20p each, they have to decide on the type of calculation to do, and choose whether to estimate the answer, to calculate it exactly using mental methods, to calculate it exactly using pencil and paper, to use a simple calculator, or to use a spreadsheet. Their choice will depend on their levels of ICT capability and numeracy (as well, of course, as the affordances of the setting they are in – the tools available, the help they can get from others, and the teacher's aims for the activity).

We can thus see how higher order skills and concepts are used to combine knowledge of and techniques in number and in ICT in order to solve even quite simple number problems (see Figure 5.3).

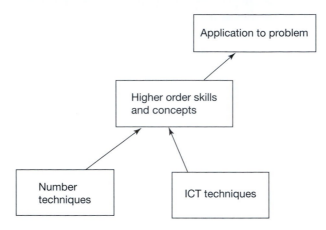

Figure 5.3 Combining numeracy and ICT

Thus if children develop the ICT and number techniques in isolation, then both their ICT capability and their numeracy will be to that extent impoverished. It will be more difficult subsequently for them to solve more complex problems which require generic higher order skills to plan their entry to the problem, monitor progress and evaluate solutions.

Developing an integrated approach to teaching ICT in the primary curriculum

The role of ICT in the primary classroom is as a complex but potentially powerful tool. Although the principles of good teaching in primary schools apply to ICT as much as to other subjects, if teachers are to integrate ICT effectively into the curriculum rather than add it on as an extra activity, they will need a good understanding of ICT concepts and their relation to other areas of the curriculum.

We have highlighted the value of planning to focus on the importance of clear objectives for each classroom activity. Moseley and Higgins (1999) find that teachers plan to develop pupils' ICT capability prior to using ICT in other subject learning, so that pupils can focus on specific subject objectives. But any ICT activity has a context, and it would be difficult to introduce spreadsheets, for instance, without involving number activity. There are close relationships between ICT capability and knowledge, skills and understanding in other subject areas, and we do not think it is helpful to see their development in isolation. The ITCD project found that the most effective learning *of* and *with* ICT involved a *shift of focus* between ICT objectives and other learning objectives during the course of an activity, and this is effected through planned teacher interventions. With this approach, an ICT-capable primary teacher can foster learning strategies that emphasise higher order skills and provide an effective foundation for the challenges of a disjointed secondary curriculum.

Key issues

1   Systems must be in place for regular access by all pupils.
2   Planning, monitoring, resources, assessment and record keeping are so closely related that they must be considered together.
3   A clearly defined purpose for a task sharpens the focus of intervention during the activity.
4   A briefing to the whole class or group prior to an ICT activity, and a plenary discussion of results after pupils have carried out the activity, enables the teacher to help pupils develop concepts and higher order skills.
5   ICT activities are not isolated from the rest of the curriculum, and they can contribute to numeracy and literacy as well as to other subjects.
6   The use of ICT for communicating information predominates in most schools, and the potential for ICT in activities that develop pupils' higher order skills is not widely exploited.

Points for reflection

•   How can teachers who are confident technically be made aware of how ICT can develop independent learning and higher order skills?
•   What training is needed to give teachers who are reluctant to use ICT the confidence to introduce new skills to a large group or the whole class? What would help them to identify the educational purpose of the activity?
•   What advantages do activities with generic software have over specific teaching and learning software for improving pupil attainment in literacy and numeracy? What does the internet have to offer?

6 ICT in the secondary classroom

Teaching someone else's subject?

We now move into the secondary school, and look first at the teacher of subjects other than ICT. Each curriculum subject has its own characteristics, and it is difficult to generalise about planning, organisation, teaching or assessment. We thus focus on teachers, their beliefs and practices in relation to ICT capability, and the sort of pedagogy which is developing in ICT-capable schools.

Subject culture

The culture of the secondary school is fundamentally different from that of the primary school. Whereas primary school teachers regard teaching as pedagogical practice and the school as their organisational unit, secondary school teachers tend to frame their teaching in terms of their subject and their organisational unit as their department (Siskin and Little 1995). At their best, subject departments form closely knit teams of collaborative and mutually supportive teachers with common approaches to teaching their subject. When they work well, such teams routinely share discussions about pedagogical issues and difficulties, forming a sound basis for professional development and the achievement of high standards of learning.

However, from another viewpoint they are sometimes seen as 'bastions of curricular conservatism', with professional self-interests that are often at odds with the interests of pupils (Siskin and Little 1995: 2). For example, the subject department model is poorly suited to deal effectively with cross-curricular themes, key skills, social education and vocational education. All of these cross-curricular issues are in danger of being viewed by subject teachers as both outside of their responsibility and, indeed, as *someone else's subject* which is encroaching on their own subject's precious time allocation. Hargreaves and Macmillan (1995) use the term 'balkanised' for schools in which subject boundaries have grown to be so strong that they impact negatively on education.

The power which the subject culture holds over the secondary school teacher is considerable. In a real sense, the professional ambitions and material interests of teachers in secondary schools are inextricably bound up with the status and fate of their subject. The relative success of a subject in gaining curriculum time, attracting high-ability pupils and achieving success in formal examinations influences its status within the school. High-status academic subjects tend to be granted more time and are more likely to be compulsory than are low-status practical subjects (Hargreaves and Macmillan 1995: 61). This inequality in subject status often leads to a political battle for valued territory within the school, such as senior level courses (Goodson and Marsh 1996). The secondary teacher's career is often played out within the subject department and the relative status of the subject department is believed to be influential in career development (Ball 1987; Goodson 1992). Encroachment by one subject, for example ICT, on the territory of another is likely to be strongly resisted within a highly balkanised school. The reaction to innovation in such schools is often based on an assessment of which subjects are to be winners and which losers rather than on the overall educational gain for pupils.

What we know and believe about teaching and learning often depends on our subject. Few secondary school teachers identify with more than one subject grouping and, as many of the opportunities for professional development occur through discourse within the subject subgroup, what teachers within a school know and believe often varies considerably between subjects (Hargreaves and Macmillan 1995). Furthermore, the whole process of becoming a teacher, through university, teacher training and then school, may be seen as induction into the common beliefs, attitudes and values held by teachers of that subject. Induction into subject teaching encourages the development of a shared set of understandings, assumptions and values relating to teaching, learning, pupil grouping and assessment (Hargreaves and Macmillan 1995). Significant elements of the identity of a secondary school teacher are formed by the subject subculture.

Subject subcultures find expression not just through their content but through their different styles of teaching and classroom organisation. For example, Goodson and Mangan (1995) report that in some subjects lessons are typically characterised by a lecturer-like delivery and the dictation of notes, followed by a practical exercise which emphasises the correct execution of the prescribed instructions. Individual coaching of learners occurs, but there is a fairly formal relationship between teachers and learners. In other subjects, there is less emphasis on content and lecture style, a greater emphasis on individuality and creativity, a higher frequency of individual coaching and a less formal classroom atmosphere (Goodson and Mangan 1995: 616).

The style and content of teaching activity in the classroom are framed by the cultural characteristics of the particular subject combined with a teacher's personal characteristics. However, individual teachers succeed in developing their own teaching approaches according to their personal beliefs and styles. In any case, subject cultures change over time as a result of professional discussion (Goodson and Mangan 1995). The introduction of ICT into subject teaching may initially create a mismatch between the teacher's normal style and the way in which ICT is used. What is an effective ICT activity for one teacher may thus be ineffective for another.

The impact of computers on subject culture

Given opportunities for professional discussion and learning, however, the subject culture should be able to accommodate to the integration of ICT. Furthermore, patterns of balkanisation are not inevitable, and reforms aimed at developing an ICT-capable school may in themselves encourage a more extended form of professionalism. The introduction of ICT challenges subject subcultures in three major ways: as a rival subject, as a key skill, and as a challenge to the established norms of organisation, pedagogy and belief within subject subcultures.

If ICT is established within the curriculum as a subject in its own right, with its own assessment objectives and examinations, it presents a challenge through its demands on curriculum time and resources. The subject-based structure of the secondary school pushes ICT teachers to demand subject status to secure their own position within the system. Once a subject has justified inclusion in the curriculum on the basis of vocational or personal development, subject teachers inevitably seek to drive up their subject's academic status (Goodson 1992; Siskin 1994). ICT co-ordinators require such status to facilitate their negotiations with subject heads of department so as to achieve their cross-curricular objectives for ICT as a key skill and for the use of ICT in subject teaching. Unfortunately the disadvantage of this increased status is that they may then be viewed as rival barons in the political battle for valued territory within the curriculum, reinforcing objections to the encroachment of ICT key skills on limited subject time. In a balkanised secondary school the negative effects associated with such subject rivalries may severely limit the potential to develop an ICT-capable school.

The introduction of ICT into subject teaching may act as a catalyst for reform by focusing the attention of subject teachers on a new pedagogy which challenges traditional subject practices and beliefs. We have found, however, that for many teachers the challenge of using ICT in their teaching would not be a minor innovation, the co-opting of a new technique, but rather a root-and-branch change in teaching style. We believe that it is the extent of the change demanded by the use of ICT in subject teaching that has led to the low level of penetration into schools reported by surveys (e.g. Lovegrove and Wilshire 1997).

The way in which pupils work in the subject classroom varies considerably according to the use made of the technology, but the introduction of ICT often seems to demand a considerable change in teaching. Often, the introduction of computers into subject teaching pushes classroom organisation towards a more individualised model in which children proceed at their own rate, sometimes working individually on different tasks (Goodson and Mangan 1995). This form of organisation sits more easily with some subject cultures than with others, and in many cases would represent a major change in practice.

Integrated learning systems (ILS) are based on such a form of organisation. They take an instrumental stance (Skemp 1976) to instruct pupils about correct methods which must be followed exactly, with little room for personal interpretation or initiative. Control of learning is in the hands of the management system and not the pupil. Although many teachers, perhaps even the majority, would regard the pedagogy assumed by such systems as unproblematic, many others would find it to be old-fashioned and so different from the subject subculture as to be almost unusable.

> The last time I tried to have a go with ICT, I can't say it was terribly successful. At the time, the packages available commercially in French insisted on total

accuracy, which we do not insist on when children write their work. It just didn't work with all these machines beeping at children all the time, for leaving off accents – all the fun element was gone.

(French teacher)

If we reflect back on the nature of ICT capability as discussed in Chapter 2, it is clear that such systems would be unlikely to teach the higher order knowledge and processes required. However, ICT in subject teaching tends more commonly to be associated with an increase in individual control, personal responsibility for learning and free exploration by pupils. Certainly, the activities suggested by subject advisers, university researchers and government guidance show a tendency to move pedagogical style in this direction (e.g. Tanner and Jones 1995). The emphasis in such activities is often on the development of higher order knowledge and processes in both the subject and in ICT itself. Unfortunately, it is clear that for many teachers, a move in this direction would represent a major change in their teaching style. Fortunately, it is also the case that the majority of teachers care deeply about their pupils and are interested in opening up new opportunities for them (Goodson and Mangan 1995). Although teachers identify very closely with their subject subculture, many are prepared to exhibit flexibility in style and make significant efforts to adapt to the demands of new technology.

Adoption of ICT

The take-up of computers is variable across subject departments within schools, and it is clear that the innovation required is easier to achieve in some subjects than in others. Goodson and Mangan (1995: 624) claim that 'if an individualised classroom environment already exists, the introduction of computers is fairly unproblematic'. Uptake of computers is also closely influenced by teachers' views about their subject and the nature of appropriate content, and Selwyn (1999a: 36) reports that when ICT use is 'inherently congruous with the nature and content of their subject', using a computer is viewed as 'unproblematic if not inevitable'. When the existing culture is pupil-centred, the introduction of ICT into subject teaching is likely to be seen as less problematic, whereas in subjects with a more teacher-centred culture ICT might be viewed as a threat to traditional classroom processes of teaching and learning (Selwyn 1999a). Moseley and Higgins (1999), working with successful primary teachers, report that those who favour ICT are likely to value collaborative working, enquiry and decision making by pupils. On the other hand those with reservations about the use of ICT are likely to exercise a higher degree of direction or to prefer pupils to work individually.

Pedagogy is highly resistant to change. Very few teachers change their pedagogy on introducing ICT; they just modify their existing practice. They tend to describe the computer as *just a tool* and maintain their original lesson structure and objectives largely as before. The introduction of computers is greeted most enthusiastically when no change is required (Goodson and Mangan 1995).

Goodson and Mangan (1995) also describe how a minority of teachers react to the innovation, not by trying to fit the computer to what they already do, but by overthrowing their existing practice, surrendering their subject to vocationalism and becoming technical trainers rather than subject teachers. We are concerned, however, that in such cases the change may be superficial and transitory. ICT capability, like other key skills, shows in its application to a meaningful task. Although it is sometimes appropriate to modify the objectives of a subject to take account of the potential of ICT, it would not be right for the key experiences and values of subject disciplines to be replaced by those of technology, or by a false vocationalism. The higher order skills and processes characteristic of high ICT capability are seen when pupils and teachers recognise opportunities to make *appropriate* use of the technology. When the technology is the sole focus of the activity, the ICT use is most likely to be *inappropriate* and superficial. In the longer term, such uses prove to be transient, and are often dropped at the end of the curriculum development projects that introduced them, having failed to mesh with the underlying values and beliefs of the subject. During the ITCD project we saw many examples of the superficial use of ICT in subject teaching, uses which lacked educational value and were unlikely to stand the test of time.

For example, we saw English lessons in several schools in which writing, which had been drafted and re-drafted until perfect, was typed up on the computer to produce a neat copy. The value of such an activity to the development of the pupils' abilities in English was marginal, at best. As the drafting and re-drafting had occurred away from the computer, little of value was gained in the development of ICT capability. Activities such as this give the outward appearance that computers are making inroads into subject teaching, but the use is superficial. There is no educational value added by such use of the technology.

Becoming ICT-capable teachers

Teachers new to ICT are like novice teachers in their first year of teaching. Even experienced teachers swing from permissiveness to excessive strictness, focusing on class management and control issues and superficial features of the situation (Mevarech 1997). As might be expected, after their initial focus on discipline, their concerns focus next on how they would behave if all the screens went blank. Their attention is often focused on the technology rather than the pedagogy. They often increase their direction of pupil activity considerably and follow a transmission model of teaching (Selinger 1999). At first they follow teacher guidance blindly and fail to base decisions on their own pedagogical knowledge. In consequence, standards often decline at first (Mevarech 1997).

In order to become ICT capable, teachers must become aware of the affordances of the technology for learning within their subject. In order to be able to use ICT effectively, teachers must develop metacognitive knowledge and skills which enable them to control the computer as a tool and spot the opportunities for appropriate use as they occur. Gaining this higher level knowledge requires significant effort on the part of the teacher as learner. Teachers are unlikely to make such an effort unless they see a purpose for the activity which is relevant in their own terms. 'All meaningful learning must involve the kind of production over which the learner feels a *sense of responsibility*, *relevance*, and *empowerment*' (Stables *et al.* 1999). An externally imposed development is unlikely to generate such a sense.

Unfortunately, access to computers by subject teachers and ownership of computers by subject departments can often be very limited. ICT co-ordinators have a curriculum role with their own subject content to teach and their own agenda for development. Within a highly balkanised school, ICT will always be seen to some extent as a rival department raising the possibility of territorial disputes. Selwyn (1999a) reports that there is often a disagreement between ICT co-ordinators and subject teachers about the value of centralising ICT resources in computer labs. ICT co-ordinators were enthusiastic about 'the control and easy access to machines that the labs afforded' whereas non-ICT subject teachers felt that the lab system 'disenfranchised them of a right to use computers' (Selwyn 1999a: 41). This is an example of balkanisation and territorial disputation, but one which also reflects issues of curriculum policy and planning.

The organisation and distribution of computers in an institution should reflect the curriculum needs of that institution, for example, the need to service examination courses in ICT or generic ICT lessons. However, once such courses have been prioritised, there are knock-on effects in other curriculum areas. The teachers in the ITCD project spoke often of their difficulties in accessing computers because resources were tied up with ICT classes. Subject teachers also made it clear that they wanted access which was local to their department and under their own control, allowing them to create their own subject ambience around the facility, their own forms of organisation which permitted informal last-minute bookings for *ad hoc* use.

> I don't want a computer room. We do carousel activities, and if I had a couple of machines in my classroom they could run two of my activities; but what I cannot do is send a group off to the computer room or library unsupervised.
>
> (French teacher)

> I suppose I could book in advance, but I cannot book in September for March – I don't know what my needs are going to be. I need to book today for tomorrow and that's difficult.
>
> (German teacher)

One of our case study schools was moving towards this form of devolved control by placing a suite of ten computers in the locality of each large department. Another had allocated one large computer room solely for other subject use and allowed bookings to be made no more than one week in advance. It is clear that centralised systems that must be booked months in advance do not meet the criterion of practicality for the many teachers who plan on a more day-to-day basis. Unless issues of access and ownership are solved, there is a danger that subject teachers will regard the resources as *someone else's computers*. Furthermore, if the computers are sited in an environment with the ambience of a different subject area, this is likely to reinforce the negative attitude that they are to be used only when *teaching someone else's subject*.

Managing change in the subject department

The introduction of ICT into subject teaching is posited on a *root-and-branch* change.

> It requires *branch changes* through the demand for significant changes of practice in the use of computers but also demands *root changes* through changes in underlying beliefs about pedagogy and the nature of traditional subjects. Root changes are unlikely to occur unless teachers are fully involved in the process. The involvement of teachers in educational change is vital to its success, especially if the change is complex. . . . And if this involvement is to be meaningful and productive, it means more than teachers acquiring new knowledge of curriculum content or new techniques of teaching. Teachers are not just technical learners, they are social learners too.
>
> (Hargreaves 1994: 11)

Teachers are social learners, and change is likely to remain superficial unless it is based on their own desires for change arising from within the subject culture. Pedagogy in secondary schools is driven to a large extent by the examination system. This is especially true in KS4 and post-16. Under pressure to perform against external criteria, teachers' and pupils' aims for education become focused on a well-defined goal: *the grade*. The subject teacher asks two key questions, in such situations, when the use of ICT is suggested. First, is the use of ICT a syllabus requirement? For most subjects, this immediately produces a negative response. Second, does the use of ICT produce a better grade in my subject? This may elicit a more positive response, but the belief may be based primarily on the motivational aspects of computer use.

Teachers and their pupils impose conditions of practicality which dictate the limitations of use for ICT in the upper secondary school. This leads to *defensive teaching* (Selwyn 1999a). For some pupils on examination courses *defensive learning* may also apply as they react negatively to activities that are not in the examination.

> Perhaps we should use computers more, but we are working with children who can't do the basics of adding up, taking away, etc., and one has to strike a balance. It isn't in any exam syllabus, and that's what counts! Graph plotting, for example, gives a pretty picture, but we haven't found it particularly useful. We achieved more by the traditional methods – paper and pencil and tracing paper.
>
> (Head of mathematics)

This particular teacher was not likely to be impressed immediately by the computer's affordances in relation to pupil exploration and trial-and-error working, when his pedagogy was essentially based on high direction, emphasising dictated notes, copied examples followed by practice in the mechanical routines. A movement from teacher-centred instruction towards more pupil-centred constructivist approaches to learning may be desirable, but beliefs about teaching and learning are deeply rooted and involve far more than just the use of ICT.

The introduction of ICT into subject teaching includes a number of separate elements: the development of technical skill; the use of new materials; the use of new teaching approaches; and possible changes in pedagogical beliefs. The justification for such changes in practice at national level seem to have been based largely on the possibly unwarranted assumption that computers in the classroom are *inherently a good thing*. Furthermore, until quite recently, training in the use of new technology has not been substantial. It is perhaps not surprising, then, that uptake by subject teachers has been limited. It was expecting too much of most teachers to develop in all four of these areas without clear leadership or substantial training.

> Almost all educational changes of value require new (i) skills; (ii) behaviour; (iii) beliefs or understanding . . . changes, to be productive, require skills, capacity, commitment, motivation, beliefs and insight, and discretionary judgement on the spot. If there is one cardinal rule of change in human condition, it is that you cannot make people change. You cannot force them to think differently or compel them to develop new skills.
>
> (Fullan 1993: 22–3)

To be successful, any educational innovation must address issues that are regarded by teachers as priority needs (Fullan 1991). Although teachers have often reported to researchers that they require training in the use of ICT in their subject, it is unlikely that they were suggesting this as a priority need. Many of the teachers interviewed on the ITCD project admitted a need for training, but also referred to the use of ICT in their subject as *the icing on the cake* rather than as a priority issue. Teachers are unlikely to engage in a root-and-branch reform of their practice if they are not dissatisfied with their current situation. It is clear that for many teachers, the first stage of development should be to convince them of the value of the innovation for their own identified needs (Jennings 1994). For subject teachers, the introduction of any innovation must be practicable and must improve pupils' performance in that subject. The first condition implies ready access, software which is user-friendly and reliable, and secure knowledge of their own skills in the computer environment – implying regular use. The second condition is probably more difficult to satisfy, as it requires the teacher to believe that the introduction of new technology – and perhaps a new pedagogy – will produce more than just isolated examples of effective learning. They must expect a significant improvement in examination performance.

If the introduction of ICT into subject teaching is to be more than superficial, teachers must change their thinking about their goals, their strategies for attaining those goals and the essential nature of their discipline in relation to changing technology. However, when dealing with complex change, such as that associated with a change of teaching style, many issues emerge only during implementation. Teachers will become clearly aware of their real needs only after they have begun to introduce the technology and have become more familiar with its use. However, the double bind is that teachers are likely to persist with their efforts to change only if their early needs are met during the initial stages of implementation (Fullan 1991).

Teachers' attitudes

Fortunately, teachers' attitudes to ICT are generally found to be positive. During the ITCD project we gave attitude questionnaires to an opportunity sample of teachers in twelve Welsh secondary schools: 289 teachers responded and their mean attitude was 3.4 on a scale with a mid-point of 3.0. Analysis revealed significant differences between subgroups of teachers according to their sex, their teaching subject and whether or not they had access to a home computer. Men's attitudes were on average slightly more positive than women's attitudes. Teachers from the numerate disciplines (mathematics, science, design & technology, business studies and information technology) were better disposed to ICT than were those from the non-numerate disciplines. Teachers with home computers had a more positive attitude than those without home computers.

Factor analysis revealed six main factors. These were characterised, in order of importance, as:

1   worries about their own competence with computers;
2   the efficiency of teaching with computers;
3   the quality of learning achieved when using computers;
4   computers and professionalism;
5   enjoyment;
6   the impact of computers on presentation.

Teachers' *worries about their own competence* with technology were typified by agreement with statements like: 'I worry about what to do when pupils get stuck with computer work' and 'I think I might make mistakes when I use a computer in my teaching.' This was the only factor on which there was a difference by sex, with men showing more self-confidence than women. Fewer concerns about competence were expressed by teachers with a home computer or from a numerate discipline.

The *efficiency factor* was typified by agreement with such statements as: 'Computers help me to encourage pupils to make decisions for themselves' and 'When I teach with computers I can get better work out of pupils.' Teachers with a home computer had a more positive attitude on this factor than did those without. There was no significant difference by sex or subject.

Quality of learning was typified by agreement with such statements as: 'If pupils learn about computers, they won't learn as much in other subjects' and 'The use of computers to help pupils learn is overrated.' There were no differences by sex, subject or access to home computers on this factor.

Professionalism was typified by agreement with such statements as: 'I would like to use computers more often in my teaching' and 'You don't have to know about computers to get on in teaching.' There were no differences by sex, subject or access to home computers on this factor.

Enjoyment was typified by agreement with such statements as: 'I enjoy using computers myself' and 'I enjoy lessons where pupils use computers.' There were no differences by sex on this factor, but teachers with home computers or from numerate disciplines were slightly more positive than were those from non-numerate disciplines.

Quality of presentation was typified by agreement with such statements as: 'Pupils' work is better presented if they have used a word processor' and 'Pupils will improve the quality of their work if they learn to use computers.' There were no differences by sex or subject on this factor, but teachers with home computers were more positive than were those without.

Impact of home computers

The positive impact of a home computer on key factors of teachers' attitudes is clear. When teachers have a practical means of accessing technology over an extended period, they are able to develop and practise skills, and they eventually begin to appreciate the affordances of the technology, its potential for improving the efficiency of teaching and learning processes, enjoying its use and beginning to overcome stereotypical reactions due to gender or subject background. This is in line with the findings of BECTA (Harrison *et al.* 1998) on the impact of providing 1,150 teachers in 575 schools with portable computers. The confidence and competence of the teachers improved, and their knowledge of ICT increased substantially. More importantly, teachers changed their ways of working, and there were positive benefits for teaching and learning. The conditions for success in implementation included:

* initial and immediate success with the technology;
* personal ownership and exclusive use over an extended period;
* the portability of the equipment, and formal and informal support (Harrison *et al.* 1998: 4).

The portables gave teachers a practical means of accessing technology which they could then practise with over an extended period, effectively providing them with both a home computer and practical access to a computer in school.

Many of the more ICT-capable subject teachers interviewed in the ITCD project had computers at home and claimed to have been *self-taught*, having experienced no need to go on courses to learn new ICT skills. They were often able to see new opportunities for appropriate ICT use in their subject teaching.

> I actually learned to use IT when I acquired a computer and I just made myself sit down and do it. Whenever I did INSET before then the skills were immediately forgotten because I didn't have a chance to use them straight away. But now I just use the computer as another tool in the classroom.
> (Special educational needs teacher)

Interestingly, many of the more ICT-capable teachers were unconcerned that their pupils might sometimes know more than they themselves did:

> I don't worry about children knowing more than me – you learn from one another. As long as you're willing to work in partnership with children, they respect that. It gives them a lift, the same as if they have read something you haven't. They see that you're learning all the time, never stop, for life. I don't mind saying I don't know.
>
> (Science teacher)

They regarded themselves as lifelong learners in partnership with their pupils and fellow-teachers. Furthermore, their view of education and of the school was not as balkanised as those of many of their colleagues.

> I don't feel that ICT is taking time away from science. We give a broad and balanced education, and ICT is cross-curricular.
>
> (Science teacher)

They also tended to be more willing to work in a collegial and collaborative way with their colleagues:

> I'm a firm believer in working in each other's classrooms, sharing teaching styles, how to tackle problem groups. We have done a lot of sharing of ideas recently, adopting a cross-school approach and sharing good practice.
>
> (German teacher)

One of the most successful lessons we saw using ICT in subject teaching involved this German teacher. He had set his group the task of producing an advertising leaflet in German to promote holidays in the Rhineland. He had decided not to use a German spell-checking facility as he wished the pupils to practise their skills with dictionaries. The ICT co-ordinator had offered in-class support in the early stages of this teacher's ICT development, and although her help was no longer really needed, she dropped in occasionally to offer moral support and talk to some pupils about their ICT portfolios as they worked. The pupils worked on their text on paper before moving to the computer, but on the computer they used the word-processor to draft and re-draft, as the teacher circulated discussing the language that was being used. Pupils scanned in appropriate pictures, using frames to illustrate their text. Some of the class were not skilled in this, and 'class experts' supported their less-capable peers during this procedure. These experts appeared to be well trained to explain how to perform processes without actually taking over the task. Metaphorically, they 'kept their hands in their pockets'. The ethos of the classroom was one of collaborative learning – those who knew how to do something explained to those who did not, whether pupil or teacher, German or ICT. The lesson achieved its subject goals: the pupils wrote creatively in German, the target language, and were coached in their performance as they proceeded. The lesson also achieved its goals in ICT as the teachers in the classroom, German or ICT, made general points about how these processes might be used elsewhere. The transition from teacher of German to teacher of ICT appeared seamless.

Stages of development

During the ITCD project we observed teachers in four different stages of development as they moved towards the effective integration of ICT into their teaching.

1 The end-of-term treat stage. At this early stage of development, teachers are focused on the technology rather than its use. An activity may have the potential to support their subject teaching, but they have not yet made the connection between their subject pedagogy and aims and their use of ICT. Because the link has not been made, the tendency is for the lesson to be superficial. Coaching by a trusted colleague is probably necessary for a lesson to reach its potential. At this stage, the lesson is probably only a special event and likely to be dropped from the repertoire.

2 The lesson is in the scheme of work, but it's really someone else's subject. At this stage, the teacher often says things like: 'We're going to do spreadsheets in maths for the ICT department. There is obviously a link between my subject and the activity, but I haven't had the time to think it through yet.' The aims of the lesson are ICT aims. The potential is still not fully realised, but experience is being gained, and with reflection the task and the teaching might be adapted to achieve subject specific goals. Collaborative planning within the subject department might lead to further development.

3 'I understand the affordances of the technology, which I can use as a tool. I am always looking for opportunities to use ICT to support my subject teaching.' At this stage, ICT is beginning to realise its potential for improving subject teaching. Teaching styles have begun to change as practices are changed to take account of the affordances of the new tool. The teacher recognises what ICT capability pupils will develop and plans accordingly.

4 'We are an ICT-capable school, and we all regard ourselves as teachers of the ICT Key Skill alongside literacy and numeracy as a natural part of our jobs.' At this stage, subject walls have been weakened and the focus of our attention has moved more towards the needs of the pupils than the needs of the subject. Lesson aims might relate to ICT in addition to the more usual subject aims. There is monitoring and planned progression in ICT as there is with all key skills throughout the school.

Approaches to professional development

Professional development occurs when teachers engage in an action research cycle, using classroom activities as a catalyst for professional growth (Ridgway 1997). First, they have to decide to take a risk by modifying their current practices, attempting to use new techniques or approaches. Second, they reflect on their classroom experiences, evaluating their success, perhaps discussing the issues with trusted colleagues. Third, they modify their beliefs and begin the cycle again. Clearly, for this approach to move forwards, success in the form of satisfying classroom experiences must begin in the first part of the cycle. Two conditions are thus necessary if the subject teacher is to engage with ICT: a desire on the part of the teacher to change; and a set of activities that can reasonably be expected to produce success, which is judged as such by the teacher at his or her current stage of development (Ridgway 1997).

The subject teachers who we hope will introduce ICT-based approaches may already be operating very successfully according to their own standards and according to the usual norms of the school. Asking such teachers to attempt to teach in another way is to ask them to take a risk with their professional reputations. Ridgway (1997) presents us with the case of Jim, an imaginary teacher of mathematics:

> Asking Jim to teach in different ways is asking him to expose his mathematics, his professional competence, his classroom credibility with children and the respect which the school has for him. The costs to us of his classroom failure would be tiny; the costs to Jim might be very great indeed.
>
> (Ridgway 1997: 7)

Why should Jim play the ICT game? Continuing in established patterns is the safe option. The challenge to curriculum managers and ICT co-ordinators is to create systems and provide tasks during the critical early stages of innovation which will ensure that Jim's reputation is not exposed to unacceptable risk and yet will demonstrate that the affordances of the technology can produce improved learning on Jim's terms. The most successful ICT co-ordinators we saw on the ITCD project worked collaboratively with subject teachers to generate lesson ideas that were acceptable within their current pedagogical beliefs and then supported their implementation in the classroom to ensure that technical difficulties were minimised.

There is much evidence that supportive relationships among teachers are a prerequisite for successful school-based curriculum development. In fact, it is often claimed that curriculum development and teacher development are brought together through collaboration and collegiality (Hargreaves 1994: 186). The implementation phase of curriculum development is best served by a collaborative culture that encourages trust, support and open channels of communication (Fullan 1988). Such collaborative cultures are usually spontaneous, voluntary, development-oriented and unscheduled (Hargreaves 1994: 192). Unfortunately, Hargreaves (1994: 189) claims that the forms of collaboration which support curriculum development are comparatively rare. However, the best subject departments exhibit precisely these characteristics (Tanner and Jones 1999b). In fact, one of the major strengths of the subject subculture is that collaborative teams evolve that are often able to support novices in the critical early stages of attempting to implement innovative approaches.

In the case of ICT, however, it may be the case that the subject department is initially unable to offer skilled support and that this must be provided by the ICT co-ordinator. In the ITCD project, the most successful ICT co-ordinators were able to operate as trusted friends and collaborators in the classroom, providing any necessary technical support, companionship and professional feedback to support the early stages of implementation.

Even the most socially skilled and persuasive ICT co-ordinators required the support of the senior management team and in particular of the headteacher to encourage significant numbers of teachers to take the risk and commit themselves to the innovation. However, successful implementation of a complex development requires persuasion rather than compulsion if the change is to be more than superficial.

> The more complex the change, the less you can force it . . . ideas acquired with ease are discarded with ease. New ideas of any worth to be effective require an in depth understanding, and the development of skill and commitment to make them work. You cannot mandate these things. The only alternative that works is creating conditions that enable and press people to consider personal and shared visions and skill development through practice over time.
>
> (Fullan 1993: 22–3)

Goals must be communicated clearly by the senior management team, but if these are over-simplified superficial change results. A false clarity may be presented and superficial goals generated if the more difficult aspects of innovation are avoided (Fullan 1991). ICT capability requires the development of higher level knowledge and processes, not just the practising of low-level skills and techniques. Unless the goals of the reform are focused on higher level processes, difficult issues of pedagogy and beliefs about learning, there is a danger that context-based technological skills will become the sole focus of teaching activities. Teachers will *do* spreadsheets in mathematics and will *do* word-processing in English, while failing to make a link between the use of the technology and their subject aims and so failing to change their beliefs about learning. It is unlikely that either subject knowledge or ICT capability would develop in such a context, as higher order knowledge and processes would be ignored.

For example, during the ITCD project, we observed several superficial lessons in different schools on the theme of designing a poster to prevent litter. This activity was conducted during English lessons with classes whose ages varied from 6 to 14. We were informed that this was 'writing with a sense of audience' – an essential element of the National Curriculum for English. Unfortunately, in very few of the lessons we observed was there any discussion of the relative merits of the language used with regard to the intended audience. In many cases, no progress was observed against any targets to do with English as a subject. Nor, in most cases, did we observe much progress in ICT capability, as the focus of the lesson was usually on the exact commands required for a particular clip-art package. It is possible that some of the more insightful pupils did subsequently reflect on their experiences. However, in most cases, because the teachers were novices with ICT and were working on an essentially superficial level, they failed to teach in a manner that would gain maximum educational value from the task. These lessons did not possess the characteristics either of effective ICT lessons, which would have considered different concepts and techniques for presentation in different contexts, or of effective English lessons, which would have considered the use of the medium for expression appropriate to different genres.

In one case, however, we observed a teacher whose main aim for the lesson was to develop transferable knowledge about the use of frames for organising text and images. In this case the teacher had a clear sense of purpose for the lesson, and used discussion during the activity and a plenary session at the end to encourage pupils to generalise from their experiences using frames, with the intention of developing their ICT capability. The teacher asked the class to brainstorm the advantages and disadvantages of using frames and to suggest other contexts in which they might be used. We believe that this act of collective reflection would be likely to encourage the development of metacognitive knowledge about the affordances of the technology.

This reflective teacher also focused on the language used, and during the plenary got the class to articulate valuable points about the appropriate use of formal and informal language. In the superficial lessons, novices with ICT were quite naturally focusing on the mechanics of the task itself, whereas in the reflective lesson the task was a context in which to reflect on experiences, and to generalise from them and develop higher level knowledge. The teacher of this lesson was reasonably experienced in the use of ICT, and was addressing the difficult questions about its contribution to teaching and learning rather than just adding another task to the curriculum.

Although the reflective teacher succeeded in drawing some valuable points about language and audience from the task, the activity is not one rich in potential for work about language. Another teacher had devised a task that was richer in its use of language and thus addressed aims associated with the teaching of English more directly. The pupils were required to produce a web page reporting on a book they had enjoyed reading. The audience for the pages was comprised of other pupils in the class who might be interested in reading the book. Writing book reports is a common feature of English lessons, but the use of ICT added the demand that the pupils write in the genre of the web page, with consequences for design and language use. The task used ICT not just as a tool for producing an attractive product, but as an integral element of the activity. This teacher also used questioning effectively during the task and a reflective plenary at the end to draw out generic features within both English and ICT, which had a clear focus on higher level processes. The pupils were motivated by what they saw as a real-life task and produced a product of which they were proud.

For teacher development to occur, the complex relationship between the affordances of the technology, the ICT capabilities of the pupils and the subject aims of the lesson must be made explicit and subject to reflection. Planning and evaluation of the use of technology as a tool are required, not just dabbling with activities for their own sake.

In order for teachers to understand the interaction between subject aims and the affordances of the technology, they actually need to use ICT in the classroom. It often seems to be the case that a change in behaviour must precede a change in beliefs (Fullan 1991). However, teachers can be very efficient learners. If they view an innovation as practicable and if sufficient support and appropriate conditions are provided, they will endure the turbulence and anxiety associated with change for the good of their pupils (Fullan 1991; Huberman 1992).

Any worthwhile change will involve significant effort, and even pain, as long-held beliefs and practices are overturned (Fullan 1991). There must be some benefit for teachers to encourage them to participate. Fortunately, one of biggest motivators for teachers is the belief that the effort they are making will help them become better teachers! If the proposed activities meet teachers' practicability tests in terms of support, access, respect for their current teaching style and a reasonable expectation of improved pupil learning, they are likely to be willing to experiment with the use of ICT in their teaching. If their early experiences are positive, they are then likely to persevere, eventually changing their beliefs about learning and their attitudes to their use of ICT.

Key issues

1   Secondary teachers' identities are built around allegiance to subject cultures.
2   The nature of subject cultures can inhibit integration of ICT, and the strength of the allegiances can form a barrier to cross-curricular collaboration on key skills such as ICT capability.
3   Although teachers are predisposed to the use of ICT by pupils, this may not be enough to stimulate their own continued use. Their early attempts to exploit ICT should thus be planned to ensure success in subject teaching.
4   Developing an ICT-capable classroom often means a fundamental change in teaching style, and this can take time.

Points for reflection

•   To what extent is your school balkanised? What strategies might help overcome barriers to a whole-school approach to ICT capability development?
•   Is there a potential ICT representative in each department who has sufficient credibility in teaching his or her subject to lead others forward?

7 The ICT specialist

Establishing a new type of subject culture

Having considered the potential and the challenges of ICT for teachers of other subjects, we now pursue the question of the role for specialist teachers of ICT. These staff can have a great effect on the success of a whole-school initiative on ICT capability, and the senior management of secondary schools need to consider it carefully in relation to their strategies for whole-school ICT capability development.

This chapter is both incomplete as a study of the field and necessarily somewhat subjective given the paucity of relevant published research on the specialist role. The ITCD project did not survey the roles, practices or attitudes of ICT specialist teachers in relation to their subject, and there is only a very small literature base concerning pedagogy in the subject. We do have some understanding of the issues concerning how the ICT specialist teacher influences whole-school ICT capability, however, and to explain these we start with a look at the nature of ICT as a specialist subject, and how this has developed in the curriculum.

The nature of ICT as a subject

We can identify a number of fields of knowledge whose content or methods are used by researchers and practitioners in the field of ICT:

- *engineering*: for methods of selection of materials, tools and techniques with properties required for particular purposes, and for the design, construction and configuration of devices and systems;
- *mathematics*: for the structures and relationships of logic and algebra which underlie information storage, retrieval and processing;
- *psychology*: for the ways in which humans interact with machines;
- *sociology*: for the broader impact of ICT on human activity and relationships.

Are there important concepts and methods of enquiry that characterise ICT as a discipline in its own right? There seem to be a number of fundamental concepts and methods that make the discipline academically distinctive and characterise professional practice:

- data: binary values which may represent text characters, numbers, colours, vectors, storage locations, etc.;

- instructions: such as arithmetic operations, comparisons, movement of data;
- structures: such as tables, lists, stacks, links, networks;
- procedures: such as search, sort, evaluate, insert, delete, locate, transfer, exchange;
- information systems: comprising collection, entry, storage, processing and communication of data to provide information for users;
- hardware subsystems: input, output, storage, communications;
- software subsystems: BIOS, DOS, applications;
- systems development: strategies such as analysis, design, implement, test.

The list is not immutable, of course, and new items may be added to any of these categories when sufficiently accepted by the research and development community.

Such a high level of content completeness is relevant primarily to the researcher or developer. In analysing the concepts and methods which characterise ICT, it is important to distinguish the *user* of ICT from the *developer* of ICT systems, each of whom requires a particular level of understanding. For the user, the fundamental concepts will be those of Table 2.1 (see p. 22), and the methods can be characterised in the form of the strands of progression in ICT (see p. 16). Again, these are not fixed, and new ideas at user level will also be generated by the research and development community.

These concepts and processes make up the *content* of ICT as a subject. However, the study of ICT in schools concerns primarily the ways in which ICT is applied to various *contexts*, particularly:

- curriculum;
- business;
- leisure;
- school administration.

The General Certificate of Secondary Education (GCSE) IT syllabus of the Welsh Joint Education Committee (WJEC 1998), for instance, specifies that candidates will be expected to be familiar with ICT applications in:

- shops and money services;
- the Electronic Office.

The National Curriculum, on the other hand, explicitly states that studies in other curriculum subjects should be the main context for the study of ICT, and the change in context for GCSE represents a progression from the familiar context of school to the less familiar context of commerce and work. It appears at first sight to represent a shift from academic to vocational emphasis. Indeed, there are GCSE syllabuses with a genuine vocational bias (RSAEB 1996). Further analysis of the WJEC syllabus, examination papers and mark schemes reveals, however, that the knowledge expected is a quite abstract and idealised model of real-world practice. While learning prior to GCSE is generally based on practical tasks and problems that are real for the pupils, for pupils taking the WJEC and similar syllabuses, the shift at GCSE is in fact towards the academic.

Development of ICT as a subject

The process by which a domain of knowledge becomes a school subject has been studied extensively by Goodson and colleagues (Goodson 1995; Goodson and Marsh 1996), who identify four processes which are involved:

(a) invention;
(b) promotion;
(c) legislation; and
(d) mythologisation.

Goodson draws on Layton's 1972 analysis of the development of science as a school subject since the nineteenth century in terms of three stages:

1   The subject is initiated on the basis of utility, and it is its perceived relevance that attracts students to it.
2   Academic status starts to accrue as more scholarly work is carried out in the field. The subject develops conceptual structure as its basis, and attracts students by its reputation.
3   The subject becomes an academic tradition, which students passively choose and study because it is the norm.

Goodson (1995) also suggests, however, that many school subjects are barely disciplines, because they are unsure about their most fruitful concepts, explanations and characteristic methodologies. There is much evidence for this in the case of ICT as a subject: not just in the lack of literature, but in the range of pedagogical practice that we have observed. Yet we can already perceive the same pattern of development emerging for ICT as for science. Stage 3 would seem to be inappropriate for an ICT-capable school, however, and headteachers should take steps to prevent that situation being reached.

From our observations during the ITCD project, we can identify four main strands (see Figure 7.1) that have influenced the current nature of ICT as a subject in UK secondary schools.

Each of these strands represents a body of educational practice for which ICT is an important tool or focus, and the influence of each has waxed and waned over the relatively short period of time since ICT first entered the educational arena – which itself was remarkably soon after the invention of digital technology. The predominant influence on the authors of the National Curriculum seems to have been the information/study–skills field, despite the initial placing of ICT in the design & technology domain (see Chapter 1). In secondary schools, however, the computer science and business studies fields had already established territorial claims over ICT resources, and we have seen that these curricular influences still

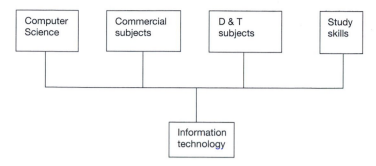

Figure 7.1 Influences on the development of specialist ICT courses

dominate the practice of ICT teaching at KS3. The advent of the National Curriculum led many schools to turn away from the computer science influence, as they switched resources from specialist examination courses to the provision of an ICT entitlement for all pupils. GCSE syllabuses in the early 1990s were, in any case, required to be compatible with the National Curriculum, but the influence of the computer science interest group remains strong in most examination boards, and the more recent changes in government policy have allowed the boards to return to a more theoretical content base for their schemes.

This brief analysis highlights the socially constructed nature of the ICT curriculum, and we now consider how the social unit of the department impacts upon the ICT capability of the school.

ICT departments

ICT is quite a recent addition to the curriculum, and it is perhaps surprising that ICT departments have developed so rapidly. The explanation for this lies in the importance of subject departments in the professional life of teachers, for which we have reviewed the evidence in Chapter 6.

Most of the secondary schools involved in the ITCD project had an identifiable department of ICT, although their characteristics varied considerably according to the following three factors:

- *The size of the department.* In large schools, there could be three or four teachers whose main allegiance was to the ICT department. Where the departmental head was a successful leader, they were able to share a vision, share ideas, share responsibilities and form a team that could achieve more than the individual teachers could in isolation. In small schools, however, often only the head of ICT could really be identified as a specialist teacher of ICT. Other teachers who taught some ICT owed primary allegiance to other departments, and relied very much on the head of ICT for detailed guidance on what to do. The effectiveness of this arrangement depended largely on the qualities of the head of ICT as a teacher and as a producer of learning materials for pupils.

- *The importance of departments in the management and ethos of the school.* There was some variation in the status of the individual subject departments in the management structures of the schools. In a school where departments were influential in the management structure, there was pressure on the head of ICT to make ICT an important subject in its own right. In this situation, it is perhaps inevitable that teachers of other subjects view ICT as *not our problem*, and leave it exclusively to the specialists. In schools that were less balkanised (see Chapter 5), there was more opportunity to support other subject teachers in their contribution to pupils' ICT capability.
- *The role and status of the head of the ICT department.* In most cases, the head of ICT was the school ICT co-ordinator as well. The difference in roles was usually somewhat blurred. The head of department role was concerned primarily with examination courses; the co-ordinator role was concerned primarily with resource management; and the management of ICT capability development was the area with least clear specification of responsibility and was consequently the role least effectively carried out. In some cases, the head of ICT was not the school ICT co-ordinator and did not have responsibility for KS3 National Curriculum ICT.

It was clear from our observations and interviews for the ITCD project that being a teacher of ICT, with full or partial membership of the ICT department, was an important factor in influencing teachers' perspectives on the development of ICT capability and their practices in teaching ICT as a subject. Although ICT teachers' perspectives and practices varied from school to school to a greater extent than for teachers of any other subject, we observed more similarities within ICT as a subject in different schools than we have seen similarities between ICT and any other subject in the same school. We thus feel that ICT has developed its own subculture.

The most successful departments worked to try to develop some consistency in the approaches of staff. The head of department encouraged members of staff to observe each others' classes, either formally at agreed times or by dropping in when convenient. Teaching approaches were discussed in departmental meetings, as well as schemes of work, resources, assessment and scheduling issues.

Pedagogical practices and representation of concepts for teaching

In characterising common practice within subject departments and variations in practice between teachers within a department, Ball and Lacey (1995) differentiate between subject *paradigm* and subject *pedagogy*. They note that particular pedagogies tend to be associated with particular paradigms.

ICT seems to be rather complex in this respect, and there may be more than one paradigm in the same school when there is no clearly defined department. At KS4, the choice of GCSE syllabus is perhaps the main indicator of the subject paradigm for ICT in a school. We can distinguish two main paradigms or cultures of specialist ICT teaching: the *academic* culture and the *capability* culture.

It is characteristic of an *academic* ICT culture that lessons are divided into the *theoretical* and the *practical*. At its best, this reflects an expectation that, in lessons away from the computer, pupils will reflect on their practical activities and on their experiences outside of school, and that they will contribute to discussion of the principles behind them. They are then given opportunities to apply the principles in context. These expectations are developed from the beginning of Year 7.

At its worst, the non-computer lessons are scheduled because of a shortage of resources, and there is little pupil talk and much pupil writing (by hand), which is resented by pupils. There is little relation between these lessons and the practical work, which involves a combination of highly structured activities designed for the learning of techniques, and very open tasks ('projects') which may be unlike any tasks met by pupils before the stage of examination assessment. Pupils have difficulty organising their project work, but teachers feel unable to provide scaffolding for pupils who are working on projects, because it must be the learner's own work that is assessed for examination purposes.

A *capability* ICT culture, at its best, is characterised by:

(a) project- and resource-based learning, with theoretical principles discussed as necessary to solve problems and explain relationships, as they are met;
(b) work in groups, on and off the computer, involving discussion and reporting;
(c) direct experience of the need for information and for practical ICT solutions in the world of work;
(d) assessed project work to be carried out when pupils have sufficient higher order skills, and knowledge of processes and techniques, to be able to work largely independently.

The capability culture is clearly supported by Crawford (1998b). He feels that only a constructivist view of knowledge and learning is appropriate to ICT, and suggests that many traditional beliefs and teaching approaches are therefore ineffective. Teachers can never be a comprehensive source of information and explanation – indeed, they should learn alongside their pupils, or from pupils who know more than they do about the particular software being used. The National Curriculum for ICT does not tell them what to teach, but does require that pupils have access to a range of tools. Pupils can attempt real tasks, as they have access to the same software as is used by professionals, and the teacher should not direct their focus through the use of set mechanical tasks.

These ideas are echoed by Selinger (1997), who provides also some principles that should be the basis of ICT teaching:

- It is OK to make mistakes.
- Collaborative learning is positively encouraged.
- Peer support is as valuable and as legitimate as (if not more so than) teacher support.
- Students are empowered through taking control of the technology.
- The locus of control moves away from the teacher.

Effective teaching of ICT

Drawing on Crawford's (1998b) suggestions, together with our analysis of ICT capability and our own observations of specialist ICT teaching, we can suggest a number of valuable principles concerning the development of concepts and skills.

Plan and seek opportunities to develop each component of ICT capability

1   *Routines*. The conversion of techniques to routines may be left to natural processes in the course of tasks set in lessons. Pupils who are slower to learn routines will make slow progress with curriculum tasks, however, if they continually need help with basic operations such as selecting items and undoing mistakes. If pupils do not meet these important techniques sufficiently frequently, focused practice tasks may be given for homework.

2   *Techniques*. Pupils need to associate the actions involved in a technique with the effect it achieves. Having a name for the technique and/or the effect is helpful (e.g. copy-and-paste, minimise-a-window, undo, find-and-replace); the name should be seen not as something extra to learn but as a means of communicating and thinking about the action and its effect. This is especially so if the name is used in menu options, but is also helpful where mouse movements, buttons or shortcuts are used.

3   *Processes*. Whenever possible, discuss with pupils what it is they are doing at the process level rather than just identifying the next technique. Draw on relevant images and analogies where it is helpful, in order that pupils gain a feeling for the whole process. They should then be able to identify useful techniques themselves. For example, when searching a flat-file database, pupils need to keep in mind, right from the start of the process, the information they wish to be displayed and the criteria which limit the search. If they then think of the database as a stack of record cards, then the computer looks at each card in turn, checks the criteria, and writes down the required information in a list. This will clarify how they should proceed with a search.

4   *Higher order skills*. Initially, the teacher will manage the planning, monitoring and evaluation of pupils' work, involving pupils in the process through whole-class teaching. Increasingly, pupils should take over some of the thinking about their work and about their learning; this can be achieved by asking strategic and evaluative questions, encouraging pupils in groups to ask these questions of each other, and then expecting individuals to ask these questions of themselves.

Focus on concepts behind the skills

Whole-class teaching can be used to discuss examples and non-examples of a concept, both with and without ICT, in order to highlight the important features of the concept. For example, a poster is not a 'message', as it is not communicated to a particular person. Table 7.1 provides some further suggestions which can be used as the basis of questioning and activities away from the computer.

Table 7.1 Representing concepts

ICT concept	Examples	Non-examples and analogies
Electronic document	Powerpoint presentation, word-processed report, poster produced by DTP	Handwritten transparencies, printed book, drawing on paper
Message	An e-mail	Phone call, letter, poster
Hypertext	Web pages, multimedia authoring	Electronic document, printed book, videotape
Model	Spreadsheet	Table in document, printed accounts
Database	Pupil record system	Spreadsheet, card file
Database query	Finding all Year 10 pupils who are studying ICT	Visually identifying pupils in ICT classes, looking through card file
Sequence of instructions	Logo program	An apprentice, robot

Naïve ideas about handling particular tools should be challenged, both in whole-class teaching, where appropriate, and when monitoring the progress of individuals. For example:

- When pupils use spaces to spread out text on a line or page, the teacher could show the effect of adding extra text so that the spaces move to a different position in the line.
- If they use the back space key to delete back to an earlier mistake and re-type, the teacher could set a task requiring the editing of previously composed text to achieve a different goal.
- When pupils type calculations in a spreadsheet using values directly rather than formulae containing cell references, the teacher could change the values in the cells, and point out the incorrect result from the calculation based on the previous values.
- When displaying the results of a database search, if pupils select only the search field for display, the teacher could remind them of the manual process with a card file to focus on the distinction between search criterion and information display.

Reflection is a vital element in concept development, and a reflective write-up activity (Deadman 1997) can be used to focus pupils' thinking on the principles they have met. Research or discussion activities carried out in groups can be reported to a plenary session using an ICT tool such as presentation software. Reflection is also an important aspect of their higher order skills, and pupils should be expected to use the technique as a matter of course in all subjects as they progress in secondary school.

Use a range of ways of supporting pupils

Choose methods carefully for supporting pupils' learning in order to meet their needs. When the focus is on techniques, the following may be used successfully in appropriate situations:

- demonstration with descriptive or explanatory commentary (mainly used in introducing the ideas to a group or the whole class);
- monitored instruction (the teacher gives instructions step-by-step and checks that the pupils are following);
- monitored repetition (the pupils try to repeat the technique, with the teacher filling in what the pupils can't do);
- guided discovery (the pupil tries to work out the steps, with the teacher providing questions/prompts to help them recognise relevant cues, concepts and familiar techniques);
- guided repetition (pupil tries to repeat the technique, with the teacher providing questions/prompts to help the pupil recognise relevant cues and concepts);
- quick fix (the teacher solves a problem without explanation to enable the pupil to focus on the intended objectives).

As we saw in Chapter 2, when focusing on higher order knowledge and processes, pupils should be expected to think about their actions, to talk about their work and to write plans and reports. Both whole-class and small-group work can be used effectively to support pupils as they are developing metacognitive knowledge and skills.

Use a careful combination of criteria in making assessments of attainment

A judgement of capability will depend on the appropriateness of task outcome, the techniques/processes/strategies observed, the resources available, the time taken and the support provided. But be careful not to assess other subject knowledge rather than ICT capability, and do not attempt to achieve a level of precision that is unrealistic and unnecessary.

For example, the science department may set pupils the task of producing a poster to encourage young children to eat healthful foods as a context for the application of science knowledge in ICT lessons as well as for the development of their ICT capability. We cannot separate out pupils' ICT capability from their knowledge of children and food, but we do not want to prevent pupils from achieving their potential with ICT because of inadequate contextual knowledge. They will thus need an initial discussion, and subsequent intervention on design features suitable for young children and on the nutritional knowledge needed, building on work they have carried out in science lessons. There will be particular matters to look for while they are working on the task. For instance, if they choose inappropriate foods in their illustrations, consider whether this is because:

- they have not understood the requirements of the task;
- they have misunderstood the nutritional content of the foods;
- the clip-art available is limited;
- they are unable to locate or insert the appropriate images.

The first three should not affect the assessment of ICT capability. At the end of the activity, a plenary evaluation will enable the teacher to focus pupils' thinking on what makes a poster effective, using science criteria concerning nutrition and ICT criteria concerning the selection of techniques and visual effects.

During examination courses, integrate practical work with teaching the concepts and terminology of information systems

Real contexts should be used, and a case study approach can be employed in which a scenario for ICT application is studied in terms of

- the need for information;
- data collection and entry;
- data communication;
- data storage;
- data processing;
- information display.

By considering the purpose of the information system, each aspect can be analysed and evaluated in terms of design issues, techniques used and hardware/software tools needed (see Figure 7.2).

For project work, a clear briefing is given and careful monitoring is carried out, and when intervention is needed, just sufficient questioning and prompting is given to enable pupils to continue. Specific help is noted and taken into account when assessing formally.

The ICT department's contribution to the ICT-capable school

We have provided some pointers towards an effective pedagogy for ICT as a subject. How, then, are ICT specialist teachers to respond to the development of an ICT-capable school? If ICT use pervades the curriculum, what is the role of a specialist teacher?

We have presented a view of ICT as a subject in which the concepts are drawn out from experiences of the practicalities of life. This is in contrast to the traditional view of a subject as a fundamental knowledge structure which must be carefully developed in pupils during their schooling. Most of the rest of the curriculum, however, is set out in a highly detailed way, subject by subject, with particular content at particular ages, reflecting the traditional view of subjects. Attempts to

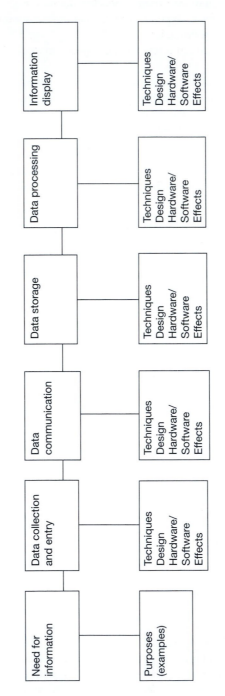

Figure 7.2 Principles of information systems and corresponding matters to be taught

promote linking themes have not been supported by the UK government during the 1990s. The recent initiatives concerning literacy and numeracy are also based on the belief that teaching these skills should be separated out from other activities, even in the primary curriculum. This makes it particularly difficult to pursue an alternative approach with ICT.

Nevertheless, we see possibilities in the secondary schools that retain the strengths of a specialist department while still promoting and exploiting the whole-curriculum approach. Where there is no ICT department, the full integration of ICT capability development across the curriculum *can* be successful, particularly in a small school with good communications among the staff. In this situation, however, ICT may become an *unreal* subject, and there is a danger that pupils' ICT learning is accorded little status unless an accredited course is provided. Where an ICT department has attained an academic status, a whole-school model should build on its strengths by giving specialist teachers a support role in the development of ICT in other subjects.

In the ITCD project, we observed three particular approaches (see also Chapter 4) that were already demonstrating some success in schools which had a typical level and range of pupil performance generally. Summary details are given below:

(a) School 1

- large school;
- three full-time ICT teachers;
- discrete KS3 delivery, with aim of covering most of the GCSE short-course syllabus in KS3;
- full GCSE courses a popular option in KS4, with provision restricted to around half the pupils only;
- staff working on applying ICT capability throughout the curriculum through regular meetings of departmental representatives.

(b) School 2

- medium-sized school;
- one full-time ICT specialist/co-ordinator;
- cross-curricular KS3 delivery, with various subjects contributing to the teaching of all or part of a strand;
- all pupils take a GCSE short course in ICT, with specialist teaching;
- staff working on developing the effectiveness of cross-curricular delivery by the ICT specialist co-teaching with other subject specialists.

(c) School 3

- small school;
- one full-time ICT specialist/co-ordinator;
- mixed KS3 delivery, with some discrete units scheduled in Year 7 and some in Year 9, and various subjects contributing further teaching and application in liaison with the ICT specialist;
- full GCSE courses available in KS4 as options;

- staff working on broadening the range of subjects and teachers who are using ICT effectively.

We identified in these schools particular strategies designed to generalise pupils' learning and foster transfer of ICT capability across the curriculum. The strategies were similar irrespective of the approach adopted:

1   alert pupils to the key ICT teaching points;
2   challenge inefficient, naïve methods of achieving goals during a task;
3   draw out general principles from their experiences in a particular context;
4   discuss the possibilities for application of the concepts and processes in other contexts;
5   model the higher order skills needed to plan, monitor and evaluate the activities.

The most effective ICT teachers were clear that they were teaching *processes*, not merely how to use particular *programs*. They had developed policies for consistency in teaching concepts and processes, and in promoting the development of routines. Where teachers want pupils to do things in a different way from the standard approach, they discussed why, in a particular context, the new way is more appropriate than the familiar one. Issues considered in such policies included:

- use of frames and tables in word-processing and desktop publishing;
- access to clip-art libraries;
- use of names and cell references in spreadsheets;
- database design and development;
- web page access and the use of search engines.

In addition, there are issues concerning the availability and culture of computer rooms. We noted in Chapter 6 the difficulty that teachers of other subjects expressed concerning access to ICT resources in computer rooms which seemed to be under the control of the ICT department. Furthermore, teaching in a computer room has a significant effect on the balance of activity in a teacher's lesson structure, with a shift from whole-class to individual and small-group work.

We observed how pupils also have a computer room culture, so that many pupils feel more confident to work autonomously there than in conventional classrooms. They are also more inclined to work collaboratively, and this factor can be exploited by setting group tasks which enable pupils to learn from each other as well as from the teacher. But pupils' ICT culture is based on home use, and it is also necessary to set clear policies about acceptable behaviour in the school computer room, and to establish particular routines for pupil entry, seating and movement. It is important that rigid adherence to such rules does not inhibit beneficial changes in learning style, however. They must still be encouraged to try out new ideas and explore the tools available, subject to the principles of ethical ICT practices.

In general, policies on the availability and use of resources should be driven by a school plan to provide for pupil learning. The intention should be to facilitate access to resources and improve their use. The resources must be considered as the pupils', not the ICT department's. The specialist ICT teacher should help develop the confidence of other staff concerning use of the computer room, and should not act as the *gatekeeper to a secret garden*.

The role of a specialist teacher of ICT

The specialist teacher, then, has a key role to play in any approach to organising the curriculum for ICT. This role is different from that of the ICT co-ordinator, as it involves direct teaching of pupils. It may be organised as a standard teaching timetable, with the same classes scheduled throughout the year; as a series of modules with different year-groups at different times of the year, to fit in with the application in other subjects; or as the collaborative teaching of particular lessons in other subjects where significant learning objectives concern ICT.

The ICT specialist should be able to contribute aspects of the pupils' learning needs not generally expected of other teachers:

- awareness of capability developed during KS1, KS2 and outside of school, and planning to build on this progressively during KS3 and KS4;
- developing concepts and challenging naïve ideas at key points in capability development;
- ensuring new developments are incorporated into the curriculum;
- providing specialist ICT courses leading to examinations.

This list of roles also provides a starting-point for the identification of ICT specialists' own staff development needs. In addition, the ICT specialist should be able to help set high expectations of pupils in their application of ICT and contribute to developing generic higher order skills in other areas of the curriculum.

A strong specialist ICT department can avoid the isolation of ICT teachers and help develop the practice of members. But such a department can easily become politically protective, and so make it more difficult to develop the teaching of ICT within other areas of the curriculum. In order to overcome this, we identified in Chapter 3 the value of a wider group, representing all departments, to plan staff and curriculum development. The ICT specialists should not be marginalised, however, and should have a parallel involvement in planning their own contribution to the process. Teachers of other subjects must recognise ICT teachers' status in terms of a whole-school contribution, rather than purely on examination results, and senior management has an important role to play in initiating and fostering this recognition.

Key issues

1   ICT has developed a status as a subject in its own right in the school curriculum, and this may create a barrier to a whole-school approach to ICT capability.

2   There is wide variation in teaching approaches for ICT, depending on the background of the teacher and of the subject in the school.

3   There are several principles which characterise effective teaching strategies for ICT.

4   The ICT specialist teacher or team can make a positive contribution to the ICT-capable school without loss of status, provided other departments recognise their special role.

Points for reflection

•   What role does the specialist ICT teacher/team play in your school? Does this support or inhibit the development of ICT capability across the school?

•   Will there be a need for any ICT specialist teachers once all teachers become ICT capable?

8 Pupils' perspectives on ICT education

A clash of cultures?

There is much justification for the claim that the use of ICT in schools has not yet achieved its potential to enhance learning and teaching, and has yet to make any significant impact on educational standards (Lovegrove and Wilshire 1997). The hardware in use has often been technologically outdated, with very variable penetration across schools and considerable variation in usage (Stevenson 1997). However, outside of schools it is clear that during the last twenty years technology has made great inroads into the lives of ordinary people and now impacts significantly on pupils and their families.

This chapter examines the role of pupils in developing the ICT-capable school. Pupils spend only a relatively small part of their time in school, and we need to consider the other arenas in which their ICT capability develops.

Access to ICT at home

The homes of many of our pupils contain a broad range of information and communication technology. Many pupils are now avid users of mobile telephones. Televisions are no longer used only as passive receivers but are becoming interactive devices, connected to satellite or cable decoders, video recorders and games consoles. We cannot be precise about the extent of access to computers in homes, because of differences between children's and adults' perceptions as to what constitutes a 'computer'. In 1997, the UK government estimated that 40–50 per cent of households would have at least one home computer by 2000 (Timmins 1997), and at the time of writing this seems likely to be an underestimate. Certainly, a considerable proportion of our pupils inhabit a technologically rich environment, controlling far more advanced electronic multimedia equipment in their homes than they find in their schools.

However, there also exists a substantial group of pupils who have no such access at home. The issues of equity in relation to pupils' access to home computing are complex and challenging. The rapidly changing nature of technology seems likely to amplify the gap between the information-rich and the information-poor; only the economically advantaged homes can afford to keep up with the most powerful devices and media. As we redefine learning in the twenty-first century to take account of the possibilities offered by expanding technology, equality of opportunity to develop the new literacies will become ever more significant (Downes 1997a). Pupils without home access to appropriate technology will suffer not only through their lack of the range of tools with which to learn, prepare and present work outside of school, but because of their under-exposure to the computer-rich culture existing in the homes of their more fortunate peers.

Most previous research has shown that pupils who have access to computers at home have more positive attitudes towards computers in schools than those who lack such access (see e.g. Martin 1991; Kirkman 1993; Coley *et al.* 1994; Selwyn 1997c). These results are unsurprising given the relatively small amount of computer use experienced in school. Averages sometimes disguise wide variations, but Kirkman in 1993 reported that for the average 12-year-old, over 90 per cent of computer experience was gained at home. Any bias by gender, race or class for access to computers outside of school should, then, be regarded as a serious issue in terms of equity.

Attitudes towards technology may in themselves prove to be a significant aspect of ICT capability, on the assumption that pupils with a positive attitude towards ICT are more likely to seek out applications for their ICT knowledge and skills and will therefore have a tendency towards lifelong use and learning. However, from the discussion in Chapter 1 it is clear that there are also techniques, processes and higher level skills and knowledge which must be attained. Furthermore, the differences between ICT usage at home and at school may lead to problems of transfer between the two environments. Nevertheless, there is reason to suspect that use of a computer at home is likely to improve performance in ICT in school (Underwood *et al.* 1994; Selwyn 1997c; 1997d).

Gender and class effects

Research conducted during the 1980s suggests that attitudes to computer use are greatly affected by gender. Sutton (1991: 488) offers a comprehensive summary for the period and reports either a more positive attitude to computers by males, or no difference between males and females in all cases. In no case did the research indicate a more positive attitude to computers by females rather than males.

A number of factors may have contributed to these gender differences, but exposure to computers either at home or in school appears to be the major factor and, when controlled for, differences in attitude have often been removed (see e.g. Chen 1986; Levin and Gordon 1989). However, the research suggests that boys are far more likely to have access to computers than girls. For example, Culley (1988) reported that boys were twice as likely to have access to home computers than girls and that computers were six times more likely to be bought for boys than for girls.

Research in the 1990s confirmed some of the findings of the 1980s, but also indicated that conspicuous changes may have occurred in some areas. Male pupils were still reported to be likely to have the greater access to computers outside of school but with smaller though still statistically significant differences in numbers (Reinen and Plomp 1997; Selwyn 1998). On the other hand, drawing on research in Australian primary schools, Downes (1995) suggested that gender differences were related mainly to video game ownership with no gender differences in family ownership of computers. There is also evidence that during the 1990s boys and girls used computers differently, with boys using the computer more frequently than girls and playing games more often (Kirkman 1993; Selwyn 1998), whereas girls preferred word-processing, placing games as their second most common usage (Selwyn 1998). This echoed earlier findings that girls are more likely to use computers in a productive tool-like way rather than for entertainment (Sanders 1984) and more recent interview-based research by Millard (1997), who reported that when girls are allowed free access to technology, they adapt it to their own purposes and interests.

Social class is also likely to be a factor in the availability of computers outside of school, although the relationship between class and attitudes to computers appears to be a complex one. It seems intuitively obvious that wealthier families would have access to the best equipment, and Downes (1997b) confirmed this. Similarly, Millard (1997) reported that more affluent middle-class homes are more likely to own a PC that is used for homework. However, she also suggested that girls' access is likely to be affected by class, with middle-class homes having a family machine and working-class homes a personal computer which was 'the personal property of the boys in the family' (Millard 1997: 7). Kirkman (1993) found differences between enthusiasm, confidence, self-assessed ability and home usage in three social classes, with girls in 'the lowest group' having 'the least enthusiasm for computers and the lowest self assessed academic ability'. However, boys from this low group were the most enthusiastic about computers, used them the most often and rated their abilities highly.

The ITCD project developed and trialled a questionnaire which was given to a stratified sample of 2,001 pupils in Years 6, 7 and 10, in 34 schools. The questionnaire addressed four major areas: home use of ICT, school use of ICT, self-assessment of ICT capability; and attitude to ICT. The attitude questionnaire included 32 statements and employed a 5-point scale ranging from 'strongly disagree' to 'strongly agree'. A simplified version of the questionnaire was also given to a stratified sample of 445 Year 2 pupils in 21 schools using a 3-point scale for attitude.

Overall, 61 per cent of pupils from all years claimed to have a computer at home that was not just a gaming machine. A supplementary question asked for the make and model to provide a check on the validity of the classification. The difference between boys (63 per cent) and girls (59 per cent) claiming access to a home computer was not statistically significant. The proportion of pupils with a home computer increased slightly with age, from 57 per cent in Year 2 to 64 per cent in Year 10.

For the pupils in Years 6–10 an approximate classification of socio-economic class was made by asking pupils the name of any national newspaper read in their household. These were then grouped as follows: class 1 (the red-tops): *Sun, Mirror,* etc.; class 2 (the middleweights): *Mail* and *Express,* and class 3 (the broadsheets): *The Times, Guardian,* etc. This is the same approach as used by Kirkman (1993) and in

NHS surveys (e.g. Balding 1986) as an easy and inoffensive way of collecting data about the social and cultural background of pupils. For educational purposes it has the advantage of considering the culture of the home directly, rather than through more traditional and indirect approaches based on the income or occupation of parents. However, it limits the sample used for purposes of comparison to those pupils (less than half) claiming that their household takes a national newspaper.

Table 8.1 shows that there are far fewer children in social class 1 with access to a home computer than would be expected by chance. There are far more children in social classes 2 and 3 with a home computer than would be expected by chance. The differences between the social classes are statistically significant, in contrast to the small differences between boys and girls.

Table 8.1 Percentage of pupils with a home computer by sex and class

Sex	Class 1 (F = 322, M = 243)	Class 2 (F = 123, M = 89)	Class 3 (F = 88, M = 63)	Total (F = 533, M = 395)
Females with computer				
Count	150	95	76	321
Expected value	194	74	53	321
% within class	47	77	86	60
Males with computer				
Count	130	73	51	254
Expected value	156	57	41	254
% within class	54	82	81	64
Total with computer				
Count	280	168	127	575
Expected value	350	131	94	575
% within class	50	79	84	62

There was no significant difference in the range of uses that pupils claimed for their home computers. The following uses were reported: games 90 per cent; word-processing 82 per cent; retrieving data from a CD-ROM 64 per cent; revision programmes 44 per cent; internet 26 per cent. Large numbers of both sexes and all classes reported playing games, although more boys (92 per cent) played games than girls (89 per cent). There were no other gender differences in usage overall, although there were differences by class. Social classes 2 and 3 claimed a wider range of uses than social class 1. Pupils in social class 1 used the internet much less than would be expected by chance (class 1: 21 per cent; class 2: 29 per cent; class 3: 34 per cent).

Our results suggest, then, that issues of equity about access to computers at home should now largely be focused on class and culture rather than gender. It seems likely that the children in class 1 who also have less than expected access to computers at home are the same children who lack literature and other intellectually challenging cultural experiences in the home.

Learning to use ICT in and out of school

Strack (1997) reported that a majority of pupils and parents believe the use of computer results in better marks and that computer skills are important for good marks. Certainly there was evidence in our interviews that pupils perceived their lack of access to a computer outside of school as placing them at a serious disadvantage. The aphorism 'Bill Gates doesn't do my homework' was well known in some schools; and, although often said with a degree of bravado, it implied a sense of injustice.

Pupils described learning to use a computer at home and in school differently, with the word *play* appearing frequently in interviews even when the activity described would not normally be seen as a game. So, for example, pupils reported *playing* at retrieving information from their encyclopaedia CD-ROM, *playing* on the internet, *playing* at drawing graphs or *playing* at using word-processing to write stories. This was particularly true of younger pupils. The interviews echo the findings of Downes (1998), who noted that the play aspect of home computing related to the amount of control the children had over the activity and its purpose. The pupils we interviewed talked about producing pictures and graphical designs, and attaching them to stories and e-mails to their friends for fun. On probing, it seemed that when using computers at home they enjoyed a creative freedom often denied them at school:

> You don't have a teacher looking over your shoulder and bossing you around about what to do and how to do it all the time.
>
> (Year 7 girl)

Older pupils talked about using computers in their coursework. Boys in particular seemed to find that the computer motivated them to write longer and more detailed pieces of work than usual.

> You can find stuff on the web that really gets you into it. Like when I was doing my history homework on Roosevelt, I got into the White House web site and found all kinds of stuff about his life, his dog and so on. I spent hours on that. The teacher said I must have copied it.
>
> (Year 10 boy)

Several pupils preferred to work on computers at home rather than in school. As might be expected, reasons given in interviews included disparaging comments about the old equipment used in school compared with the more modern technology in use at home.

> I have better graphics at home, so the teacher has given me special permission to do the work there.
>
> (Year 7 boy)

> I'm better at using the computer I have at home – it's a PC with Windows and that, they have old Acorns here. They're not reliable, the software is slow and they haven't got enough memory.
>
> (Year 10 boy)

Some pupils commented on school computers always being busy and said they were able to concentrate more at home than they could at school:

> The library computers are always busy and you have to wait your turn. I can work for longer at home, I don't get distracted by all the talking and so on.
>
> (Year 10 girl)

There are other sources of learning in the home as well: one Year 6 girl commented that she 'learned about using the internet from *Blue Peter* and that programme on BBC2'.

Although attitudes expressed about computers were generally positive, some older girls expressed the opinion that they didn't use computers for pleasure, but to do a job well. The work done in ICT lessons was less valued by such pupils:

> I wouldn't go to a computer club. I'm not *interested* in computers – I just use them to present my work better.
>
> (Year 10 girl)

> The stuff you learn in IT lessons might be useful later on, but it's not much use to you now.
>
> (Year 10 girl)

Other pupils recognised the value of structured ICT teaching, whether or not they had computers at home:

> I built my own PC, and I use a lot of different software, so I don't do many new things in the IT lessons. But when Mr Jones explains things, I understand what I'm doing better.
>
> (Year 10 boy)

> I don't have a computer at home, but on the IT course I learn things that I'll have to use when I leave school.
>
> (Year 10 girl)

Most pupils expressed a desire to use ICT more often in their learning, commenting on how much more interesting it was to retrieve information from CD-ROMs and the internet than from books or normal lessons. Computers were sometimes described as more forgiving, perhaps more human, than teachers tend to be: 'Teachers shout a lot. Computers don't tell you off for something you didn't do' (Year 10 boy).

Unfortunately, most pupils reported that teachers made little use of ICT across the curriculum. Sometimes this was seen as being due to a lack of expertise on the part of teachers from an older generation, who didn't understand about the technology in use today. On other occasions, it was attributed to laziness on the part of teachers who saw no need to change with the times:

> Most of them are too old – they don't understand about computers.
>
> (Year 7 girl)

> It's a lot of hassle for them. Every year they give out the same old worksheets – so why change it?
>
> (Year 10 boy)

Pupils with little experience of computers outside of ICT lessons could not see the opportunities which might be presented for teaching and learning in other subjects. A minority of pupils described using computers to draw graphs in mathematics or science lessons, but many just could not see how computers could be used in those subjects. Considering that ICT in schools often grew from the work of enthusiasts in mathematics and science departments, it is depressing to find that these are the subjects most often volunteered by pupils as being unsuitable for the use of ICT.

Learning to use computers at home was seen as a much more pleasant activity than learning from teachers in school. Pupils with home computers often indicated that they were far more independent in their learning, both *about* ICT and *with* ICT. The majority of pupils with computers expressed a willingness to have a go at learning how to use a new piece of software by themselves. Echoing the results of Downes (1998) in Australia, *Dad* (40 per cent) was the most likely person to sort it out if the computer went wrong, with *myself* (28 per cent) the second most popular choice. *Mum* was likely to be consulted by only 10 per cent of pupils, perhaps reflecting traditional stereotyping.

The confidence to sort out possible problems by oneself may be seen as an aspect of ICT capability. That 28 per cent of pupils with home computers should see themselves as the most likely person to sort out problems is an indication of the self-confidence with ICT expressed by many pupils.

Pupils' attitudes towards ICT expressed in the interviews were generally very good, and included comments about ICT being the thing of the future and necessary for employment:

> My Dad says: 'Get into IT now, 'cos there won't hardly be any jobs when we're older otherwise.'
>
> (Year 7 boy)

All the interviewees were asked which subjects were the most important in school. All pupils mentioned mathematics and English as the two most important subjects.

If a third subject was mentioned, it was usually science, but sometimes Welsh, geography or computers. To the question, 'If you were to put the subjects in order of importance, where would IT go?', answers varied between 'Pretty high up' and 'Number four'. A small minority of older girls expressed a lack of interest in computers and made disparaging remarks about other (male) pupils in their class who liked using computers, saying: 'Oh them, they're just nerds – they should get a life.' However, for the vast majority of the interviewees, the negative comments about ICT in school were about lack of use of ICT in curriculum subjects. A number of pupils felt that they had not yet gained enough experience using ICT, and expressed a desire for more school use and greater availability. This was particularly true for those without computers at home.

Attitudes

The responses of Years 6, 7 and 10 to the attitude questionnaire were above the arithmetical mid-point of the scale (3) and represented a positive attitude (see Figure 8.1).

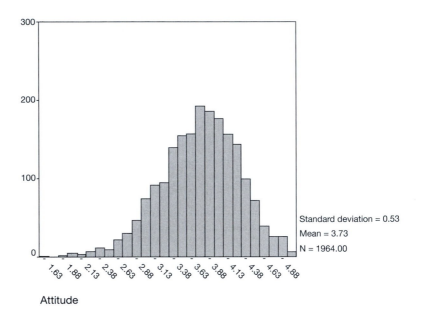

Attitude

Figure 8.1 Attitudes for Years 6, 7, 10

Similarly, the attitude questionnaire which was answered by Year 2 pupils showed a very positive attitude towards ICT (see Figure 8.2). These pupils answered on a 3-point scale coded 0, 1 and 2.

However, again there were gender differences. In Years 6, 7 and 10 combined, the boys' mean attitude score was significantly higher than the girls'. However, this was not true for the Year 2 pupils, where boys' and girls' scores were not significantly

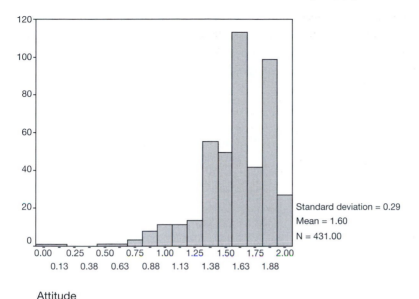

Attitude

Figure 8.2 Attitude for Year 2

different from each other. Attitudes varied significantly according to year. Pupils in Years 6 and 7 had more positive attitudes than did those in Year 10, possibly reflecting an increasing emphasis on ICT in schools and a better ICT experience in primary schools for the younger pupils.

Factors contributing to pupils' attitudes

The attitude scale for Years 6, 7 and 10 was subjected to factor analysis, and six factors were found to contribute 50 per cent of the variance in the scale. These factors were:

- enjoyment of the computer as a tool;
- frustration with inhuman machines;
- the future importance of computers;
- fear or nervousness;
- social aspects of computing;
- the utility of computers.

Three key statements from each factor are listed below to typify the attitude.

Enjoyment of the computer for its own sake or as a tool

- I enjoy using computers.
- A computer could make learning fun.
- Computers help you learn.

Frustration with machines

- Computers don't let me think for myself.
- Computers aren't as useful as they are made out to be.
- Computers take up too much time.

The future importance of computers

- Every home should have a computer.
- Everyone will have to use computers in the next century.
- Computers should be used in all subjects.

Fear or nervousness about computers

- I am worried about making mistakes on the computer.
- Sometimes I worry that all my work will disappear from the screen.
- Some of the words used in computing make me nervous.

Social aspects of computers

- I prefer to work on a computer with a friend.
- I don't like working by myself on the computer.
- When I leave school, I should like to use a computer in my job.

Utility

- Using a word-processor makes your work look neat.
- Computers are useful for finding out information.
- I feel confident in using a computer.

Gender differences in factors

When the responses of boys and girls are compared on the factors of attitude which have been identified, some interesting results arise. Boys were much more inclined to enjoy using the computer for its own sake and scored significantly higher than girls on the factor 'enjoyment of the computer as a tool'. Boys were much more inclined than girls to see computers as the thing of the future.

Girls were more nervous about computers than boys and scored significantly higher on the factor associated with 'fear of computers'. On the other hand, girls had a more positive attitude, and perhaps more patience than boys on the factor associated with 'frustration with technology'. This was the only factor in which girls scored more highly than boys.

Interestingly, there were no significant differences between the attitudes of boys and girls on the factors of attitude to do with both 'the social use of computers' or the 'utility' of computers. In the interviews they gave in school and in their responses to the attitude questionnaire, both boys and girls indicated that they were aware of the power of ICT to improve the presentation and quality of their work. Both boys and girls expressed their pleasure in working with their friends on a computer in the interviews, and this is confirmed by the attitude questionnaire.

As might be expected, access to a computer at home influences attitude towards ICT. Pupils with access to a home computer have better attitudes towards ICT than those without such access. Although having a home computer is not significant with respect to the 'enjoyment' or the 'future importance' factors, it is a more powerful fixed factor than is sex for all the other aspects of attitude. Thus pupils without a home computer are aware of the importance of what they are missing both in terms of the potential of the computer to help them enjoy their learning and in terms of its significance for their future lives. However, their responses to the statements in the other factors suggest that they may have difficulty making up the deficit in school. In particular, both girls and boys are more likely to express attitudes associated with 'frustration' or 'fear' if they have no access to a computer at home. Similarly they are less willing to work on a computer alone ('social factor') and are less aware of the potential opportunities offered through the 'utility' of ICT.

Both sex and access to a home computer are significant factors affecting attitude for Years 6, 7 and 10 (see Tables 8.2 and 8.3). Neither was a significant factor for Year 2.

Table 8.2 Attitude of Year 6, 7 and 10 pupils to ICT using sex and access to a home computer as factors

Sex	Home computer	Number	Mean attitude	Standard deviation
Girl	No	421	3.60	0.55
	Yes	645	3.75	0.48
Boy	No	320	3.65	0.55
	Yes	572	3.84	0.54

Table 8.3 Tests of significance for effect of sex and access to a home computer on attitude in Years 6, 7 and 10

Factor	Sum of squares	F-value	Significance	Power
Sex	2.381	8.62	0.003	0.86
Home computer	13.088	47.38	0.000	1.00
Interaction	0.254	0.92	0.338	0.16

Attitude varies according to the sex of the pupil and whether they have access to a home computer. The interaction between these two effects is not significant. Table 8.2 shows that while there is an underlying attitudinal advantage to boys, both boys' and girls' attitudes improve if they have access to a home computer. It should be noted also that the mean attitude of girls with a home computer is better than the mean attitude of boys without a computer, so the effect of gender stereotypical attitudes may be compensated to a significant extent through access to a computer in the home.

Attitude towards ICT is one aspect of ICT capability. Other aspects depend on the skills and knowledge to apply ICT in other subject areas, as opportunities are presented. Following common practice (see e.g. Millard 1997), we asked pupils to self-assess their capability in ICT. Pupils were invited to grade their competence as 'good', 'OK', or 'no good' in using a computer in a range of eleven situations. Clearly this approach has suspect reliability, as pupils may overestimate or underestimate their capability when making a self-assessment, and there is reason to suspect that boys may be more inclined to overestimate their capabilities than are girls (Tanner 1997).

Analysis of variance for self-assessed ICT capability shows no significant effect for sex, or for social class. However there is a significant advantage to those pupils who have access to a home computer above those who do not. Tables 8.4 and 8.5 show that while there are no significant differences between boys and girls for self-assessed ICT capability, there are significant advantages to the ICT capability of boys and girls in having access to a home computer.

Table 8.4 Self-assessed capability by pupils in Years 6, 7 and 10 using sex and access to a home computer as factors

Sex	Home computer	Number	Mean claim	Standard deviation
Girl	No	418	1.66	0.65
	Yes	645	1.83	0.63
Boy	No	320	1.55	0.66
	Yes	571	1.84	0.68

Table 8.5 Tests of significance for effect of sex and access to a home computer on self-assessed ICT capability for pupils in Years 6, 7 and 10

Factor	Sum of squares	F-value	Significance	Power
Sex	1.094	2.55	0.110	0.36
Home computer	24.894	58.05	0.000	1.00
Interaction	1.532	3.57	0.059	0.47

Use of ICT across the curriculum

In order to focus on the impact of school computing and to compare the extent to which computers were being used across the curriculum, we asked pupils about the frequency with which they used computers in a range of eleven subjects. A further question asked for the frequency of use of school computers at lunchtime and after school. Responses were on a 5-point scale: never, not often, monthly, weekly, daily.

For every subject area in secondary schools, the most common response was 'never'. This provides a measure of the extent to which ICT has failed to penetrate subject teaching, a measure that does not emerge from figures based on teacher reports. Even the median choice was 'never' in all cases except for English and D&T, in which it was 'not often'.

In primary schools, however, the pattern was very different, with much greater use being made of ICT in the teaching of subjects (see Table 8.6). We cannot make a direct comparison because of the different patterns of teaching used in the two phases, but the contrast is striking.

Table 8.6 The percentages of secondary and primary pupils choosing *Never* or *Not often* for use of computers in curriculum subjects

Curriculum subject	Secondary pupils	Primary pupils
English	81	34
Welsh	92	59
Mathematics	85	49
Science	87	58
Geography	89	64
History	88	53
Modern languages	91	n/a
Design & technology	65	64
RE	92	79
PE	97	87
Music	90	71
Lunchtime or after school	70	75

Given the concerns expressed above about the disadvantage suffered by pupils without access to a home computer, it might be hoped that pupils would be able to make up for their relative deprivation at home by using school computers at lunchtime or after school. However, this does not seem to be the situation. Only a small minority of pupils make use of such facilities (29 per cent). In fact, pupils without a home computer are significantly less inclined to make use of school facilities at lunchtime and after school than those with computers at home. The proportion of pupils using such facilities at least monthly are 31 per cent for those with a home computer and 25 per cent for those without a home computer. There was no significant difference between boys' and girls' use overall. However, boys with a home computer were much more likely to use such school facilities during lunchtimes or evenings than boys without a home computer, whereas there was no such split between girls.

In all the subjects considered, those pupils with access to computers at home claimed more frequent use in lessons than did those without. The differences were significant only in English, science, geography and modern foreign languages. It appears, then, that the use of ICT in curriculum subjects or in optional lunchtime or evening sessions is unlikely to make up the technological deficit suffered by pupils without home computers; indeed, it seems to be widening the gap.

In secondary schools many pupils gain their main experience of ICT through dedicated ICT lessons. In our sample, this mode of organisation was experienced by 60 per cent of Year 7 and 42 per cent of Year 10 pupils. In Year 10, analysis showed that having a specialist ICT lesson was a significant factor with approximately equal power to having access to a home computer for attitude, self-assessed ICT capability and written test of ICT capability. However, this was not unexpected, as most Year 10 pupils who report having specialist ICT lessons have *chosen* to study ICT as a GCSE subject (the National Curriculum for ICT is not compulsory in Wales at KS4).

In Year 7, neither sex nor having a specialist ICT lesson significantly affected attitude or self-assessed capability, but having a home computer was a significant factor.

Dealing with the issues

Thus the problems of equity considered at the beginning of this chapter are not being met currently in schools. The school population is divided into two groups: the technologically rich and the technologically disadvantaged. Those in the new underclass are most likely to be drawn from backgrounds which are already culturally disadvantaged in comparison to their peers in the technologically rich classes. At the moment it appears that pupils gain much of their ICT capability outside of school, and little is being done to redress the balance inside school. If 'Bill Gates does the homework' of a large proportion of the school, strategies must be developed to give the other pupils the same support. We must organise our teaching so that *all* children can benefit from the technological skills which many now bring to school. We need to develop strategies for homework and coursework that will exploit the resources which exist in the homes of some of our pupils while not further disadvantaging the technologically poor.

The low level of penetration into subjects reported above indicates that ICT as a teaching resource remains seriously under-exploited. Teachers of all subjects should capitalise on the obvious enthusiasm for ICT displayed by pupils and should utilise more effectively the prior knowledge and skills of our more advanced pupils. Our research has enabled us to identify a number of strategies for improvement, and we suggest that schools should:

- Develop a classroom culture in which all pupils feel valued and are able to participate using whatever resources they are able to bring to bear from outside school.
- Group pupils for work so as to take account of the higher prior learning of some pupils, who might sometimes be used as *classroom experts* to assist the others.
- Recognise the fear and frustration felt by some pupils, and accounted for within grouping arrangements, and take care to ensure that all pupils experience success with ICT.
- Vary groupings regularly to ensure that long-term reliance on complementary expertise cannot develop – all pupils should experience being the *expert* and the *team leader* (see Hoyles and Sutherland 1989; Downes 1998).

- Organise the curriculum so as to maximise the pupils' *sense of control* of the technology, and thus exploit the sense of learning through play.
- Teach ICT processes and terminology explicitly, especially for those pupils from technologically deprived backgrounds.
- Organise plenaries in which pupils are asked to articulate their experiences and provide opportunities for collective reflection about the processes and affordances of ICT.
- Collect data about the extent and nature of ICT resources in the pupils' homes.
- Organise and *monitor* easy access to ICT outside the teaching day, and set targets for ICT use.
- Encourage teachers to set homework and coursework that assumes the availability of ICT.
- Nurture links between home and school, helping parents in homes with computers to develop the ICT knowledge of their children and supporting those who do not have computers by ensuring that good information is available about the resources in the community or provided by the school out of hours (see Downes 1998).

We have deliberately focused this list on actions that may be taken within the school. However, it is clear from our research that the significance for life-long learning of ICT in the home is so great that those deprived of it may form a new technological underclass. Access to ICT facilities should be an issue for the wider community and not just for the school. Part of the solution may be through open access provision in libraries and community centres, but the power of the computer in your own home should not be underestimated.

Key issues

1   There is wide variation in pupils' access to ICT, and this amplifies existing educational disadvantage.
2   Pupils' attitude to ICT is more dependent on their access outside of school than on their curriculum use, or on fixed factors such as sex.
3   Pupils are positive about all aspects of learning ICT, but boys are more enthusiastic about ICT itself, whereas girls are more concerned with the purpose for which it is used.
4   Secondary school pupils are conscious of the lack of ICT in their lessons and aware of a culture gap between themselves and their teachers.

Points for reflection

- How can schools make up for the lack of worthwhile ICT activity in many homes? Which other organisations might be able to help?
- Do pupils take more seriously those subjects that use ICT in lessons, or do they see ICT as *playing*?

9 Sharing perspectives across the phases of schooling
Promoting continuity and progression

The issues of continuity and progression in ICT concern the promotion of effective learning experiences throughout pupils' school life. The transition from primary to secondary phases of schooling has long been recognised as a difficult time for pupils, both socially and cognitively. Many do not make the progress expected during the early stages of KS3. The reasons suggested for this include the sudden change in classroom style, the variation in what is expected in different curriculum areas, and boredom and demotivation resulting from repetition of work. Clearly, there has to be a process of induction into the culture and practices of secondary classrooms for the new intake, and ICT is no exception to this. But this induction should be managed so as to *contribute* to ICT capability rather than imposing another barrier to progress. In this chapter we propose a number of procedures that will enable schools to improve their strategies for cross-phase transition.

Bridges between primary and secondary schooling

All pupils look upon the move from primary to secondary school with mixed feelings. There is the stimulation of being in new surroundings that offer exciting opportunities and new experiences, mixed with the apprehension that comes with meeting the unknown. As pupils mature in the primary school, they gradually gain in status. On transfer to the secondary school, while the physical and mental maturation processes continue, their status as pupils within the new establishment is considerably reduced.

Schools have done a great deal to aid the transition process in recent years, either because the secondary school wished to maintain its pupil intake when pupil numbers are falling, or because of a genuine desire to reduce pupils' worries about moving up to the 'big school'. The main focus of many schools' work has been with helping pupils to settle into the secondary environment quickly and alleviating any fears that they may have. However, there are a number of interrelated problem areas that need to be addressed when looking at the overall transition process. In order to clarify the situation we have chosen to adopt a framework proposed by Rudduck *et al.* (1998), where the major hurdles involved in the transition process have been identified. They propose five bridges that schools need to build to support cross-phase continuity.

1 *The bureaucratic bridge.* To a large extent, schools have managed to solve many of the bureaucratic problems associated with transfer. Senior staff in the primary and secondary sectors meet frequently to exchange information at whole year-group level. These meetings are helping staff to appreciate what other schools in the cluster are trying to achieve with their pupils. They help to foster a greater understanding of the problems associated with transition.

2 *The social bridge.* This bridge has probably received the greatest attention in recent years. It is common for secondary staff to visit the cluster primary schools to talk to their Year 6 pupils. Pupils are invited to secondary school induction days at which they are offered a variety of activities centred mainly around the experiences that will be new to them, e.g. working in a laboratory, using specialised sport equipment, using high-powered computers. Some secondary schools' pupils go back to their primary school to talk to Year 6 classes about their experience of the transition. Such meetings can have significant benefits in helping pupils overcome their fears. Parents play an important role in supporting the social side of the transition process but it can also be a time when some parents significantly reduce their involvement in their child's education. Schools will benefit from trying to take parents across the transition into the new roles required of them in the secondary school.

3 *The curriculum bridge.* At this point, the business of transfer begins to get difficult, and there is the tendency for some schools to shy away from the issue, believing that any form of curricular continuity is an impossibility. We believe that it is possible; indeed, it is essential in order to sustain effective learning.

4 *The pedagogic bridge.* This is concerned with the extent to which we prepare pupils for new ways of teaching and learning. Methods of teaching in both sectors are changing. To a large extent, however, pupils in primary classes are taught by one teacher and experience only his or her particular teaching style. In the secondary school pupils have to come to terms with a multitude of teaching styles and expectations of how they should work and behave.

5 *The management-of-learning bridge.* As the pupils move to a new phase of education they require news tools for learning. They need to think about how they are going to deal with new knowledge. As learners they need to mature and develop the strategies and vocabulary for consolidating their knowledge and dealing with new situations. In many primary schools pupils are given a significant degree of autonomy over their learning, but on transfer they may experience a diet of mainly, if not entirely, teacher-directed learning.

The importance of continuity and progression in ICT

As with any other subject that is taught in both primary and secondary schools there is a need to ensure that pupils experience a curriculum that allows them to develop their knowledge and skills as they grow older and mature. If work is duplicated there is a danger of pupils stagnating in their learning, and that can lead to disruptive behaviour. But ICT capability is more than just a subject on the curriculum: it is a tool for learning that permeates all subject areas. It is therefore important both to consider continuity in the allotted slots for ICT in the timetable and to recognise that the new intake of pupils need to develop ICT skills to support their learning in all subjects. Just as pupils need to expand their vocabulary to understand increasingly complex concepts, so they also need to use more sophisticated software and techniques to support their learning as they progress through school.

Continuity is a process that involves the sharing of views on aims and objectives, the content of the curriculum and how it is taught and assessed. The remaining sections of this chapter are concerned with methods of developing continuity in terms of the curriculum, pedagogy and the management of learning.

In Chapter 2 we introduced the factors involved in considering progression in ICT. Here we analyse progression further in order to help teachers facilitate cross-phase planning. First, we believe it is important to untangle the words *continuity* and *progression* which are often glibly joined together in conversations on cross-phase transfer. As we have seen, the term 'continuity' refers here to the nature of the experiences offered to pupils. It is achieved by presenting pupils with tasks that are designed to follow on from one another with no sudden jumps and no repetition. Progression is more concerned with an individual's learning. It is about how a pupil can learn concepts and skills of increasing difficulty. Continuity in curriculum planning does not guarantee progression in learning. Planning for progression requires the teacher to have a good level of knowledge of each pupil's capabilities. It implies that some sort of differentiated approach should be used in order to cater for the different learning needs in any one class.

ICT aids differentiation by providing pupils with opportunities to

- work on challenges appropriate to their abilities;
- take a more active role in their own learning;
- try out things without fear of being humiliated in front of their peers;
- follow a flexible route towards the learning goals;
- maximise their independence as learners.

As we have seen, discussions of progression in ICT are complicated by having to consider progression in subject knowledge (science, maths, French, etc.) alongside the progression in ICT. To a certain extent the two should move along together (see Figure 9.1) and every subject teacher should see it as part of their job to help pupils to improve their ICT capability. Progression in ICT will occur as each pupil is required to work on increasingly complex situations that arise from subject curricula. When developing new concepts, pupils find it easier to use the skills that are familiar to them. They can then go on to apply these ideas using more sophisticated computer techniques if this is appropriate.

The challenges

Galton and Willcocks' study of pupils undergoing transfer, carried out in the early 1980s, revealed a number of problems:

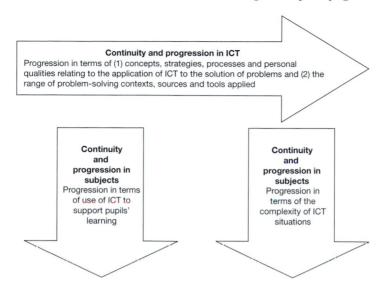

Figure 9.1 The two-dimensional nature of continuity and progression

- Almost all the children in the survey made good progress in tests of basic skills in the last two primary years. One year after transfer, only 63 per cent had continued to make progress, and for the majority the rate of progress was reduced – 7 per cent of pupils marked time in their new schools and 30 per cent actually regressed.
- Pupils experienced a decline in achievement in their first year of secondary school, lost motivation and found school less enjoyable.
- Most staff in the secondary schools differed markedly in their general style of teaching from staff in the contributory schools. These new teaching styles became a dominant influence on pupils' behaviour and performance: the decrease in the individualisation of the learning process in favour of whole-class teaching created a cohort of 'easy riders'. The researchers suggested that, in science, some 48 per cent fell into this category (Galton and Willcocks 1983).

There is little to indicate that the situation has changed significantly since the introduction of the National Curriculum. In a recent Ofsted report (1999a: 3) it was noted that 'Pupils who enter secondary school with some ICT capability too often continue to operate at levels which are hardly more advanced than those they have been using in the primary schools.' Many teachers remain uncertain about the value of liaison, which they see mainly as a mechanism for helping pupils to settle in at secondary school more easily rather than as a means of supporting their learning and progress. Uncertainty about the potential benefits could be one of the main threats to effective curriculum-focused liaison.

The National Curriculum

The National Curriculum was designed to help sustain curricular continuity, with its Programmes of Study for the different phases of education. However, many teachers do not see continuity in the terms intended by the architects of the National Curriculum, and still show uncertainty about classroom practice in the other phase of schooling. There is evidence to suggest that in at least one subject (history) the National Curriculum alone has made no improvements to the transfer process (Huggins and Knight 1997). Schagen and Kerr (1999) report that the introduction of the National Curriculum may have had a negative effect on cross-phase transfer due to the extra burdens of implementing its requirements and its assessment procedures, and dealing with open enrolment and competition from other schools.

The ICT National Curriculum (DfEE/QCA 1999) is written in general terms and gives a very broad picture of what pupils should be able to do at a particular key stage. As a consequence, there is little standardisation concerning practice in different schools. It does, however, indicate that during KS2, pupils should use a wider range of ICT tools than at KS1, and that as pupils progress through KS3 they should 'become *increasingly independent* users of ICT tools and information sources' (our italics). During the ITCD project, we found few schools where these features of the key stages were evident, and they can thus provide an initial basis for cross-phase planning.

The lack of time problem

Lack of time is a frequently used excuse for avoiding something that has been given a low priority. Yet time spent on planning for continuity would save time that is currently being used to repeat work in the secondary school. Spending the time in the short term should reap benefits in the long term.

There are too many contributory schools

In some urban areas secondary schools receive pupils from a large number of contributing primaries. There are secondary schools with more than twenty link primary schools, some of which may lie in another LEA (Jones and Jones 1993). Clearly, this is a significant problem, and one that requires LEAs and schools to work together to produce guidance and agree core schemes of work.

Not appreciating the value of cross-phase continuity

Some teachers believe that it is best to assume that pupils new to secondary level have little or no knowledge of their subjects and that it is best to start from scratch. They may do this because they wish to neutralise the problem of the variety of teaching that the pupils have previously experienced, or they may feel that pupils should be allowed to begin secondary school with a 'clean sheet'. Stillman and Maychell (1984) point out that this *fresh start* philosophy is untenable, at least in curricular terms. While there might be a case for pupils' experience of curriculum change to be sharp rather than smooth – see, for instance, Kennewell (1993) – this should be planned in full knowledge of what has gone before, rather than left to chance and circumstance.

The quantity and nature of the information transferred

Some teachers are not clear about what information to get from the primary school and what to do with the information once they have received it. Often the sheer volume of information can be so overwhelming that the teacher finds it difficult to decipher and select material that is important in providing continuity and progression for individual pupils. Some guidance is given later (see pp. 146–9) about the nature and level of information that is worth transferring, but the key to success is making sure that the information is sent to someone who is in a position to do something with it.

Rhetoric rather than reality

It is common for secondary schools to have statements referring to continuity in their aims or policy statements, but all too often these aims are not put into practice effectively. A statement such as 'the school aims to continue to develop and refine the curriculum between Key Stages 2 and 3' is of little value unless the idea is followed up by specific action items.

The gender issue

There is evidence to show that girls and boys respond in different ways at transfer. In Galton and Willcocks' 1983 study, the rates of achievement were virtually the same for boys and girls before transfer, but one year later 45 per cent of boys had fallen below their primary school score, while only 15 per cent of girls had done so. In history boys react more negatively than girls in Year 7 (Huggins and Knight 1997), but in science it is generally girls who are disenchanted with the teaching strategies used in the secondary school (Speering and Rennie 1996).

Change in teaching strategies

In the primary school ICT is taught mainly by the class teacher, whereas in secondary school ICT is (or should be) used by every subject teacher. Therefore in the primary school the pupils experience a consistent approach to the use of ICT; with input from a number of teachers in the secondary school, this is less likely to be the case. Although variety can be a good thing, the different approaches used by individual teachers ('But we do it *this* way in French') in the secondary school can cause some pupils to feel insecure in their own learning.

Evidence from school inspections indicates that continuity and progression in ICT is poor:

Pupils make good progress in information technology in only about one-third of schools and in a further one-third progress is unsatisfactory. The difference in achievement of pupils in these schools is widening. Progress in this subject compares unfavourably with all other subjects at both key stages. Pupils often repeat mundane, low-level work as they move up through the school. Modelling, measurement and control are often neglected in favour of presentation and communication – applications which pupils tackle well. The overwhelming majority of schools where achievement is unsatisfactory do not comply with National Curriculum requirements for information technology. In schools which do comply, pupils' progress compares well with other subjects

(Ofsted 1999a: 40)

Planning for liaison

The problem needs to be tackled at every level of the education system – from the DfEE, in supporting training for teachers and supplying funds for the hardware and infrastructure, through to the class teacher.

At local authority level

The Qualifications and Curriculum Authority (QCA 1998a) proposes that the LEA should be responsible for the following:

1   planning and delivering training;
2   supporting the transfer of the data between schools within the LEA, across LEAs and to the DfEE and QCA's National Data Collection Agency;
3   providing schools with an analysis of their data for use in relation to benchmarking and target setting;
4   supporting KS3 schools to ensure new pupils' prior attainment is acknowledged and planned for in lessons;
5   monitoring the achievement of schools in order to target advice and guidance effectively;
6   disseminating effective practice where the dip in performance at Year 7 is successfully counteracted.

Haigh (1996) emphasised the importance of LEAs in terms of long-term planning and spearheading initiatives to get the process moving. Dean (1988) commented that where LEA administrators and advisors had separate responsibilities for the primary and secondary sectors the lack of continuity was emphasised, as there was no encouragement to see education as a whole.

At school level

Headteachers must show their support for liaison through statements made in public, by their support for activities and their involvement, at least at the initial stages, in cluster-group meetings. They need to be aware of the problems and should provide advice about how to minimise them. The school should recognise the importance of liaison and make sure that cluster-group meetings are held in normal school hours, and not seen as something that teachers are expected to do in their spare time. Continuity should be a regular agenda item for departmental, whole-school and governors' meetings. Targets should be set to improve continuity not just across the two phases but throughout the time the pupils are attending school.

At subject level

In addition to being aware of pupils' prior learning, secondary subject teachers need to take advantage of pupils' enthusiasm and their enjoyment of experiencing something new. In the first few months of secondary school, a great deal can be done to create a climate for learning. This involves making pupils feel comfortable with the ICT equipment and getting them to recognise that the skills learnt will be valuable in all other areas of the curriculum. Ferguson and Fraser (1998) point out the value of the teacher generating a sense of cohesiveness or belonging to a group in which it is considered the norm that, where possible, pupils help one another to solve problems. Although a computer room is not always the best environment for subject-based ICT activity, pupils value the opportunity to work together as a class on the same activity (Kennewell 1993).

Cluster-group meetings

The first stage towards effective liaison will be to set up a cluster-group meeting comprising of representatives from all the contributing primary schools and the secondary school. The initial meeting may be at headteacher level, but subsequent meetings will involve only ICT co-ordinators. The purpose of these meetings should be to

- strengthen the conviction that all are working as partners in the education of young people;
- share expertise in teaching strategies, management of resources and knowledge of computer skills;
- discuss the impact of different teaching styles and strategies on pupils' learning;
- plan for curricular continuity in specific areas (e.g. use of spreadsheets) rather than trying to do everything at once;
- plan joint projects to *bridge* the transfer and facilitate the tracking of pupils' progress;
- decide on a policy for transfer of information (what type of information, how much, when it should be transferred, to whom it should be transferred, how it will be used);
- discuss samples of pupils' work, to reach a common understanding of standards;
- discuss how assessment data can be used to plan for progression;

- review the contexts in which ICT is used within the primary and secondary sectors;
- review schemes of work, looking for opportunities to reinforce previously learnt information and where new knowledge, concepts and skills should be introduced to pupils.

Meeting together can help bring a sense of direction and purpose to the whole curriculum, though discussion alone will provide only a sense of well-being. In order to make progress, ICT co-ordinators have to make decisions as to who will do what. They should identify key issues and give people tasks that have to be completed within a given time scale. Staging the process over a period of time allows teachers to learn about the issues that are of concern in the complementary phase and ensures that continuity is a live agenda item. Figure 9.2 illustrates such a staged approach and gives examples of issues that could be developed over a number of years. As with any development, there is a need to generate the ideas, put them into practice and then review the impact of the changes. Figure 9.3 shows this process from the point of view of improving continuity in the modelling strand. It is important that all the parties concerned should develop a shared understanding of the terms used and goals the group is aiming to achieve. The initial phase should raise questions about the existing ICT provision for pupils and how the quality of the provision can be improved.

Some schools have organised cluster groups based around particular themes, for instance language and communication skills, the use of control technology and mathematics education with significant benefits for all concerned (see e.g. MEU Cymru 1991).

A key factor in the success of all types of cluster meeting is the support of the LEA, which should provide the initial drive and the financial support to ensure that the work is maintained.

Building the curriculum bridge through schemes of work

Kennewell (1993) suggests two possible approaches that can be used to help solve the problems of discontinuity.

The first is to take advantage of the generally well-established social bridge that exists between a secondary school and its contributing primaries. For example, one large comprehensive school has invited the main cluster primary schools to use its ICT facilities on a weekly basis (Wardle 1998). This has not only helped pupils to become familiar with powerful computers but has provided in-service training for the primary staff. As a result, pupils' attainment in ICT has improved and the secondary school has altered its schemes of work to take this into account. Similar initiatives were seen in the ITCD project. Year 6 pupils in one primary school made a number of visits to the local comprehensive school, and worked on tasks designed to develop their capability. The networked software and resources, together with the specialist teaching expertise, helped them go beyond what they could achieve

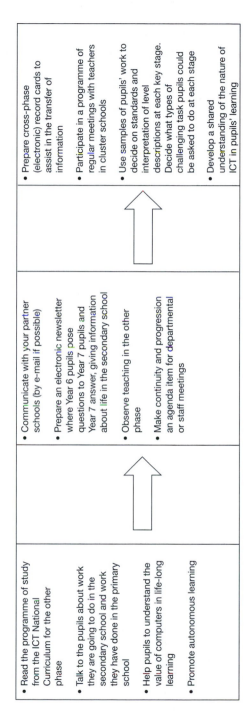

• Read the programme of study from the ICT National Curriculum for the other phase • Talk to the pupils about work they are going to do in the secondary school and work they have done in the primary school • Help pupils to understand the value of computers in life-long learning • Promote autonomous learning	• Communicate with your partner schools (by e-mail if possible) • Prepare an electronic newsletter where Year 6 pupils pose questions to Year 7 pupils and Year 7 answer, giving information about life in the secondary school • Observe teaching in the other phase • Make continuity and progression an agenda item for departmental or staff meetings	• Prepare cross-phase (electronic) record cards to assist in the transfer of information • Participate in a programme of regular meetings with teachers in cluster schools • Use samples of pupils' work to decide on standards and interpretation of level descriptions at each key stage. Decide what types of challenging task pupils could be asked to do at each stage • Develop a shared understanding of the nature of ICT in pupils' learning

Figure 9.2 Staged action that could be taken to secure greater primary–secondary continuity

---

Planning for continuity

At the meeting
The discussion based on the modelling strand could focus on a number of the following issues:

- Decide on a common understanding of modelling using ICT.
- In the current schemes of work in each of the schools identify where pupils are given the opportunity to carry out modelling.
- Does the current situation provide pupils with a curriculum that will enable them to make progress? How does one piece of work build on the previous one?
- Are there opportunities for differentiation?
- What opportunities are there for modelling with computers in the different subject areas?

Identify a small number of targets and the time-scale in which these targets should be met.

Implementation phase
Wherever possible all members of the cluster group should be involved in implementing the targets to help create a sense of teamwork and responsibility towards the common goals.

To what extent do the revised activities work in terms of:
- pupil achievement;
- pupil enjoyment;
- challenging pupils to think;
- providing pupils with the opportunity to make progress at a rate that matches their intellectual capability.

How do the changes affect other parts of the curriculum?

Review phase
Have the changes improved the continuity of the curriculum?

Figure 9.3 The three phases of cluster planning

in the primary school. The multimedia authoring work was particularly successful, as it enabled them to make electronic publications that could be accessed by younger pupils back in their primary school. However, these are isolated initiatives. In the ITCD project, we found that, although most primary and secondary ICT co-ordinators see liaison as part of their role, very few secondary ICT co-ordinators obtained information from contributing schools about their schemes of work and none received information about the level of their pupils' attainment. Most still assume that their new intake have minimal skills and know little or nothing about important concepts of ICT.

The second approach is to recognise that there will be a discontinuity, and to plan to take advantage of the strengths of the different teaching approaches in each phase. With clear planning, primary schools know how far they are expected to take the ideas in a strand, and secondary schools know what experiences their new pupils have had. Primary teachers can then focus on enabling as many pupils as possible to reach the relevant stage, knowing that secondary teachers will build from this point.

The two approaches can be combined, in fact, as each strand of progression can be treated differently. Each strand has points of consolidation and broadening in the progression through the levels, and each has significant conceptual hurdles. For *Handling Information*, the conceptual hurdle comes between level 4 and level 5, since to reach level 5 pupils will need to 'use ICT to structure . . . information'. In terms of information handling, we can interpret this to mean designing and implementing a database structure, whereas previously pupils may have merely entered and amended data in prepared structures. The consolidation and broadening comes between levels 5 and 6, where an increase in the complexity of enquiry through the use of Boolean logic is expected (Cox and Nikolopoulou 1997).

For the *Modelling* strand, however, progression from level 4 to level 5 may be seen in terms of increasingly systematic exploration of models through control of variables. The conceptual hurdle comes between levels 5 and 6, where they need to handle the *rules* in the model rather than just the *variables* – for example, entering formulae into a spreadsheet rather than just changing numbers.

For *Handling Information*, then, many pupils should be making the conceptual jump during KS2. Year 6 teachers should thus plan for their more capable pupils to work on developing their own database structures, while the less capable may continue to use a prepared structure. Year 7 pupils can then all be taught to develop database structures in a new context. For some it will be a familiar process, though the techniques may be new if the software is different. If sufficiently confident, the more capable can be asked to provide assistance to the others. This situation offers potential for an activity to develop the social bridge and promote learning. Pupils will be helped to develop the concepts by having to explain the ideas to others, rather than merely repeating particular techniques. If the software is compatible, the secondary school ICT co-ordinator can brief the Year 6 teachers in each contributing primary school concerning a database that pupils are to set up towards the end of their time in primary school. This will contain specific items of data about themselves, and will be passed to the secondary school co-ordinator who can combine them into a single file which can be interrogated during lessons in Year 7. Kennewell (1993) reports a scheme of this nature, in which the data were used in Year 7 mathematics lessons. While it is important that the files transferred have an identical structure, having entered their data into the standard structure Year 6 pupils can discuss what other fields might be added and can work on extending the data structure in order to develop or demonstrate their capability.

For *Modelling*, however, a discontinuity may be planned in that primary pupils work purely on exploring prepared models, of increasing complexity and with increasingly systematic control of variables, leaving until KS3 the work on rules and formulae for most pupils. This should reflect similar progression from number to algebra in mathematics.

As for the other strands, *Communicating Information* is one that lends itself to a continuity arrangement. There is no conceptual hurdle around transition, but there may be more sophisticated tools available in the secondary school. Year 7 pupils can be taught to use presentation software, for instance, to illustrate talks for primary pupils. Such presentations can support the social aspect of transition by increasing their awareness of the secondary environment, as well as making them aware of the possibilities created by new software tools.

Using assessment effectively

Teachers devote a considerable amount of time to assessing pupils' work, and over a key stage a large amount of data is therefore obtained. The problem is what to do with this information when the pupils transfer from one school to another. If too much information is transferred then the likelihood is that it will not be read, and vital data that are required to help pupils to progress will be ignored. The information must be condensed in some way while retaining all the key elements so that the receiving secondary teacher has a clear picture of each individual's ICT capability. In situations where there are large quantities of information being handled there is the possibility that some will get lost or misdirected. In the ITCD project we found that about half of the primary co-ordinators in case study schools reported that they passed an ICT attainment level on to their secondary schools, but none of the co-ordinators in the secondary schools in question said that they had received information from their primary schools. Three suggestions are made below that may help cluster groupings to decide what is the best way forward for their schools.

- *Portfolio of work.* Pupils frequently keep a portfolio of work containing a termly record of progress in each strand. With teacher annotations and comments this package gives a comprehensive picture of an individual's capabilities. Clearly the ICT co-ordinator in the receiving school has not got the time to sift through each portfolio and plan for continuity and progression. Schagen and Kerr (1999) report on a number of problems of using pupil portfolios, including a concern that the work provided may not reflect a pupil's ability because his or her teacher can be selective in deciding what is to be included. A more helpful approach might be for secondary schools to receive, say, three portfolios from each contributing primary, representing work considered to be at levels 3, 4 and 5. This would give the secondary ICT co-ordinator a clearer picture of the level of achievement, and along with other data could help to set the scene for further planning.
- *Record cards.* Some schools prefer the minimum amount of data on each pupil. This would result in a list of pupils against their National Curriculum level of attainment for ICT. This may be all that is required for sorting out the type of curriculum and the level of support needed for each pupil. Other schools may wish to take this one step further and devise a list of statements to give a clearer understanding of a pupil's attainment.

  What kinds of statements might these be? A focus on techniques could be unworkably detailed and would represent only one component of ICT capability; a focus on higher order skills, while providing valuable data for planning and monitoring across the curriculum, would be better if implemented generally rather than being specific to ICT. This leads us to the conclusion that it is the processes and concepts that should be the focus of statements, i.e. the National Curriculum strands, tailored to the particular schemes of work used in the school. Particularly important generic techniques could also be included in order to monitor the development of routine skills. Each pupil would then have a checklist record card similar to the one shown in Figure 9.4.

Attainment at KS2

Name: ———————————

	1	2	3
Use of word-processor and DTP to produce documents (layout, suitability for audience)			
Use of word-processor and DTP techniques (cut and paste, spell checking, tables, formatting documents, incorporating text, graphs, pictures and sound)			
Designing a database for a purpose			
Compiling a database			
Using a database to analyse ideas and information			
Exchanging messages by e-mail with identified people			
Exploring a spreadsheet model systematically			
Producing an appropriate graph from a spreadsheet			
Accessing information from the World Wide Web			
Writing Logo procedures			
Organising work – saving, retrieving, printing			
Awareness of uses of ICT in the outside world			
Aware of the advantages and disadvantages of personal information being held on computer			

Note:
1 = pupil has had some experience of carrying out this activity
2 = pupil is able to accomplish the activity but may require some help
3 = pupil is confident at using the activity and can work independently

Figure 9.4 An example of a set of statements that could be included on a pupil's personal record card towards the end of Key Stage 2

- *Pupil self-assessment.* Self-assessment is a useful life skill, and primary pupils could be encouraged to keep a record of their ICT capability during their final year. This will need to be at a more detailed level than the formal teacher assessment record so that the pupil can understand what is expected (see Figure 9.5). Because the pupil is managing the record-keeping, it should not be onerous for the teacher to add an informal confirmation of what the pupil claims to have learned. In cases of over-ambitious claims, this would stimulate a valuable conversation between teacher and pupil.

Name: _____   Teacher: _____

Word-processing	Pupil opinion	Teacher check
I can write different things using the computer		
I can make changes and correct any mistakes		
I can change font size, font type and font colour		
I can select some of the words so that I may make changes to them		
I can cut some words and paste them on another part of the page		
I can explain why I decide to make some changes		
I can save my work		
I can reload the page that I have saved		
I can print my work		
I can place a graphic on my page		
I can change the size of a graphic and change its position on the page		
I can create a table on my page		
I can make changes to work I started yesterday		
I can copy words or graphics from one piece of software and place it on a page in another		
I can create different things for different audiences		

Figure 9.5 An example of a section of a pupil's self-assessment form for use at Key Stage 2

As well as assisting the teachers involved, such self-assessment procedures can aid the reflection and development of general metacognitive skills (see Chapter 2). The record could be passed on to the secondary school and updated and extended as the pupil works through the subsequent key stages, giving the pupil a clear indication of the progress he or she is making. It could be stored, amended and transmitted electronically.

Key issues

1   Pupils' progress in secondary school is often adversely affected by unnecessary repetition and lack of challenge in tasks, and by limited autonomy in working practices.
2   Co-ordinators and teachers sometimes have inadequate information and understanding of each others' schemes and of pupils' attainment.
3   The difference in approach to teaching in primary and secondary schools means that transition cannot be seamless, but joint-planning that recognises the strengths of each approach can overcome many of the current difficulties.

Points for reflection

•   Consider pupils making the transition from primary to secondary school in your area. What ICT experiences have they had by the end of primary school? What expectations do they have of secondary school? How do their secondary school experiences compare with these expectations?
•   What liaison takes place between primary and secondary schools in your area? Is it possible to agree on

   –   core schemes of work?
   –   a format for passing on attainment information?
   –   collaborative teaching of primary pupils, involving a secondary ICT specialist?

10 The ICT-capable school
An essential vision for the future

In this chapter we draw together the strands presented in the previous chapters and set out a vision of what it means for a school to be successful in developing ICT capability. We consider the process of developing ICT capability – not just for pupils, but for teachers, classrooms, subjects, the ICT co-ordinator and senior management. We examine in more detail the role of external agencies, staff development programmes and management procedures in supporting this development. Finally, we suggest general principles which may be drawn from this focus on ICT and applied to other aspects of school improvement.

Developing ICT-capable pupils

Ultimately, this is the most important group to influence. It is by the capability of pupils that the school's success will be judged. We have found several key points emerging from our own research and from that of others:

- Pupils gain a lot of their capability from sources outside school, and some already disadvantaged pupils lose out further from their lack of access to ICT at home.
- Use in subject lessons (other than ICT lessons) is very patchy; in the same school, some pupils may be given much greater opportunity to apply their ICT capability than others.
- Extra-curricular provision focused on the technology tends to be used by those who are already confident, but situating ICT provision in general homework clubs and in the school library, rather than in computer rooms, widens access.
- Pupils' capability, gained from home and from primary school, is not always recognised in secondary specialist ICT lessons, with the result that pupils do not get a chance to demonstrate and build on their skills.
- Pupils benefit from structured teaching at appropriate points in their development of capability. Teachers, particularly in primary schools, often overestimate the extent to which pupils can develop understanding merely by working on tasks by themselves. Important learning activities need to be introduced by explanation and questioning of pupils, and concluded by further questioning and a clear summary of what has been learned. Teachers' classroom organisation for ICT does not always allow for these approaches.

- Many tasks set for pupils make insufficient demands. In secondary schools, too few tasks allow pupils to explore, make decisions and develop higher order skills.
- In primary schools, not all tasks have clear ICT learning objectives for the pupils, with the result that the work could be unfocused or repetitive.
- Pupils benefit from planned opportunities to apply their capability to different contexts in the curriculum, but they may not have the opportunity to develop higher order skills if their ICT work is limited to short units, isolated from the rest of the curriculum.

There are clear signs that children move between two distinct cultures of ICT. Home use is characterised by *bricolage* and *hard fun* (Papert 1996). Learning at home occurs through attempting to achieve personal goals, by trying out various techniques and remembering what works. This is hard, because there is often a large gap between the child's current knowledge and what they are trying to achieve. There may be no one available to provide structured help. It is fun, though, because no-one is controlling the child's efforts, risks can be taken, unexpected events occur along the way; and there is a sense of elation when frustration eventually turns to success. School use is characterised, on the positive side, by structured teaching leading to sound concepts, but, on the negative side, by fixed procedures, undifferentiated expectations and routine tasks. There will always be differences in the purposes of home and school computer use, but it makes much sense to try to bridge the cultural divide and enable pupils to use in each environment what they bring to it from the other.

There is a role for ICT-based homework in bridging school and home culture; pupils who do not have adequate resources at home should be given opportunities to use school resources outside normal school hours. Indeed, any extra-curricular opportunities in school should be homework-based rather than games/technology-based. Schools can also help to develop parents' ICT capability by providing or recommending community education courses in ICT, and providing awareness sessions concerning the software used in teaching, the tasks set and the expectations of what pupils will achieve at particular ages.

Developing ICT-capable teachers

If schools are to improve the development of pupils' ICT capability, it is through the work of teachers and other staff who support learning that it will be achieved. Unfortunately, too many teachers have opted out of the changes which have been occurring in the nature of access to and the process of handling information over the past twenty-five years. This is not really surprising: in other fields of life, management decisions have given workers at all levels little choice but to adopt new technology. In the classroom, however, the teacher has maintained a high level of control over activities, and a choice has always been available. Despite the National Curriculum requirement that ICT capability should be developed and applied in nearly every subject, teachers have received mixed messages. The proponents of using ICT in teaching have always attempted to reassure sceptical teachers that they should only use ICT when it will enhance their teaching. Indeed, in 1999, we were still reading: 'Ask yourself why you are using a computer. If the answer is not convincing, use a pencil' (Leask and Williams 1999: 206).

This is valuable advice – for teachers with some experience of ICT in their teaching. But how is a teacher who does not use ICT in the classroom expected to make such judgements? We noted that pupils need to experience some difficulty in order to learn, and the same is true for teachers. In the absence of a strong ICT culture, it takes a degree of faith for novices to overcome the difficult early stages of ICT usage and develop an understanding of why they are using a computer. If they are not supported by more experienced colleagues, teachers' initial uses of ICT may be inappropriate, and there is need, as we noted in Chapter 6, to advise and support teachers in their early experiences to ensure a positive outcome that will encourage them to go further with ICT rather than reverting to the pencil. It is only after reflection on a number of such experiences that they will be able to make effective judgements for themselves. We examine these ideas in more detail later in the chapter.

The level of in-service training for ICT received by teachers has been pitifully small to date (Harris 1999), and the quality of that provision has been described by Goldstein (1997) as being 'impoverished'. In the ITCD project we found that some successful schools had invested funds in sending teachers on long-term courses leading to vocational qualifications or qualifications at masters degree level. These courses motivated the teachers and gave them time to discuss the use of ICT resources and to reflect on the educational potential of applications.

Since our research, the government has allocated resources through the National Opportunities Fund (NOF). This gives schools an opportunity to catch up with ICT training, and to target this much-needed stimulus in support of curriculum goals. NOF will not be the end of schools' training needs, however. The rate of change of ICT is such that after the initial impetus, a sustained programme of curriculum-based training and development is vital. However, there is a danger that 'the pace of technological development involves teachers in a spiral of ongoing INSET in order to use new technologies' (Harris 1999: 46). The ICT-capable teacher should be able to exploit new resources without technology-focused training having to be provided continually.

The level of ICT capability of the individual teacher is important, and is likely to influence classroom usage in two ways:

1   *Teacher use.* There is currently little use of ICT by the teacher at the front of the whole class, even by confident teachers, owing to poor display facilities. But even those teachers confident with ICT will want to give most of their attention to the management of the pupils' learning and behaviour rather than thinking about ICT techniques. They will thus use only familiar ICT routines in this situation, and the more routines they know the wider the range of activities they can include in their repertoire.
2   *Pupil use.* The higher the level of ICT capability a teacher has the more natural it will be for him or her to scaffold pupils' learning of ICT alongside the main learning objectives.

When teachers plan to use ICT in the classroom, they need to consider pupils' ICT capability. They should recognise that not all pupils will have sufficient skills, and identify what they are expecting in terms of routines, techniques, processes, concepts and higher order skills. They can then plan to develop the relevant aspects in context, drawing on the expertise of the ICT co-ordinator and specialist teachers where appropriate, and briefing other adults who are helping in the classroom.

During the ITCD project, we noted the potential of ICT-capable classroom assistants to help monitor ICT activity and intervene to stimulate pupils' progress. We saw, too, that an ICT technician with informal teaching skills can have a considerable influence on the culture and attainment of a secondary school. Supervision of computer rooms during extra-curricular activity can be much more than merely minding the equipment: they can be transformed into resource-based learning centres if the right approach is taken.

Developing ICT-capable classrooms

The ICT-capable classroom is a combination of

- *teachers* who are prepared to use the technology as a model for pupils, even if they do not know everything about it, and allow pupils access when it might be helpful in their learning;
- *pupils* who are disposed to use ICT and can judge when it is likely to be helpful in their work, rather than just using ICT for the sake of it;
- *resources* which are easily available – either in the classroom or in a nearby resource area.

It often seems to be the case in secondary schools that subject learning work carried out in a computer room is seen as different from normal work in the subject, and has the same problems of transfer as work carried out in a different subject. This can be explained in terms of the different cultural settings, and we conclude that teachers need to provide help for pupils to link the learning located in the computer room with the activities located in the subject classroom.

There are two main ways to achieve this:

1   Provide non-ICT activities in the computer room before and/or after the ICT work, in order to reduce the cultural gap; prompt pupils to reflect on their ICT learning and identify other applications of the ideas in order to help generalise them.
2   Provide ICT resources in the subject classroom, and use them in such a way that ICT becomes part of the subject culture. Although there will still be differences in the affordances offered by the ICT and non-ICT activity settings, it will be easier to help pupils utilise each set of affordances if the cultural difference is eliminated.

The second approach is more characteristic of an ICT-capable school, as it develops the culture of the institution and the disposition of its members to use ICT. It draws on practice from the best primary classrooms, and we would encourage primary schools to continue to use the classroom as a base for resources rather than pursuing the computer room model for the ICT curriculum.

The availability of an internet link has the potential to transform the culture of most classrooms. It makes a massive range and capacity of information and activities available, facilitates direct communication with people and organisations that were previously remote and perhaps uninteresting, and allows pupils to have new audiences for their work (see e.g. Pachler and Williams 1999). In this respect, there is a great advantage to be gained from regular use in the classroom by the teacher with the whole class, or by small groups of pupils, rather than having to make special arrangements to take the whole class in a dedicated computer room for individual access. In the ICT-capable classroom, pupils will learn by watching, discussing and evaluating ICT use by others, as well as by taking their opportunity for *hands-on experience*.

Developing ICT-capable subjects

We have considered how important it is for teachers to work together in the ICT-capable school, and the role of subject leader is vital in developing a team of teachers who use ICT in the classroom. Subject leaders should keep up-to-date with ideas about links between ICT concepts and subject concepts, and should incorporate ICT into staff development activities in their subjects. They should also use ICT in analysing data concerning subject attainment by pupils.

In primary schools, the whole staff will look to the subject leader for schemes of work, activity ideas and lesson plans for ICT in each subject. It is vital for subject leaders to work with ICT co-ordinators to generate this guidance.

In secondary schools, the head of a subject department has a key leadership role, but may delegate research and planning for ICT in the subject to a more junior colleague who can work with the ICT co-ordinator to ensure the department's use of ICT fits within the whole-school scheme for teaching and applying ICT capability. They will need to consider how to overcome the potentially negative influence of National Curriculum tests and examination syllabuses. Since ICT cannot be used in these examinations, teachers must consider how pupils can learn *through* rather than *with* ICT.

The ICT-capable subject will also exploit ICT's affordances for communication and collaboration. A network in school can help staff work together, formally and informally, in developing and sharing plans and materials. Using e-mail and the World Wide Web, co-operation with teachers in other schools is much easier, and this should be of particular value in helping teachers in small primary schools and small subject departments to plan and evaluate. Internet thinking can change the way a topic is taught, increasing the 'I wonder' element. Teachers can no longer assume the role of *the* knowledge repository in the classroom, and should focus on concepts, processes and higher order skills.

Developing capable ICT co-ordinators

The co-ordinator in an ICT-capable school will have a high level of understanding of the basic ICT concepts and good higher order skills, although they will not need the depth of technical knowledge that a specialist ICT teacher should have. Perhaps most important is the understanding of how pupils learn about, with and through ICT, together with an ability to work with colleagues who may have very different teaching styles. The focus on pupil learning should drive the co-ordination of teaching, curriculum and resources, and should form the basis of advice to senior management on policy–resource development. Indeed, the job description for an ICT co-ordinator could take the form 'I am here to help children learn. This is how I do it: . . .' (Hughes 1999: 132).

The issues of continuity and progression in learning – both year-to-year and across the curriculum – will be a constant concern. The co-ordinator should be familiar with the advice concerning assessment of ICT capability that is available from the central and local government agencies (such as ACAC 1996, SCAA 1996, Bolton LEA 1999), and will have devised a system which is simple enough for all staff to be able to use, yet sufficiently focused to be informative. Goldstein (1997) has noted that information concerning pupils' attainment is rarely used to highlight weaknesses and inform developments; the capable ICT co-ordinator will use the ICT system in order both to monitor the progress of individual pupils and to analyse general patterns of attainment.

The co-ordinator may well be the ICT resource manager as well, but even if not he or she will help plan the development of a school intranet system which can support teaching, learning and curriculum management, and act as a gateway to the internet. The capable ICT co-ordinator will also, of course, use the internet for communication with colleagues in other schools, for researching ideas about new developments in technology and in teaching about–with–through ICT, and for personal staff development needs.

Developing ICT-capable management

As we have emphasised throughout the book, the role of senior management is crucial. ICT is too important to be left to those at middle-management level. ICT co-ordinators may be left isolated and impotent if they do not have the leadership, support and encouragement of the headteacher and other senior managers. Heads can support ICT co-ordinators directly in terms of:

- vision and drive;
- policy review and promulgation;
- resource planning and funding allocation, in conjunction with the governors;
- staff development planning, in conjunction with staff development leaders;
- monitoring and evaluation, in conjunction with deputy-heads;
- setting an example in ICT capability – again, deputy heads must share this commitment.

The school's vision and drive should be focused on teaching and learning, not merely the acquisition of more resources, and need to be based on understanding. There is confusion among many senior managers between the development of ICT capability and the use of ICT as an aid to learning. These two aspects of ICT in schools are closely linked, but the use of ICT for learning does not necessarily contribute to the development of capability, and each aspect needs to be planned in relation to its distinct aims.

It is still important, however, that initiatives and development are not dependent on the particular personality of the headteacher. The ICT-capable school will have systems in place, accepted and adopted by all staff, to ensure that the process of development is continuous. We look at the nature of such systems in more detail in the penultimate section (pp. 168–9).

The ICT-capable manager should also support the development of teaching and learning by effective use of management information systems to inform curriculum planning, staff development and appraisal, and pupil support.

The wider perspective

The ICT-capable school will make use of a range of external services – commercial, academic and governmental.

LEA staff are seen as a valuable filter for general findings on good practice, and their advice concerning national initiatives and research is valued. The ITCD project found that schools recognise what they have gained from advisory teachers in the past, but under financial pressure they are deciding not to devote the same amount of funding to external advice as was available when funds were centralised. In the UK, much depends on the training for teachers funded by the National Lottery (TTA 1998).

We also found that schools' inspections are a powerful force in stimulating change, but many schools take a reactive view and just attempt to fix the particular problems identified as *key issues for action*. A 'satisfactory' rating for ICT, we found, often led to complacency, although it may have concealed difficulties which were suggested in the detail of the report or highlighted in verbal feedback. The most successful schools are responding positively to any weaknesses in ICT teaching identified by inspection reports. The most capable schools did not merely react, however, but sought out advice from consultants and from colleagues in other schools, and by reading published reports from Ofsted, BECTA and other agencies concerned with developing ICT in schools.

The UK government is increasingly involving commercial concerns in the provision of managed services to schools (DfEE 1999c), and the ICT-capable school will consider seriously the possibilities of contracting out many of the non-pedagogic aspects of ICT in schools. All involved will be aware, however, of the danger of losing control of the content and processes of teaching and learning. They will view critically the idea of contracting out to external agencies this central aspect of the school's purpose.

The vision behind the National Grid for Learning (DfEE 1997a) can have a transforming effect on teaching and learning in schools, but it should not be viewed as a massive integrated learning system which enables pupils to bypass the barriers to learning created by poor teachers and poor schools. Lynch (1999) envisages the establishment of 'teaching and learning frameworks that can take full advantage of the capacity of the technology to diagnose, differentiate, demonstrate and deliver from afar'. If schools are going to provide an educational experience that exceeds the learning which can be gained from home use of computers, then such frameworks should be seen as a set of resources for pupils, teachers and managers to use in appropriate ways. Only ICT-capable schools will be able to do this effectively.

Staff development programmes for ICT capability

Staff development must also be based on teaching and learning needs, rather than being technology-driven. In-service training programmes are needed to ensure that staff have the requisite skills to make personal use of ICT equipment and that they understand how it can be used to help pupils to learn. The programme must also match the ICT policy and be in line with the school development plan. In all schools this represents a considerable challenge for those involved in providing the training. NCET–NAACE (1995) recommend that secondary schools should target specific

- *departments* in a rolling programme;
- *individuals* within departments, who then act as disseminators;
- *applications* or *programs* which have relevance to a number of departments.

There are a number of key features that help staff to become aware of the value of ICT and which provide them with the skills necessary to maximise learning opportunities with computers. M. Owen (1992: 134) contends that effective INSET for ICT should

- maintain a constant focus on classroom practice;
- take into account the radical effects that IT can have upon the teaching environment;
- take account of the organisational structure of the school climate;
- take into account the personal and professional aspirations and long-term interests of the teacher;
- address issues of progression of skills, competence and attitude;
- encourage self-reflection and professional reflection.

We suggested in Chapter 2 a framework of routines, techniques, processes, concepts and higher order skills to help analyse ICT capability (see pp. 20–24). This frame-work can be applied to teachers as well as pupils, but in the classroom it is not just teachers' personal ICT capability which must be considered. The craft of teaching, too, can be analysed in terms of routines, techniques, processes, concepts and higher order skills. When teachers adopt ICT, familiar teaching routines may no longer be appropriate, and new techniques must be adopted to implement the changes in teaching processes required to take advantage of ICT. Furthermore, some fundamental concepts may need to be restructured. But, once again, it is the higher order skills that are the most important to success, and metacognitive knowledge is paramount. Teachers' generic skills of planning, monitoring, decision-making and evaluating will not need to change in nature, but they may need to be made more explicit during a period of change.

The focus of the UK government training initiative is indeed on making these teaching skills explicit. The government is investing £230 million between 1999 and 2002 to support training in ICT for teachers and school librarians (TTA 1998). They see this as giving a major boost to the expertise of school staff and providing a foundation for further training. For many, this may be the first stage in a long line of training programmes. Figure 10.1 represents the various stages that planners need to consider when producing a development programme, and these are amplified further in the section below.

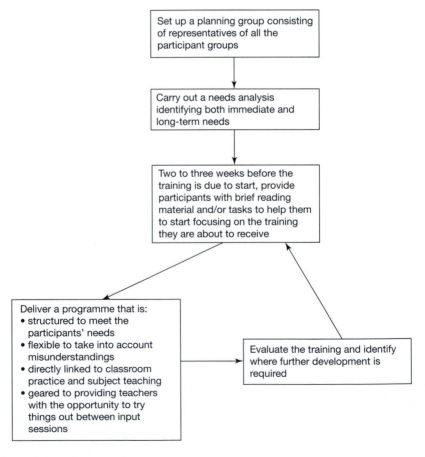

Figure 10.1 Staff development planning process

Planning the staff development programme

The planning group should, as far as possible, have representatives from

- different levels of the school's hierarchy;
- different age groups (primary);
- different departments/faculties (secondary).

The ICT co-ordinator and a member of the senior management team with responsibility for finance are essential members of the group.

Motivating teachers to learn. Teachers appreciate that their pupils' abilities to learn vary considerably in any one class, but in a situation where teachers are the learners it is quite often the case that they are treated as a homogeneous group. The ability of adults to learn about ICT will be dependent on a whole host of things that go on in their lives. Stoll and Fink (1996), in summarising the research on adult learning, point out that age, gender and stage of career influence an individual's approach to learning. The first step in planning may be a consideration of how to motivate the teachers to learn new skills when they believe that their approach to teaching is successful. There are many arguments the planners put forward to motivate the staff, and the following may be particularly important:

- Pupils enjoy working with computers and, if used in the right way, they can play a significant role in helping them to learn.
- Using computers in the classroom opens up possibilities of new ways of working with pupils or of new slants to traditional approaches; in particular they provide the teacher with new opportunities for individual and group work.
- Schools are preparing pupils for lifelong learning, and there is no doubt that computers will be used in adult learning alongside books and other traditional sources of knowledge.
- Any in-service training where teachers are given the opportunity to share experiences and learn together will enhance the quality of teaching throughout the school and help to develop a greater sense of collegiality.

This type of approach is likely to be more successful than one where teachers are presented with a view that 'ICT is something else that we have to do, so let's see how we can make it work'.

Staff development leaders need to consider whether to bring in an outside provider or to use the expertise of staff in the school. The ITCD project found that schools preferred to use in-house training provided by the ICT co-ordinator and other members of staff. The contribution of *advisory teachers* who have a greater depth of knowledge and breadth of experience was valued in primary schools, as long as they could work in school over a long enough period to influence a number of staff who could then sustain the momentum of development. Some schools registered a number of interested staff on basic ICT courses specifically designed to develop and gain accredited ICT skills. These courses covered the main ICT concepts and techniques, and enabled participants to gain familiarity with the resources and practices of a networked ICT room, and this gave them confidence in managing their own lessons involving ICT. They provided a level of ICT capability which all teachers could be expected to reach and formed the basis of planning further study more specifically designed for teachers. The accreditation provides a motivating element, and is certainly worth considering when devising the training programme.

Challenging the teacher as to the effectiveness of current practice. It is all too easy for teachers to stagnate, to become fixed in their methodology and blinkered to developments outside education. Teachers need to reflect on their current practice and consider how it could be improved. If the training is to bring about the desired improvement in teaching then teachers must be put under some sort of pressure to respond to expectations of change. Failure to do this could result in a low level of implementation of ICT and a lack of commitment to make progress. Teachers must be reassured that although there is an urgent need for them to use ICT to a greater extent, the school will support them in whatever way it can. For example, schools may

- set up teams of teachers to work together and share ideas;
- use a system of ICT mentors to support less knowledgeable colleagues;
- ensure that there is always good technical backup when things go wrong.

Preparing and carrying out a needs analysis. There are three levels of need to be satisfied: the levels of individual teacher, the faculty or department and the whole school. In order to establish a coherent structure of ICT across the school, taking into account financial restrictions, compromises will have to be made. The focus of the government's present initiative is the training needs of individuals and groups within a school, and pro-formas to aid the collection of data have been devised. These are under four headings:

- planning;
- teaching;
- assessing and evaluating;
- personal, professional use of ICT (TTA 1998).

The aim is to ensure that all teachers receive training that will enable them to meet the government's *Expected Outcomes for Teachers* (TTA 1998). These outcomes include:

- knowledge and understanding of the contribution that different aspects of ICT can make to teaching particular subjects;
- effective planning, including the use of ICT for lesson preparation and the choice and organisation of ICT resources;
- the use of ICT in whole-class teaching;
- methods for developing pupils' ICT capability;
- techniques to assist the assessment of pupils' learning of the subject when ICT has been used;

- the use of ICT to keep up to date, share best practice and reduce bureaucracy (TTA 1998).

This approach provides the individual with the chance of identifying what he or she does not know, but there is a danger that novices could ignore whole areas of ICT that are relevant to the teaching of their subjects. While a more detailed form would be helpful, it would also have the disadvantages of being more time-consuming to complete, and in any case there is still the possibility that individuals might not appreciate the value of certain aspects of ICT. The forms are likely to provide more reliable data if the participants have been involved in group discussion sessions led by the ICT co-ordinator.

The appraisal process could play a significant role in ensuring the continuing development of teachers' knowledge of using ICT in the classroom. The present government favours an accountability model of appraisal where the results of classroom observation and pupils' performance in examinations would be linked to pay and promotion. An alternative approach is to look on appraisal as a process that helps individuals to develop and which provides a supporting mechanism to ensure that targets are met. This approach is non-judgemental but is still clearly focused on improving teachers' performance. It is not a substitute for regular feedback to staff, but should be seen rather as an opportunity for strengthening existing communications by supplementing good practice and highlighting gaps where they exist. Figure 10.2 outlines some of the questions that could be used both to probe a teacher's thoughts and to judge the level of implementation of ICT in lessons, while also indicating how the review process can help to keep the teacher on track.

Prior to the main period of training it is essential to give those teachers who would class themselves as computer-illiterate some reassurance that operating computers is reasonably simple. These staff are generally reluctant to show their ignorance in front of their colleagues and would benefit from a short induction programme that teaches them the basic skills. For those who have some experience of using ICT with pupils, and for those who have some knowledge of ICT as an individual user, different types of pre-course task are useful. For example, experienced staff could be asked to report on and evaluate lessons where ICT has been used. This could look at a variety of situations, such as:

- management issues concerning the use of the computer room or using one computer in a classroom;
- pedagogical issues concerning the value of using particular types of software to teach particular concepts;
- issues to do with the assessment of pupils.

Implementing a programme

The following examples show the types of training that can take place.

(a) *Working with the whole staff in a primary school: information handling with the World Wide Web*. After an initial briefing to the staff on the purpose and outcome of the session,

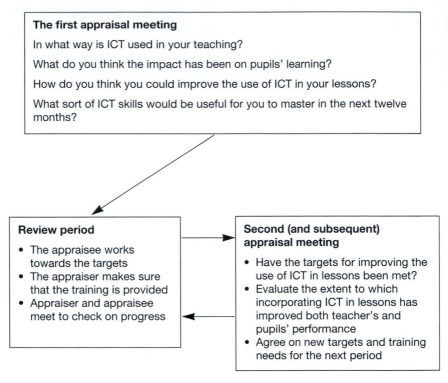

The first appraisal meeting

In what way is ICT used in your teaching?

What do you think the impact has been on pupils' learning?

How do you think you could improve the use of ICT in your lessons?

What sort of ICT skills would be useful for you to master in the next twelve months?

Review period
- The appraisee works towards the targets
- The appraiser makes sure that the training is provided
- Appraiser and appraisee meet to check on progress

Second (and subsequent) appraisal meeting
- Have the targets for improving the use of ICT in lessons been met?
- Evaluate the extent to which incorporating ICT in lessons has improved both teacher's and pupils' performance
- Agree on new targets and training needs for the next period

Figure 10.2 Incorporating an ICT focus in the appraisal process

teachers and classroom assistants work in groups, with each group based in a classroom with an internet link. They are brought back together for a plenary discussion of how they might use the ideas with pupils and an evaluation of the World Wide Web as a resource. The main purpose of the task is to improve teachers' ability to use the World Wide Web in their preparation of any topic, and in their teaching of a particular topic. They should be given the addresses of particular sites to visit, including some sites which provide a wide range of resources and some which are specific to their chosen topic. After evaluating the resources they find, they should be guided through the use of *search engines* and techniques for formulating queries.

The strengths of this approach are that

- it can build on existing work with CD-ROMs and flat-file databases;
- the structure of the session provides a model for progression in the learning which can be used with pupils;
- teachers can be taken through the information handling *process loop* (see pp. 73–4) and discuss the higher order skills that can be encouraged;
- there is a good basis for producing activity plans and assessment critiera for different year-groups.

(b) *Working with departments in a secondary school: spreadsheets in geography.* Working with all members of the geography department, the ICT co-ordinator introduces ways in which spreadsheets can be used to examine patterns and relationships in population growth. The teachers develop these ideas into teacher and pupil activities related to their learning objectives. The work could be developed further to look at how other aspects of ICT (CDROM, World Wide Web) could be used to build on the statistical data and produce a fuller picture for the pupils.

Among the strengths of this approach are that

- the teachers see the direct relevance of ICT to their subject;
- working as the geography team, any problems likely to occur will be identified and, hopefully, solved with the expertise of the ICT co-ordinator or the specialist ICT teacher;
- there is the opportunity to go beyond the initial brief, if time allows;
- the ICT specialist gains an understanding of the subject concepts underlying the ICT tasks and is, therefore, in a better position to advise on classroom implementation.

(c) *Working with individuals: data logging in science.* The ICT co-ordinator and class/science teacher plan and co-teach a lesson using a data logger to measure the drop in temperature as hot water cools. The water is contained in beakers and three different types of insulator are used. The rate of temperature loss for each insulated system is measured and drawn graphically.

The strengths of this approach are that

- working with a fellow teacher in a classroom can be very rewarding in terms of professional development: it provides plenty of opportunities for the teachers concerned to reflect on their actions – a factor identified in the effective teacher research carried out for the Teacher Training Agency (Moseley and Higgins 1999);
- it provides an opportunity for discussing how a teacher can work with a class using one computer;
- it provides an opportunity to discuss how the teacher copes with the wires, etc., from the computer peripherals, which can sometimes be a distraction, or simply annoying, when one is trying to show something to pupils;
- teachers can discuss the advantages and disadvantages in using a computer in this way for collecting data and for analysing results.

Developing classroom use of ICT

Unfortunately it is common for the outcomes of staff development exercises not to be implemented in the classroom. Many innovations remain solely in the notes taken during training. The new learning is more likely to be fully implemented when two or three people work together on tasks, sharing ideas and supporting one another's learning. This peer-coaching approach (Joyce *et al.* 1999) requires teachers to observe one another's lessons, calling on the expertise of the ICT co-ordinator when required.

There are three factors that play an important role in helping teachers to continue their development: feedback, support and reflection. These may follow on from the peer-group activities or may be used as an alternative approach when the setting up of peer groups is problematic.

Feedback

The term is used here to mean the responses the ICT co-ordinator gives to the subject/class teacher following the observation of a lesson. The focus of the observation is usually on pupils' learning with ICT.

When two teachers work together there can be problems, particularly if the observer tries to take over or if he or she is critical, either directly or indirectly, by giving advice that implies that the approach used was inappropriate. Giving feedback to a fellow professional frequently requires tact and diplomacy, and if it is not handled properly it can lead to a breakdown in relationships. The purpose of the feedback is to help the subject teacher to put into practice some of the ideas provided in previous training programmes. With the focus of the observation on pupils' learning, the ICT teacher will stand back from the main teaching role in order to observe what is going on in the classroom more clearly.

Prior planning must involve decisions as to the roles of the two teachers during the lesson (both discipline and teaching) and should ensure that the class/subject teacher conveys an understanding of the learning outcomes of the lesson to the observer. Following the lesson, the resulting discussion can

- identify gaps in competence in using the computers;
- help the subject teacher analyse what has happened and why it has happened (ways in which pupils' ICT capability has been enhanced or how the use of ICT has helped the pupils to learn the subject matter);
- assist the class/subject teacher to think about how he or she could improve on what has been taught (was the methodology used the most appropriate with this class or for this topic?).

The following questions could be posed in order to initiate the discussion.

1   To what extent is using ICT enhancing pupils' learning (over traditional methods)?
2   What kinds of learning and behaviour were you trying to promote?
3   What ICT skills are the pupils developing during the lesson?
4   Is the time spent on the computer used to the best effect? Would prior preparation by the pupils help? Is group discussion round the computer promoting learning? Why did the teacher adopt a particular course of action?
5   What other computer packages could have been used? Would they have been more or less effective?
6   How did the conditions in the room, or the circumstances generally, impinge

on your teaching and how did you take this into account when deciding what to do?

It is better to ask open questions that invite the teachers to reveal their thinking in the lesson rather than closed questions looking for confirmation or denial of what they think.

Support

'Support' describes the longer term process where the ICT teacher acts as a professional friend to the subject teacher, giving guidance on teaching techniques and software but only visiting the subject teacher's classroom on request.

In the previous chapter we mentioned the importance of the support given by the headteacher and members of the senior management. It is vital that these individuals show a keen interest in the incorporation of ICT into subject lessons and frequently talk to staff about the progress they are making. However, support will come mainly from the ICT specialist and from other subject/class teachers who are more experienced in using ICT. This is an opportunity for cross-fertilisation of ideas to all sections of the school.

Support can be helpful in a numbers of ways:

- It can reduce the isolation felt by teachers. The sharing of experiences confirms that individual teachers are not alone in having difficulties. Support meetings provide opportunities to discuss feelings and to exchange ideas about how teachers cope with the process of changing from one teaching approach to another.
- It can give encouragement and confidence to those implementing teaching approaches using ICT.
- It can provide opportunities for sharing professional knowledge. Support meetings are opportunities for sharing teaching activities, solutions to problems and the discussion of theoretical ideas.

Reflection

At some stage the teacher must become more responsible for developing the use of ICT in the classroom. Here the teacher reflects on practice and takes appropriate steps to improve.

Reflection plays an important part in teachers' professional growth. At one level it involves a brief recollection of which part of the lesson went well and what was less successful. Teachers make a mental note of their deliberations and adjust future teaching accordingly. At a deeper level the teacher starts to ask why a particular approach was a success or a failure. This type of reflection is likely to promote teachers' thinking about their classroom activities and the beliefs associated with those actions. It helps teachers to clarify existing ideas about teaching and forces them to consider new ideas or how the old ones can be modified. In some cases this type of reflection will take place immediately after the lesson, or it may require quiet consideration sometime afterwards. Groups of teachers can benefit from this process through meetings where they are asked to share their thoughts and actions with others.

While reflection should come from the teacher's own interests and actions, the following questions may be helpful in focusing on pupils' learning:

- To what extent am I catering for the abilities of all the pupils in the class?
- Are pupils able to build on prior learning?
- Have I considered common misconceptions associated with this topic?
- Are the pupils able to use what they have learnt in new situations?
- Did the pupils appreciate that they were making progress?
- Did the pupils improve their confidence in the subject and the image they have of themselves as a learner of the subject?
- Did the pupils develop good habits of work, including perseverance and a concern for correctness?
- Did the pupils use their initiative, exercise imagination and think for themselves?

Reflection can be taken further by carrying out action research. This approach requires a more rigorous look at the quality of teaching and learning. In order to make judgements teachers will have to look at a variety of evidence of classroom activity, such as:

- lesson plans and schemes of work;
- comments from observing teachers;
- a diary of classroom activity;
- the results of pupils' class and homework; and
- the results of examinations.

There are a number of stages in the action research process, which are illustrated in Figure 10.3 with an example of a modern foreign language teacher reflecting on the value of introducing ICT into her sixth-form lessons to encourage greater autonomy in pupils' learning.

Evaluating the training

The staff development programme will probably take place over a year or an even longer period and it will need to be regularly monitored to check that the training objectives are being met. The evaluation mechanism needs to be carefully thought through as it is all too easy to devise a scheme that provides a list of worthless data from which no remedial action can be devised. The first thing to consider is the nature of the thing being evaluated. Is it the software, the delivery of the in-service course, the ability of the individual to come to terms with the technology, or is it something else? Some teachers may enthuse about a wonderful piece of software

Research stage	Teacher actions
What do we want to know? (This must be clearly defined, as ambiguity here can lead to confusion later. It may be useful to break down the original question into sub-questions)	The teacher asks the question: How effective is the use of the internet in teaching the topic *L'immigration* to students in their first year of A-level?
How am I going to collect data to find out the answer to this question?	Observation of students at work, paying particular attention to student–student interactions Recording what the teacher does during the lesson (lesson plans, post-lesson review, observation by colleague) The extent of dictionary use Quality of written work produced Results of end of topic test
How much time and what other resources can be used to help answer the question?	Monitoring over 2–3 lessons Literature on students' learning, using both ICT and traditional methods
How can the data be analysed and what is the best way of presenting it?	Prepare a table of benefits and pitfalls for both the learner and the teacher Compare the results of the end of topic test and the quality of written work with other similar work How do these results compare with others in school and those described in the literature?
What changes will we carry out in the light of the findings?	Does the research suggest that I should modify: the instructions I give to the students; the way in which I manage the situation; the tasks given to the students; the amount of time devoted to this topic, etc.?
Start the review process again	Review the situation again to monitor the improvements next time the topic is taught

Figure 10.3 An example of the action research process based on a series of sixth form lessons. The teacher had searched the web to find suitable sites and had devised a series of questions which the learners would address by accessing the technology themselves

Source: Meiring and Norman (1999)

or the sophistication of the technology, and neglect the thinking about how it will support pupils' learning. The evaluator needs to be aware of this and should look for both short- and long-term gains in the teacher's attitude to computers and performance with ICT in the classroom.

Detailed questionnaires are not the best way forward unless they can be used to illustrate a teaching point concerned with the collection and manipulation of data. Three or four simple questions, similar to the following, would give some useful information:

- What did you learn?
- How will this help you in your teaching?
- How would you like to develop your ICT skills?
- Can you suggest improvements to the training sessions?

This could be carried out orally or in writing. The main advantage of talking to the teachers at the end of the course is that it gives the evaluator the opportunity to ask supplementary questions and gain an overall picture of the teachers' attitudes. The real test, though, is the extent to which ICT is used and the way it is used, and this must be monitored by the ICT co-ordinator by visits to lessons and departmental meetings.

In one of the ITCD secondary schools, for instance, the ICT co-ordinator made it her business to go to departmental or faculty meetings on a regular basis to get feedback on how ICT was being used in subject teaching. She was able to identify new training needs and, whenever possible, smooth out any technical or administrative difficulties experienced by the staff.

In the long term the effectiveness of the training must be judged in terms of

- teachers' attitudes towards ICT;
- teachers' classroom performance with ICT;
- pupils' performance in ICT and other subjects.

Resource development issues

We remarked in Chapter 1 on the interdependence of ICT capability and ICT resources. Indeed, the ICT capabilities of pupils and teachers may be reviewed as resources for learning across the curriculum, and it is natural that schools should plan resource development and capability development together.

Resource planning must be based on teaching and learning needs. There is no overriding need for standardisation in schools. ICT-capable teachers and pupils will be aware that different tools are appropriate to different tasks. They will understand the process they are going to use them for, and adapt their techniques according to the tools they are using. Indeed, the use of different resources to carry out the same process should enhance pupils' understanding of the concepts involved, provided that teachers explicitly ask pupils to reflect on their tasks and make comparisons between the resources.

Too few computers, or a predominance of older, less reliable, less powerful machines, will inhibit the development of ICT capability (Ward 1999). Teachers interviewed for the ITCD project did not find the nature or quantity of the resources an issue, however. It was their availability when needed that was the overriding consideration. The difficulty of gaining access was a major factor inhibiting ICT capability development from their point of view. If the senior managements of schools are going to expect greater use of ICT, there must be sufficient resources in the right places and at the right times for teachers to make effective use of them. This does not require a computer for every pupil or even a large number of computers in every classroom. The schools that were developing ICT capability most rapidly did not necessarily have the most equipment, but they had the clearest plans for effective distribution and the greatest level of financial commitment.

Successful schools are continually evaluating and updating resources, and in the most successful staff are confident with the types of computer, their power and their reliability. Other schools are achieving partial success despite the age of their resources. They recognise that ICT capability is dependent on the resources available, and are seeking major investment to ensure that their pupils are not disadvantaged. Schools also recognise the value of other ICT resources for teaching purposes. Hand-held devices, such as graphic calculators, are powerful tools which do not need a special room in order to provide one per pupil. Large-screen display equipment such as multimedia projectors and electronic whiteboards have the potential to transform the integration of ICT with subject teaching.

However, teachers need regular practice with the technology if they are going to make progress. It is all too easy to forget how to carry out particular functions if they are used infrequently. Teachers who have computers at home tend to use the technology more in their lessons than those who do not (Goldstein 1997; Ofsted 1999b). Some managers have recognised this as a valuable way of developing the use of ICT within the school, and have loaned teachers a computer at weekends or over the holiday periods.

> The Government's schemes for teachers in selected schools to acquire laptops over the last few years may thus have helped to improve teachers' confidence to use computers more readily and regularly in lessons. Many schools also find that making portable computers available to staff for home use is a means of raising teachers' confidence, expertise and use of ICT. This in turn has a positive effect on pupils' ICT capability.
>
> (Ofsted 1999b: 3)

Conclusion

Just as slimming aids are advertised with the caveat 'must be used as part of a calorie-controlled diet', so our recommendations are issued with the caveat *must be used as part of a general programme of school improvement.* But we feel that there are some clear messages about the types of improvement and the strategy for bringing them about.

We have set out a vision for the ICT-capable school that involves far more than simply supplementing traditional pedagogical practices with the use of computers. We also hope that while we have paid due regard to vocational arguments for the introduction of ICT, we have made it clear that we do not view the ICT-capable school as simply being better than less capable schools at teaching a few basic ICT skills and procedures. ICT capability has come to evoke a far richer notion than 'skills' and 'competences'. The focus of the ICT-capable school will be on the higher order knowledge and processes which are the key to learning across the curriculum.

Many of the ideas generated here in the context of ICT will be valuable also for numeracy and literacy initiatives. They will have even more value if used within a whole-curriculum approach to improvements in teaching and learning where the focus is on pupils' key skills – particularly the higher order skills – and their understanding of related concepts.

Our research into ICT in schools has added to the evidence that there 'has been no systemic evolution in the basic manner in which teachers approach teaching, pupils approach learning, or educational establishments approach the management of themselves' (Lynch 1999). We hope that our book will contribute to this evolutionary process. The move towards ICT-capable schooling proposed in this book demands a root-and-branch re-evaluation of views about teaching and learning. A change of this magnitude demands that teachers currently operating quite successfully by their own standards and by the norms of their school take professional risks with their reputations, experimenting with new content and new approaches. The difficulties associated with such change should not be under-estimated, but the benefits to be gained are immense.

We started by characterising ICT capability in a way that makes it clear that it is not something which can be *bolted on*. For schools, for the classrooms and the subjects in which teaching and learning take place, and for the individual teachers and pupils within them, the development of ICT capability must come from within.

However, for our pupils such change cannot come too soon. The world is dividing into the information rich and the information poor. At the cusp of the millennium, the educational equivalent of the industrial revolution has finally arrived to emancipate the human mind as dramatically as when the previous revolution freed us from reliance on the capabilities of the human muscle (Howe 1983). Schools have no choice but to embrace the ICT phenomenon and to expect teachers to develop their practice accordingly. If they do not, there are many commercial interests that can respond quickly to provide such an alternative. Such entrepreneurs view learners merely as consumers of educational products that can be delivered electronically to their homes. Schools may be excluded from such a scenario, and they must identify rapidly what it is that they can add to this bleak vision of knowledge transmission. Rather than let schools wither away, we prefer proposals for radical changes in schooling, such as those from the RSA (Bayliss 1999), which give more responsibility to learners while maintaining a strong pedagogical base. It is in this context that we offer a vision of ICT-capable schools, working in partnership with parents to develop ICT-capable citizens within a society committed to life-long learning.

Bibliography

ACAC (1995) *Consistency in Teacher Assessment: Guidance for Schools*, Cardiff: Awdurdod Cwricwlwm ac Asesu Cymru.
—— (1996) *Consistency in Teacher Assessment: Exemplification of Standards*, Cardiff: ACAC.
ACCAC (1999a) *Information Technology in the National Curriculum: Proposals for Consultation*, Cardiff: Awdurdod Cwmwysterau, Cwricwlwm ac Asesu Cymru.
—— (1999b) *Whole-School Approaches to Developing IT Capability*, Cardiff: ACCAC.
—— (1999c) *Whole School Approaches to Developing IT Capability: Executive Summary*, Cardiff: ACCAC.
ACITT (1997) *Informatics KS3*, Barking: Association for Computing and IT Teachers.
Ager, R. (1998) *Information and Communications Technology in Primary Schools: Children or Computers in Control?*, London: David Fulton.
ASE (1988) *Initiatives in Primary Science: An Evaluation*, Hatfield: Association for Science Education.
Balding, J. (1986) 'Planning the curriculum – health related behaviour studies in schools', *Health Education Journal*, 45(1): 25–7.
Ball, S. (1987) *The Micro-Politics of the School: Towards a Theory of School Organisation*, London: Methuen.
Ball, S. and Lacey, C. (1995) 'Revisiting subject disciplines as the opportunity for group action: a measured critique of subject subcultures', in L. S. Siskin and J. W. Little (eds), *The Subjects in Question*, New York: Teachers' College Press, 95–122.
Bayliss, V. (1999) *Opening Minds: Education for the 21st Century*, London: RSA.
BCS Schools Committee (1999) *Using adult helpers in the classroom*, online document, available (23 November 1999): http://www.bcs.org.uk/educat/schools/adlthelp.htm
BECTA (1998a) *IT Policy: How to Write a Whole-School IT Policy Document*, Coventry: British Educational Communications and Technology Agency.
—— (1998b) *Multimedia portables for teachers' pilot: project report*, online document, available: http://www.becta.org.uk/projects/mmportables2/final/
—— (1999) *The UK ILS Evaluations: Final Report*, Coventry: British Educational Communications and Technology Agency.
Bell, D. (1992) 'Co-ordinating science in primary schools: a role model?', *Evaluation and Research in Education*, 6: 155–71.
Bennett, R. (1997) *Teaching IT*, Oxford: Nash–Pollock.
Benzie, D. (1997) 'Information technology: is our definition wide of the mark?', in D. Passey and B. Samways (eds), *Information Technology: Supporting Change Through Teacher Education*, London: Chapman and Hall, 55–61.
Birnbaum, I. (1989) *IT and the National Curriculum: Some Fundamental Issues*, Doncaster: Resource.

—— (1990) 'The assessment of IT capability', *Journal of Computer Assisted Learning*, 6: 88–97.

Blackmore, M., Stanley, N., Coles, D., Hodgkinson, K., Taylor, C. and Vaughan, G. (1992) 'A preliminary view of students' information technology experience across UK initial teacher training institutions', *Journal of Information Technology for Teacher Education*, 1: 241–54.

Bliss, J. and Ogborn, J. (1989) 'Tools for exploratory learning', *Journal of Computer Assisted Learning*, 5: 37–50.

Bolton LEA (1999) *Bolton LEA's ICT curriculum team*, online document, available (23 November 1999): http://www.tfict.org.uk/pri/

Bowen, P. (1995) 'Secondary information technology and the Ofsted inspections – an analysis and discussion of information technology comments', *Computer Education*, 79: 2–6.

Broderbrund (1996) *The Logical Journey of the Zoombinis* (CD-ROM), Novato, California: Broderbrund Software.

Brown, A. L. (1987) 'Metacognition, executive control, self regulation and other more mysterious mechanisms', in F. E. Weinert and R. H. Kluwe (eds), *Metacognition, Motivation and Understanding*, Hillsdale, NJ: Lawrence Erlbaum.

Bruner, J. S. (1961), 'The act of discovery', *Harvard Educational Review*, 31: 21–32.

—— (1985) 'Vygotsky: a historical and conceptual perspective', in J. V. Wertsch (ed.), *Culture, Communication and Cognition: Vygotskian Perspectives*, Cambridge: Cambridge University Press, 21–34.

Caldwell, B. J. and Spinks, J. M. (1992) *Leading the Self-Managing School*, Lewes: Falmer Press.

CCW (1990) *Information Technology in the National Curriculum: Non-Statutory Guidance for Schools*, Cardiff: Curriculum Council for Wales.

—— (1992) *Fitting IT In!*, Cardiff: Curriculum Council for Wales.

Chen, M. (1986) 'Gender and computers: the beneficial effects of experience on attitudes', *Journal of Educational Computing Research*, 2(3): 265–82.

Coley, A. M., Gale, M. T. and Harris, T. A. (1994) 'Effects of gender role identity and experience on computer attitude components', *Journal of Educational Computing Research*, 10(2): 129–37.

Cooke, V. (1998), 'The role of the primary IT coordinator', *Computer Education*, 90: 17–19.

Cox, M. (1997) *The Effects of Information Technology on Students' Motivation (Final Report)*, Coventry: NCET.

—— and Nikolopoulou, K. (1997) 'What sort of information handling skills are promoted by the use of data analysis software?', *Education and Information Technologies*, 2: 105–20.

Crawford, R. A. (1998a) *IT in English state secondary schools and its impact on the initial teacher training of IT teachers*, online documents, available:
http://www.btinternet.com/~R.A.Crawford/

—— (1998b) *What is IT capability? An investigation into notions of what constitutes IT capability*, online documents, available (23 November 1999):
http://www.btinternet.com/~R.A.Crawford/

Crompton, R. and Mann, P. (1997) *IT across the Primary Curriculum*, London: Cassell.

Culley, L. (1988) 'Girls, boys and computers', *Educational Studies*, 14(1): 3–8.

Daugherty, R. and Freedman, E. (1998) 'Tests, targets and tables: the use of KS2 assessment data in Wales', *The Welsh Journal of Education*, 7(1): 5–21.

Deadman, G. (1997) 'An analysis of reflective writing within a hypermedia framework', *Journal of Computer Assisted Learning*, 13: 16–25.

Bibliography 173

Dean, J. (1988) 'Continuity', in M. Clarkson (ed.), *Emerging Issues in Primary Education*, London: Falmer Press, 90–8.

Dearing, R. (1993) *The National Curriculum and its Assessment*, London: School Curriculum and Assessment Authority.

DES (1989) *Information Technology from 5 to 16*, London: Department of Education and Science.

DES–Welsh Office (1988) *National Curriculum Design and Technology Working Group: Interim Report*, London: Department of Education and Science.

DES/WO (1990) *Technology in the National Curriculum*, London: Department of Education and Science–Welsh Office.

DfEE (1997a) *Connecting the Learning Society*, London: Department for Education and Employment.

—— (1997b) *From Targets to Action: Guidance to Support Effective Target-Setting in Schools*, London: Department for Education and Employment.

—— (1997c) *Excellence in Schools*, London: Department for Education and Employment.

—— (1998a) *Survey of Information and Communications Technology in Schools 1998*, London: Department for Education and Employment.

—— (1998b) *The National Literacy Project*, London: Department for Education and Employment.

—— (1999a) *Information and Communications Technology in Maintained Primary and Secondary Schools in England: 1999*, London: Department for Education and Employment.

—— (1999b) *The Standards Site*, online document, available:
http://www.standards.dfee.gov.uk/ (16 November 1999)

—— (1999c) *Connecting the Learning Society 2000*, London: Department for Education and Employment.

DfEE–QCA (1999) *Information and Communications Technology: the National Curriculum for England*, London: Department for Education and Employment and Qualifications–Curriculum Authority.

Downes, T. (1995) 'Children and electronic media: the home–school connection', in J. D. Tinsley and T. Van Weert (eds), *World Conference in Computer Education: Liberating the Learner*, London, Chapman and Hall, 544–52.

—— (1997a) 'The computer as a toy and tool in the home – implications for teacher education', in D. Passey and B. Samways (eds), *Information Technology: Supporting Change through Teacher Education*, London: Chapman and Hall, 310–15.

—— (1997b) *Children's Use of Electronic Technologies in the Home*, online document, available (23 November 1999): http://www.notesys.com/LinkSite/DownesStg2rep.html

—— (1998) 'Using the computer at home', in M. Monteith (ed.), *IT for Learning Enhancement*, Exeter: Intellect, 61–78.

—— (1999) 'Playing with computing technologies in the home', *Education and Information Technologies*, 4(1): 65–79.

Ferguson, P. D. and Fraser, B. J. (1998) 'Student gender, school size and changing perceptions of science learning environments during the transition from primary to secondary school', *Research in Science Education*, 28(4): 387–97.

Flavell, J. H. (1976) 'Metacognitive aspects of problem solving', in L. B. Resnick (ed.), *The Nature of Intelligence*, Hillsdale, NJ: Lawrence Erlbaum, 231–5.

—— (1987) 'Speculations about the nature and development of metacognition', in F. E. Weinhart and R. H. Kluwe (eds), *Metacognition, Motivation and Understanding*, Hillsdale, NJ: Lawrence Erlbaum, 21–30.

Fullan, M. (1988) 'Research into educational innovation', in R. Glatter, M. Preedy,

C. Reiches and M. Masterton (eds), *Understanding School Management*, Milton Keynes: Open University Press, 195–211.

—— (1991) *The New Meaning of Educational Change*, London: Cassell.

—— (1992) *Successful School Improvement: The Implementation Perspective and Beyond*, Buckingham: Open University Press.

—— (1993) *Change Forces: Probing the Depths of Educational Reform*, London: Falmer Press.

—— and Hargreaves, A. (1992) *Teacher Development and Educational Change*, London, Falmer Press.

Galton, M. and Willcocks, J. (1983) *Inside the Primary Classroom*, London: Routledge & Kegan Paul.

Gibson, J. (1977) 'The theory of affordances', in R. Shaw and J. Bransford (eds), *Perceiving, Acting and Knowing*, Hillsdale, NJ: Erlbaum.

—— (1986) *The Ecological Approach to Visual Perception*, Hillsdale, NJ: Lawrence Erlbaum Associates.

Goldstein, G. (1997) *Information Technology in English Schools – A Commentary on Inspection Findings 1995–6*, London: Office for Standards in Education.

Goodson, I. F. (1992) 'On curriculum form: notes towards a theory of curriculum', *Sociology of Education*, 65(1): 66–75.

—— (1995 2nd edn) *The Making of Curriculum*, London: Falmer Press.

——, Anstead, C. J. and Mangan, J. M. (1998) *Subject Knowledge: Readings for the Study of School Subjects*, London: Falmer Press.

Goodson, I. F. and Mangan, J. M. (1995) 'Subject cultures and the introduction of classroom computers', *British Journal of Educational Research*, 21(5): 613–28.

Goodson, I. F. and Marsh, C. (1996) *Studying School Subjects*, London: Falmer Press.

Grace, G. (1995) *School Leadership: Beyond Education Management. An Essay in Policy Scholarship*, London: Falmer Press.

Gray, J., Hopkins, D., Reynolds, D., Wilcox, B., Farrell, S. and Jesson, D. (1999) *Improving Schools, Performance and Potential*, Buckingham: Open University Press.

Greeno, J. (1994) 'Gibson's affordances', *Psychological Review*, 101: 336–42.

Haigh, G. (1996) 'No longer at cross purposes', *Times Educational Supplement*, 23 February.

Hargreaves, A. (1994) *Changing Teachers, Changing Times: Teachers' Work and Culture in the Postmodern Age*, London: Cassell.

—— and Dawe, R. (1990) 'Paths of professional development: contrived collegiality, collaborative culture and the case of peer coaching', *Teaching and Teacher Education*, 6(3): 227–41.

Hargreaves, A., Earl, L. and Ryan, J. (1996) *Schooling for Change: Reinventing Education for Early Adolescents*, London: Falmer Press.

Hargreaves, A. and Macmillan, R. (1995) 'The balkanisation of secondary school teaching', in L. S. Siskin and J. W. Little (eds), *The Subjects in Question*, New York: Teachers' College Press, 141–71.

Harris, S. (1994) *Schools' IT Policies*, Slough: National Foundation for Education Research.

—— (1999) *INSET for IT: A Review of the Literature Relating to Preparation for and Use of IT in Schools*, Slough: National Foundation for Educational Research.

Harrison, C., Youngman, M., Bailey, M., Fisher, T., Phillips, R. and Restorick, J. (1998) *Multimedia Portables for Teachers' Pilot: Project Report*, Coventry: British Educational Communications and Technology Agency.

Harrison, M. (1998) *Coordinating Information and Communications Technology across the Primary School*, London: Falmer Press.

Hayward, S. and Wray, D. (1988) 'Using Tray, a text reconstruction program, with top infants', *Educational Review*, 40: 29–39.

Heinrich, P. (1995) 'The school development plan for IT', in B. Tagg (ed.), *Developing a Whole-School IT Policy*, London: Pitman, 51–71.

Herschbach, D. R. (1995) 'Technology as knowledge: implications for instruction', *Journal of Technology Education*, 7(1): 1–8.

Hirsch, D. (1999) 'Rapporteur's conclusions', in Centre for Educational Research and Innovation (eds), *Innovating Schools*, Paris: Organisation for Economic Co-operation and Development.

Hopkins, D., Ainscow, M. and West, M. (1994) *School Improvement in an Era of Change*, London: Cassell.

Howe, J. (1983) 'Towards a pupil-centred classroom', in D. Walker, J. Nisbet and E. Hoyle (eds), *Computers in Education*, London: Kogan Page, 27–63.

Hoyles, C. and Sutherland, R. (1989) *Logo Mathematics in the Classroom*, London: Routledge.

Huberman, M. (1992) 'Critical introduction', in M. Fullan (ed.), *Successful School Improvement: The Implementation Perspective and Beyond*, Milton Keynes: Open University Press, 1–20.

Huggins, M. and Knight, P. (1997) 'Curriculum continuity and transfer from primary to secondary school: the case of history', *Educational Studies*, 23(3): 333–48.

Hughes, M. (1999) *Closing the Learning Gap*, Stafford: Network Educational Press.

—— and Greenough, P. (1989) 'Gender and social interaction in early logo use', in J. H. Collins, N. Estes, W. D. Gattis and D. Walker (eds), *Proceedings of the Sixth International Conference on Technology and Education*, vol. 1, CEP.

Jennings, Z. (1994) 'Innovations in Caribbean school systems: why some have become institutionalised and others have not', *Curriculum Studies* 2(3): 309–31.

Jones, L. P. and Jones, L. (1993) 'Keeping up the momentum: improving continuity', *Education* 3(13): 46–50.

Joyce, B., Calhoun, E. and Hopkins, D. (1999) *The New Structure of School Improvement: Inquiring Schools and Achieving Students*, Buckingham: Open University Press.

Kemmis, S., Atkin, R. and Wright, E. (1977) *How Do Students Learn? Working Papers on CAL*, no. 5, Norwich: University of East Anglia.

Kennewell, S. (1993) *Changes in Strategies for Teaching and Learning across Primary/Secondary Transfer*, Swansea: Department of Education, University College of Swansea.

—— (1995a) 'Information technology capability – how does it develop?', in J. D. Tinsley and T. Van Weert (eds), *World Conference in Computer Education: Liberating the Learner*, London, Chapman and Hall, 419–28.

—— (1995b) 'Education for information technology capability: progress and barriers in South Wales' schools', *The Welsh Journal of Education*, 4(2).

—— (1997) 'The integration of information technology into teachers' decision making', in D. Passey and B. Samways (eds), *Information Technology: Supporting Change through Teacher Education*, London: Chapman and Hall, 169–75.

——, Parkinson, J. and Tanner, H. (2000) 'A model for the study and design of teaching situations with ICT', in D. Watson and T. Downes (eds), *Learning in a Networked Society*, Dordrecht: Kluwer Academic Publishers, 129–38.

Kennewell, S. and Selwood, I. (1997) 'The professional development needs of secondary school IT co-ordinators', *Journal of Information Technology in Teacher Education* 6(3): 339–56.

Kirkman, C. (1993) 'Computer experience and attitudes of 12-year-old students: implications for the UK National Curriculum', *Journal of Computer Assisted Learning*, 9: 51–62.

Lawley, P. (1999) *Target Setting and Bench Marking*, Dunstable: Folens.

Layton, D. (1972) 'Science as general education', *Trends in Education*, 25: 6–15.

Leask, M. and Williams, L. (1999) 'Whole-school approaches: integrating ICT across the curriculum', in M. Leask and N. Pachler (eds), *Learning to Teach Using ICT in the Secondary School*, London: Routledge, 194–209.

Levin, T. and Gordon, C. (1989) 'Effect of gender and computer experience on attitudes toward computers', *Journal of Educational Computing Research*, 5(1): 69–88.

Lovegrove, N. and Wilshire, M. (1997) *The Future of Information Technology in UK Schools*, London: McKinsey.

Loveless, A. (1995) *The Role of IT: Practical Issues for the Primary Teacher*, London: Cassell.

Lynch, O. (1999) 'Teaching and learning for the next decade: Is ICT indispensable? Is it sustainable?', keynote speech to BETT '99, London, 14 January 1999, online documents, available: http://www.becta.org.uk/information/bett99_speech/bett99_speech1.html

Martin, R. (1991) 'School children's attitudes towards computers as a function of gender, course subjects and availability of home computers', *Journal of Computer Assisted Learning* 7: 187–94.

McGuinness, C. (1999) *From Thinking Skills to Thinking Classrooms*, London: Department for Education and Employment.

Meiring, L. and Norman, N. (1999) 'Planning an integrated topic', in N. Pachler (ed.), *Teaching Modern Foreign Languages at A-Level*, London: Routledge.

Mellar, H., Bliss, J., Boohan, R., Ogborn, J. and Thomsett, C. (eds) (1994) *Learning with Artificial Worlds: Computer-Based Modelling in the Curriculum*, London: Falmer.

MEU Cymru (1991) *Links: Primary Secondary Continuity and Progression in IT*, Cardiff: Microelectronics Education Unit Cymru.

Mevarech, Z. (1997) 'The U-curve process that trainee teachers experience in integrating computers into the curriculum', in D. Passey and B. Samways (eds), *Information Technology: Supporting Change through Teacher Education*, London: Chapman and Hall, 46–51.

Michael, I. (1999) 'Managing of staff development for ICT to support teaching and learning in the secondary school', unpublished MEd thesis, University of Wales, Swansea.

Millard, E. (1997) *Differently Literate: Boys, Girls and the Schooling of Literacy*, London: Falmer Press.

Moseley, D. and Higgins, S. (1999) *Ways Forward with ICT: Effective Pedagogy Using Information and Communications Technology for Literacy and Numeracy in Primary Schools*, Newcastle-upon-Tyne: University of Newcastle.

Murray D. (1992) 'IT capability in primary schools: a case of something lost in the translation?', *Journal of Computer Assisted Learning*, 8(2): 96–103.

NCC (1990) *Non-Statutory Guidance: Information Technology Capability*, York: National Curriculum Council.

NCET (1991) *Focus on IT*, Coventry: National Council for Educational Technology.

—— (1995a) *Approaches to IT Capability at KS3*, Coventry: National Council for Educational Technology.

—— (1995b) *Making Sense of Information*, Coventry: NCET.

—— (1996) *Delivering Capability in IT*, Coventry: National Council for Educational Technology.

—— (1998) *IT Coordination in Secondary Schools*, Coventry: National Council for Educational Technology.

NCET–NAACE (1995) *Inspecting IT*, Coventry: National Council for Educational Technology–National Association of Advisers for Computers in Education.

—— (1997) *Implementing IT*, Coventry: National Council for Educational Technology–National Association of Advisers for Computers in Education.

Ofsted (1995a) *The OFSTED Handbook*, London: Office for Standards in Education.

—— (1995b) *Information Technology: A Review of Inspection Findings 1993/94*, London: Office for Standards in Education.

—— (1999a) *The Annual Report of Her Majesty's Chief Inspector of Schools 1997–98*, London: Stationery Office.

—— (1999b) *Standards in the Secondary Curriculum 1997/98: Information Technology*, London: Office for Standards in Education.

OHMCI (1996) *Framework for the Inspection of Schools*, London: Central Office of Information.

—— (1999) *Information Technology and the Final Evaluation of the WOMPI Project*, Cardiff: Office of Her Majesty's Chief Inspector.

Owen, G. (1992) 'Whole-school management of information technology', *School Organization* 12(1), 29–40.

Owen, M. (1992) 'A teacher-centred model of development in the educational use of computers', *Journal of Information Technology for Teacher Education*, 1(1), 127–38.

Pachler, N. and Williams, L. (1999) 'Using the internet as a teaching and learning tool', in M. Leask and N. Pachler (eds), *Learning to Teach Using ICT in the Secondary School*, London: Routledge, 51–70.

Papert, S. (1980) *Mindstorms: Children, Computers and Powerful Ideas*, Brighton: Harvester.

—— (1996) *The Connected Family: Bridging the Digital Divide*, Georgia, GA: Longstreet Press.

Passey, D. and Ridgway, J. (1992) *Coordinating National Curriculum IT: Strategies for Whole-School Development*, Lancaster: Framework Press.

Pea, R. D. (1985) 'Beyond amplification: using the computer to reorganise mental functioning', *Educational Psychology*, 20(4): 167–82.

Pelgrum, W. and Plomp, T. (1993) *The IEA Study of Computers in Education*, Oxford: Pergamon.

Piaget, J. (1977) *The Grasp of Consciousness: Action and Concept in the Young Child*, London: Routledge & Keagan Paul.

—— (1978) *Success and Understanding*, London: Routledge & Keagan Paul.

Prawat, R. (1989) 'Promoting access to knowledge, strategy and disposition in students: a research synthesis', *Review of Educational Research*, 59(1): 1–41.

Proctor, N. (1987) 'Bullock refreshed: the five languages for life', *Reading*, 21(2): 80–91.

QCA (1997) *Expectations in Information Technology at Key Stages 1 and 2*, London: Qualifications and Curriculum Authority.

—— (1998a) *Building Bridges: Guidance and Training Materials for Teachers of Year 6 and Year 7 Pupils*, London: Qualifications and Curriculum Authority.

—— (1998b) *Primary Schemes of Work: IT*, London: Qualifications and Curriculum Authority.

—— (1999) *Review of the National Curriculum in England*, London: Qualifications and Curriculum Authority.

—— (1999b) *Information Technology: the National Curriculum*, London: Qualifications and Curriculum Authority.

Ranson, S. (1994) *Towards the Learning Society*, London: Cassell.

Reinen, I. and Plomp, T. (1997) 'Information technology and gender equality: a contradiction in terms?', *Computers & Education*, 28(2): 65–78.

Ridgway, J. (1997) 'Vygotsky, informatics capability and professional development', in D. Passey and B. Samways (eds), *Information Technology: Supporting Change through Teacher Education*, London: Chapman & Hall.

Robertson, J. (1998) 'Paradise lost: children, multimedia and the myth of interactivity', *Journal of Computer Assisted Learning*, 14: 31–9.

RSAEB (1996) *Information Technology: 1998 Syllabus*, Coventry: RSA Examinations Board.

Ruddock, J., Gray, J. and Galton, M. (1998) *Times Educational Supplement*, 20 November, 19.

Russell, T. (1995) 'IT and education: where have we gone wrong?, *Computer Education*, 81: 2–4.

Salomon, G. and Globerson, T. (1987) 'Skill may not be enough: the role of mindfulness in learning and transfer', *International Journal of Educational Research*, 11(6): 623–37.

Sanders, J. (1984) 'The computer: boy, girl or androgynous?', *The Computing Teacher* 4: 31–4.

SCAA (1995) *Consistency in Teacher Assessment: Guidance for Schools*, London: Schools' Curriculum and Assessment Authority.

—— (1996) *Consistency in Teacher Assessment: Exemplification of Standards*, London: Schools' Curriculum and Assessment Authority.

Schagen, S. and Kerr, D. (1999) *Bridging the Gap? The National Curriculum and Progression from Primary to Secondary School*, Slough: National Foundation for Educational Research.

Schein, E. H. (1997) *Organisational Culture and Leadership*, 2nd edn, San Francisco, CA: Jossey-Bass.

Schoenfeld, A. H. (ed.) (1987) *Cognitive Science and Mathematics Education*, Hillsdale, NJ: Lawrence Erlbaum.

Selinger, M. (1997) 'Defining a pedagogy for IT', *ITTE Newsletter*, autumn 1997.

—— (1999) 'ICT and classroom management', in M. Leask and N. Pachler (eds), *Learning to Teach Using ICT in the Secondary School*, London: Routledge, 36–50.

Selwood, I. and Jenkinson, D. (1995) 'The delivery of information technology capability in secondary schools in England and Wales', in J. D. Tinsley and T. Van Weert (eds), *World Conference in Computer Education: Liberating the Learner*, London, Chapman & Hall, 419–28.

Selwyn, N. (1997a) 'Assessing students' ability to use computers: theoretical considerations for practical research', *British Educational Research Journal*, 23: 47–59.

—— (1997b) 'Teaching information technology to the "computer shy": a theoretical perspective on a practical problem', *Journal of Vocational Education and Training*, 47(3): 395–408.

—— (1997c) 'The effect of using a computer at home on students' use of IT', *Research in Education*, 58: 79–81.

—— (1998) 'The effect of using a home computer on student's educational use of IT', *Computers and Education*, 31(2): 11–27.

—— (1999a) 'Differences in educational computer use: the influence of subject cultures', *The Curriculum Journal*, 10(1): 29–48.

—— (1999b) 'Why the computer is not dominating schools: a failure of policy or a failure of practice?', *Cambridge Journal of Education*, 29(1): 77–91.

Siskin, L. S. (1994) *Realms of Knowledge: Academic Departments in Secondary Schools*, London: Falmer Press.

—— and Little, J. W. (1995) 'Introduction. The subject department: continuities and critiques', in L. S. Siskin, and J. W. Little (eds), *The Subjects in Question*, New York: Teachers' College Press, 1–22.

Skemp, R. R. (1976) 'Relational understanding and instrumental understanding', *Mathematics Teaching*, 177: 20–6.

Smith, M. (1991) 'Curriculum models for the effective delivery of information technology capability in secondary schools', *Computer Education*, 69: 2–5.

—— (1995) 'The IT audit', in B. Tagg (ed.), *Developing a Whole-School IT Policy*, London: Pitman, 27–50.

Speering, W. and Rennie, L. (1996) 'Students' perceptions about science: the impact of transition from primary to secondary school', *Research in Science Education*, 26(3): 283–98.

Stables, A., Morgan, C. and Jones, S. (1999) 'Educating for significant events: the application of Harre's social reality matrix across the lower secondary school curriculum', *Journal of Curriculum Studies*, 31(4): 449–61.

Stevenson, D. (1997) *Information and Communications Technology: An Independent Inquiry*, London: Independent ICT in Schools Commission.

Stillman, A. and Maychell, K. (1984) *School to School*, London: NFER–Nelson.

Stoll, L. and Fink, D. (1996) *Changing Our Schools*, Buckingham: Open University Press.

Strack, G. (1995) 'Curriculum constraints and opportunities', in B. Tagg (ed.), *Developing a Whole-School IT Policy*, London: Pitman, 9–26.

Straker, A. (1997) *National Numeracy Project*, Reading: National Centre for Literacy and Numeracy.

Sutton, R. (1991) 'Equity and computers in the schools: a decade of research', *Review of Educational Research*, 61(4): 475–503.

Tanner, H. F. R. (1991) 'The information technology curriculum and mathematics', *Institute of Mathematics and its Applications*, November: 87–91.

—— (1992) 'Developing the use of IT within mathematics through action research,' *Computers and Education*, 18(1–3): 143–8.

—— (1997) 'Using and applying mathematics: developing mathematical thinking through practical problem solving and modelling', unpublished PhD thesis, University of Wales Swansea.

—— and Jones, S. A. (1994) 'Using peer and self-assessment to develop modelling skills with students aged 11 to 16: a socio-constructive view', *Educational Studies in Mathematics*, 27(4): 413–31.

—— (1995) *Better Thinking, Better Mathematics*, Swansea: University of Wales Swansea.

—— (1999a) 'Dynamic scaffolding and reflective discourse: the impact of teaching style on the development of mathematical thinking', *Proceedings of the 21st Psychology of Mathematics Education Conference, Haifa, Israel*, 4, 257–64.

—— (1999b) 'Schools that add value: raising standards in mathematics', *Proceedings of the British Educational Research Association (BERA-99), Brighton*, online documents, available (23 November 1999): http://www.leeds.ac.uk/educol/bera99.htm

TCT (1997) *Managing IT at Key Stage 3*, London: Technology Colleges Trust.

Taylor, R. (1980) *The Computer in the School*, New York: Teachers' College Press.

Tharp, R. and Gallimore, R. (1988) *Rousing Minds to Life*, Cambridge: Cambridge University Press.

Thomas, G. (1986) 'Education and technology in the third wave', *Oxford Review of Education*, 12(3): 223–31.

Timmins, N. (1997). 'Schools' IT a national priority says report', *The Financial Times* (CD-ROM), 20 March 1997, story 557.

TTA (1998) *The Use of ICT in Subject Teaching: Expected Outcomes for Teachers*, London: Teacher Training Agency.

Twining, P. (1995) 'Towards an understanding of the links between conceptual understanding of computer systems and information technology competence', *Journal of Information Technology for Teacher Education*, 4(3): 377–91.

Underwood, J. and Underwood, G. (1990) *Computers and Learning: Helping Children Acquire Thinking Skills*, Oxford: Blackwell.

Underwood, J., Billingham, M. and Underwood, G. (1994) 'Predicting computer literacy: how do the technological experiences of schoolchildren predict their computer-based problem-solving skills?' *Journal of Information Technology for Teacher Education*, 3(1): 115–26.

Vygotsky, L. S. (1962) *Thought and Language*, Cambridge, MA: MIT Press.

Ward, C. (1999) 'Using and developing information and communications technologies in a secondary school', *Computer Education*, 93: 9–17.

Wardle, H. (1998) 'The way forward: IT secondary/primary liaison', *Computer Education*, 90: 8–12.

Webb, R. (1994) *After the Deluge. Changing Roles and Responsibilities in the Primary School: Summary and Recommendations of Research Commissioned by the Association of Teachers and Lecturers*, London: Association of Teachers and Lecturers.

Wellington, J. (1989) *Education for Employment: The Place of Information Technology*, Windsor: NFER–Nelson.

—— (1990) 'The impact of IT on the school curriculum: downwards, sideways, backwards and forwards', *Journal of Curriculum Studies*, 22(1): 57–63.

Whitaker, P. (1993) *Managing Change in Schools*, Buckingham: Open University.

Williams, R. and Moss, D. (1993) 'Factors influencing the delivery of information technology in the secondary curriculum: a case study', *Journal of Information Technology for Teacher Education*, 2(1), 77–88.

WJEC (1998) *Information Technology: 2000 Syllabus*, Cardiff: Welsh Joint Education Committee.

Wood, D. and Wood, H. (1996) 'Contingency in teaching and learning', *Learning and Instruction*, 6(4): 391–7.

Yeomans, D., Williams, R. and Martin, A. (1995) 'From vertical to horizontal? A longitudinal study of information technology in ten schools', *Journal of Information Technology for Teacher Education*, 4(3), 329–50.

Yukl, G. A. (1989) *Leadership in Organisations*, 2nd edn, Englewood Cliffs, NJ: Prentice-Hall.

Index

182 *Index*

concept 20–21, 23, 27, 30, 57, 74, 86, 110–111
conceptual hurdle 145
confidence (in using ICT) 17, 19, 25, 30, 42, 69–70, 75, 77, 82–83, 87, 96–97, 117, 121, 125, 165–166, 169.
constraint 25–26
content-free 81–82
continuity (in learning) 4–5, 39, 41, 45, 57, 59, 68, 134–137, 138–146, 155
co-ordination (ICT) 47–48, 50–54, 62–64, 66
Cox, M. 6, 145
Crawford, R.A. 109–110
creativity 19, 89, 98, 123
credibility 49, 100, 103
critical thinking 19, 33
cross-curricular 48, 50, 53–55, 59, 80, 88, 90, 98, 103, 115
cross-phase 134–149
curriculum delivery 53–54, 115
curriculum development 49–50, 92, 100, 117

data: collection 2, 74, 105, 113, 122, 133, 140, 146, 160, 163, 168; logging 163; processing 85, 113–114, 166; structure 22, 145
database 9, 11, 29–30, 70–71, 75, 81, 83, 85, 110–111, 116, 145, 147, 162
Daugherty, R. 75
Dean, J. 140
Dearing, R. 7
decision making 14, 17, 19, 28–29, 81, 85, 91–92, 96, 151, 158
demonstration (by teacher) 10, 19, 26, 29–30, 34, 61, 71, 79, 112.
department 10, 34–36, 43, 48, 51, 55, 59, 61–62, 88–91, 93–94, 99–100, 103, 107–108, 112, 115–118, 125, 141, 154, 157, 159–160, 163, 168; head of 48, 51, 108
deputy head 34, 61, 155
design & technology 7, 75, 107, 131
desktop publishing (DTP) 7, 21, 73, 81–83, 111, 116, 147
development: cycle 3, 41–42; plan 37, 39, 42, 44
discrete (ICT teaching) 53–56, 59, 115
discussion (classroom) 17, 23, 26–27, 29–30, 78–79, 83, 87, 101–102, 109–112, 145, 154, 164
disposition 13, 18–19, 153.
dissemination 14, 43, 48, 52, 66, 140, 157

Downes, T. 70, 79, 120–121, 123, 125, 132–133
draft (with ICT) 28–29, 33, 58, 71, 76, 83, 98
drawing (with ICT) 70, 81, 123, 125
drive 39, 42, 44, 47, 65–66, 142, 155–156

electronic whiteboard 78, 169
e-mail 25, 69, 111, 123, 147, 154
emancipation 9, 69, 170
empowerment 33, 36, 93, 109
English 7, 75, 92, 101–102, 125, 131
enquiry (with ICT) 17, 74, 81, 91, 145
enthusiasm 10, 25, 39, 42, 50, 62, 66, 70, 85, 91, 93, 121, 132–133, 141
entitlement 54, 107
entrepreneur 170
equal opportunity 39
equity 119–120, 122, 132
ethics 17, 116
ethos 15, 33, 64, 98, 108
evaluation 4, 43, 50, 56, 60, 62–63, 72, 75–80, 99, 154–155, 158, 160, 166–169
examination 10, 14–15, 38, 88, 90, 94–95, 105, 107, 109, 117, 154, 161, 166; courses 50, 93–94, 107–108, 113
expectation 3, 29, 52, 58, 60, 62, 71–72, 80, 103, 109, 117, 151
explanation (of ICT concept) 21, 23, 27, 112, 145
extra-curricular 38, 45, 70, 131, 150, 153

factor analysis 96, 127
feedback 3, 28, 60, 64, 68, 71–72, 76, 101, 156, 161, 164, 168
finance 33, 35, 38, 142, 156, 159–160, 169
firefighting 53
Flavell, J. H. 23–24
form tutor 60
Fullan, M. 33, 35, 95–96, 100–101, 103
fun 25, 91, 123, 127, 151
future proofing 17

Galton, M. 137, 139
games 119, 121–122, 151
GCSE 105–108, 115, 132
gender 39, 79, 97, 120–122, 126, 128–129, 139, 159
generalisation 14, 20, 25, 102, 116, 153
genre 102
geography 84, 126, 131, 163
Gibson, J. 26